Ethnographies and Exchanges, edited by A. G. Roeber, is published as part of the Max Kade German-American Research Institute Series. This series provides an outlet for books that reflect the mission of the Penn State Kade Institute: to integrate the history and culture of German-speakers in the Americas with the major themes of early modern scholarship from the sixteenth to the early nineteenth century.

ETHNOGRA
AND
EXCHAN

ETHNOGRAPHIES AND EXCHANGES

Native Americans, Moravians, and Catholics in Early North America

Edited by
A. G. ROEBER

THE PENNSYLVANIA STATE UNIVERSITY PRESS
UNIVERSITY PARK, PENNSYLVANIA

Library of Congress Cataloging-in-Publication Data

Roeber, A. G. (Anthony Gregg), 1949–
Ethnographies and exchanges : Native Americans,
Moravians, and Catholics in
early North America / A. G. Roeber.
    p.   cm. — (Max Kade German–American
        Research Institute series)
Includes bibliographical references and index.
ISBN-13: 978-0-271-03346-4 (cloth : alk. paper)
1. Indians of North America—Missions.
2. Indians of North America—Cultural assimilation.
3. Indians of North America—Historiography.
4. Moravians—Missions—North America.
5. Moravians—North America—Historiography.
6. Jesuits—Missions—New France.
7. Jesuits—New France—Historiography.
8. North America—History—17th century.
9. North America—History—17th century—Historiography.
I. Max Kade German–American Research Institute.
II. Title.

E98.M6R58 2008
970.004'97—dc22
2007042096

Copyright © 2008
The Pennsylvania State University
All rights reserved
Printed in the United States of America
Published by The Pennsylvania State University Press,
University Park, PA 16802-1003

The Pennsylvania State University Press is a member of the
Association of American University Presses.

It is the policy of The Pennsylvania State University Press to
use acid-free paper. This book is printed on Natures Natural,
containing 50% post-consumer waste, and meets
the minimum requirements of American National Standard
for Information Sciences—Permanence of Paper for
Printed Library Material, ANSI Z39.48–1992.

For Professors Emeriti

MICHAEL McGIFFERT
GORDON S. WOOD
JOHN M. MURRIN
HERMANN WELLENREUTHER

from a grateful student

CONTENTS

Preface
A. G. Roeber   ix

"This Much Admired Man":
Isaac Glikhikan, Moravian Delaware
David Edmunds   1

I. TEXTS AND INTERPRETIVE PERSPECTIVES

Moravians and the Development of the Genre of Ethnography
Christian F. Feest   19

The Succession of Head Chiefs and the Delaware Culture of Consent:
The Delaware Nation, David Zeisberger, and Modern Ethnography
Hermann Wellenreuther   31

Zeisberger's *Diaries* as a Source for Studying Delaware
Sociopolitical Organization
Robert S. Grumet   49

II. MISSIONS AND EXCHANGES

The Impossible Acculturation: French Missionaries and
Cultural Exchanges in the Seventeenth Century
Dominique Deslandres   67

The Holy See and the Conversion of Aboriginal Peoples
in North America, 1760–1830
Luca Codignola   77

Policing Wabanaki Missions in the Seventeenth Century
Christopher J. Bilodeau   97

The Moravian Missionaries of Bethlehem and Salem
Rowena McClinton   115

"Incline Your Second Ear This Way":
Song as a Cultural Mediator in Moravian Mission Towns
Walter W. Woodward   125

III. INDIGENOUS PERSPECTIVES

Munsee Social Networking and Political
Encounters with the Moravian Church
Siegrun Kaiser 145

The Gender Frontier Revisited:
Native American Women in the Age of Revolution
Jane T. Merritt 165

Debating Missionary Presence at Buffalo Creek:
Haudenosaunee Perspectives on Land Cessions,
Government Relations, and Christianity
Alyssa Mt. Pleasant 175

IV. CONCLUSION

Translation as a Prism:
Broadening the Spectrum of
Eighteenth-Century Identity
Julie Tomberlin Weber 195

Index 208

PREFACE

A. G. ROEBER

A generation ago, standard histories of early North America presented a geographic vision of European settlers arriving from the right-hand side of conventional maps of a "New World." Only passing acknowledgment recognized the critical role the "First Peoples" played on the left-hand side of this picture, one that in fact made possible any European survival anywhere in the Americas. Students today cannot be expected to recognize just how extraordinary have been the labors of historians, archaeologists, anthropologists, ethnographers, and literary scholars in the past quarter-century. Their efforts tell us far more about the American natives' first impressions of, and exchanges with, the European arrivals than we once believed it possible to recover. Nor do we quite see the mapping of the Atlantic world the way we once did.[1]

The title chosen for this collection of essays might also deserve a word or two of explanation. Although "ethnography" is a recognized discipline today, its roots actually lie in the period, and in the labors of the peoples these essays explore. At its simplest, the word means to write about or to describe a "people" or "nation." But to do this correctly, the ancient Greeks knew, depended on being able to penetrate the language, and through that, the understanding a "people" had about themselves, the known world, and perhaps a world or life beyond this one. We need to be careful especially in distinguishing how the early moderns understood this word from the associations it has since acquired. Only in the 1830s and 1840s did the Greek come to be translated as "race" rather than "nation" or "people," and "ethnology" as a study of "races." This "turn" to a pseudoscientific "race" study would not have been understood by the Europeans of the seventeenth and eighteenth centuries, though in some unintended ways their labors may have led those who benefited from their pioneering efforts to turn toward a "race" explanation of "peoples."[2] The two European settlement peoples whose interactions with Native Americans we

---

1. For a useful survey of many directions in "colonial" American scholarship—with the odd exception of a treatment of Atlantic history—see Daniel Vickers, ed., *A Companion to Colonial America* (Malden, Mass.: Blackwell Publishers, 2003).

2. On this point, see Steven Conn, *History's Shadow: Native Americans and Historical Consciousness in the Nineteenth Century* (Chicago: University of Chicago Press, 2004), 168. I am indebted to Gregory Dowd for the reference.

explore in this volume were German-speaking Moravian Protestants and French-speaking Roman Catholics. Neither group played the part of providing Europeans with formative descriptions of the peoples of the Americas. Both Portuguese and Spanish accounts had spread in translation across Europe by the time the French, or the Swedish and Dutch, settlements emerged in the north and middle Atlantic by the 1620s. The Mediterranean world had already shaped exchanges with Africa, and then the Caribbean, setting in motion many of the ecological, political, and religious patterns of exchange that later emerged on the North American continent. Material goods and the unintentional mixing of plants and animals hold pride of place in the timing of "exchanges" (which were still predominantly a "one-way" imposition upon the Americas). The Atlantic world the French, and later the German-speaking Moravians, inherited had already been refashioned by those late fifteenth- and early sixteenth-century contacts. But how people came to interpret exchanges by the later seventeenth and eighteenth centuries is really the focus of this collection of original essays. That focus emerged because of an intensified interest on the part of both Moravians and Jesuits in the language, religion, and political organization of the First Peoples they encountered in North America.[3]

That interest has piqued our own. Experts in many disciplines have recognized how "scholars of literature and art join and compete with historians and anthropologists to draw out the many meanings embedded in texts broadly defined."[4] The essays collected in this volume do not pretend to sort out all the complexities of European–Native American exchanges. They do build upon fine recent efforts to recapture the voices of both Europeans and Native Americans in neglected or forgotten areas of North America.[5]

The essays began as presentations at the Max Kade German-American Research Institute Conference, "David Zeisberger, Native Americans, and

---

3. On the "imposition" of European flora and fauna, the classic essay remains Alfred W. Crosby, "Ecological Imperialism: The Overseas Migration of Western Europeans as a Biological Phenomenon," *Texas Quarterly* 21 (1978): 103–17. For a lively overview of much recent literature on precontact American societies, cultures, and ecologies, see Charles C. Mann, *1491: New Revelations of the Americas Before Columbus* (New York: Knopf, 2005).

4. Karen Ordahl Kupperman, "Introduction: the Changing Definition of America," in *America in European Consciousness, 1493–1750*, ed. Karen Ordahl Kupperman (Chapel Hill: University of North Carolina Press, 1995), 4.

5. See, for example, William A. Pencak and Daniel K. Richter, eds., *Friends and Enemies in Penn's Woods: Indians, Colonists, and the Racial Construction of Pennsylvania* (University Park: Pennsylvania State University Press, 2004); Daniel K. Richter, "A Framework for Pennsylvania Indian History," *Pennsylvania History* 57 (1990): 236–61; and James H. Merrell, *Into the American Woods: Negotiators on the Pennsylvania Frontier* (New York: W. W. Norton, 1999).

Cultural Exchanges in Early Modern North America," held at Penn State University in September 2004. That conference recognized the appearance of the critical edition (in English translation) of the Moravian missionary David Zeisberger's diaries. It also, sadly, honored the memory of one of the editors of that volume, the late Dr. Carola Wessel. Carola provided much of the preparatory work for participants in several disciplines on both sides of the Atlantic.[6]

Students will find here a fresh perspective from which to carry out the exploration of how people interpreted the exchanges among Native Americans and Europeans from the 1670s to the decades just after the American Revolution. Despite the broader perspective that newer surveys of the early modern Atlantic provide us, many of our deepest impressions about these first exchanges continue to be guided by the Spanish contacts in the Caribbean, Meso, and South America, or English experiences in Virginia and Massachusetts. The Chesapeake and New England stories, especially, have long dominated accounts of early English North American contacts.[7]

Dates and contexts for the middle and northern Atlantic areas where exchanges unfolded take most students into unfamiliar territories. The "Moravians"—or, to use the more accurate self-description they favored, "the Unity of the Brethren"—traced their roots to the 1457 aftermath of the wars between the Catholic emperor and the Hussites of Bohemia and Moravia. But this memory bears the marks of remembered religious myth. The brutal truth was that by 1648 the Thirty Years' War had probably destroyed all, or nearly all, original Protestant communities as well as an additional center in Leszno or Lissa in present-day Poland.

The reconstitution of the Brethren in the 1720s under the protection of Nicholas Count von Zinzendorf in Saxony brought them, within a decade, into contact with British North America. There, Moravian interests in converting both enslaved Africans and Native Americans from the Caribbean and on the North American mainland catapulted them into an uneasy relationship with other Protestant groups and often tense relations with European colonial regimes. Their own fragile existence in the midst of European empires contributed to a

---

6. David Zeisberger, *The Moravian Mission Diaries of David Zeisberger, 1772–1781*, ed. Herman Wellenreuther and Carola Wessel, trans. Julie Tomberlin Weber (University Park: Pennsylvania State University Press, 2005).

7. For examples of the more recent approaches, see Karen Ordahl Kupperman, ed., *Major Problems in American Colonial History*, 2d ed. (Boston: Houghton Mifflin, 2000), 1–56; T. H. Breen and Timothy Hall, *Colonial America in an Atlantic World* (New York: Longman, 2004), 1–13; Peter Charles Hoffer, *The Brave New World: A History of Early America* (Boston: Houghton Mifflin, 2000), 1–42.

somewhat more chastened and humble attitude that Moravians brought to their contacts with non-European peoples and their beliefs.[8]

The Catholic French are likely to be recognized because of the accounts that survive in the *Jesuit Relations*. We need to remind ourselves immediately, of course, that not all French Catholic missionaries were Jesuits. Indeed, some very shrewd ethnographic descriptions penned by French Catholics were done by Franciscans, Suplicians, and secular clergy. Still, the Jesuits do hold a kind of pride of place in the tale of European–Native American exchanges in Canada. It seems especially appropriate, therefore, to mention the famous collection of texts compiled by the Jesuits. One of the conference participants, Allan Greer, had already provided an accessible selection of excerpts for students from this seventy-three-volume work. Greer alerted students to the issues of texts, translations, religious worldviews, and ethnographic reporting that are the subjects of the essays in this volume. And, whatever the limitations of the French Jesuit reporters and compilers, Greer's judgment remains sound: "the Jesuits knew what they were talking about . . . [and] because they lived in native villages for years on end, learned the local languages, got to know the people, and took their place on the margins of Amerindian society, they came to know native peoples as few other Europeans did."[9]

That Jesuit accomplishment seems to encourage a comparison between French Jesuits and German-speaking Moravians. Greer has provided a case study of his own to illustrate some of the challenges that surround texts, terminology, religious worldviews, and sociopolitical organization among Native Americans, as reflected in the career of Kateri Tekakwitha. Only recently have scholars begun to probe this Mohawk woman's life and "the contradictions or paradoxes she may have struggled with as she embraced an alien faith."[10]

But not only do our impressions and interpretations of Huron, Mohawk, Montagnais, or Mahican peoples continue to require revision. The Jesuits themselves, once portrayed as either Catholic heroes or the bogeymen of Protestant nightmares, in more recent years have again suffered at the hands of

---

8. For an excellent summary that places the Moravians and their significance in a transatlantic context, see Craid D. Atwood, *Community of the Cross: Moravian Piety in Colonial Bethlehem* (University Park: Pennsylvania State University Press, 2004), 21–40.

9. Allan Greer, ed., *The Jesuit Relations: Natives and Missionaries in Seventeenth-Century North America* (Boston: Beford Books, 2000), 1. For an assessment of the French colonies and the role of the Jesuits, 1600–1660, students with a command of German should also consult Hermann Wellenreuther, *Niedergang und Aufstieg: Geschichte Nordamerikas vom begin der Besiedlung bis zum Ausgang des 17. Jahrhunderts* (Münster: LIT Verlag, 2000), chapter 7, 191–237.

10. Daniel K. Richter, *Facing East from Indian Country: A Native History of Early America* (Cambridge: Harvard University Press, 2001), 81.

both secular and some Native American scholars to serve as the paragons of "Christian missionaries as a malevolent force." Greer's subtle interpretation of these missionaries, and of the Native Americans, outlined in his contribution to the conference, are best followed in his full-length study of Tekakwitha.[11]

These essays look both east and west from parts of the North Atlantic world that are less familiar. Because we are interested in the issue of texts, translations, and the challenge multiple languages posed in European–Native American exchanges, European religious leaders interested in these issues play a somewhat exaggerated role in that story. The middle Atlantic British settlement area where German Moravians encountered the Lenape and others, and the St. Lawrence River and Great Lakes region where the French met Huron, Algonquian, and Haudenosaunee, probably still remain slightly out of focus in our mind's eye. We do not instinctively look there for the main outlines of the story of European–Native American contacts. But the French Catholic and German Moravian experiences provide important correctives to some received wisdom about the language, religion, and political structures of Europeans and First Peoples. Their exchanges require us to integrate them into more familiar tales and areas of Native American–European meetings.

Most of the serious study of Native American languages and culture took place among European Christian clerics. The authors of these essays made no attempt to survey all of those efforts. For example, the insights into Native American kinship relations gleaned from the 1661 Sulpician manuscript dictionary of Algonquian still awaits the full attention of anthropologists, linguists, and ethnohistorians.[12] Exchanges about language, political organization, and gender roles do figure in our essays within the broad context of religious objectives and interpretive lenses provided by both Moravians and Jesuits, Lenape, Haudenosaunee, Wabanaki, and Cherokee.

The first task we would urge on students is to keep the geography of the middle to northern Atlantic and the St. Lawrence River in mind. This seems important because the perspective of most of the writers differs slightly from that advanced by scholars who have tried to talk of a "middle ground" where Europeans and First Peoples met. Both the French Jesuits and the German Moravians might qualify as inhabitants of what Richard White called "the

---

11. Allan Greer, *Mohawk Saint: Catherine Tekakwitha and the Jesuits* (New York: Oxford University Press, 2005); x; see also his bibliography of the shifting assessments of the Jesuits, 207–8n4.
12. See Heidi Bohaker, "*Nindoodemag:* The Significance of Algonquian Kinship Networks in the Eastern Great Lakes Region, 1600–1701," *William and Mary Quarterly,* 3d ser., 63 (January 2006): 23–52, 33, 34n10.

place in between: in between cultures, peoples, and in between empires and the nonstate world of villages." The same might have been true for many of the Lenape, Mahican, Haudenosaunee actors. But the interior of the continent where White explored this notion of a "middle ground" had its own regional characteristics and posed its own problems. Both Catholics and Moravians penetrated into the Great Lakes and Ohio country, and southward among the Cherokee as well. But, at least from the European perspective, the relative weakness of many of those missionary efforts delayed, or made more difficult, extensive probing of Native American languages and cultures.[13]

Nearly all scholars in related disciplines share White's objective of providing an imaginative framework for examining "an elaborate network of economic, political, cultural, and social ties" among various groups. At the same time, because of the conference's focus on issues of language, religion, and political organization, our essays probe religious belief systems more deeply than White did in his discussion of the importance of dreams and visions. Questions about political organization among Native Americans could not be asked by Europeans without a struggle with terms and relationships that demanded a real grappling with indigenous languages. Those grapplings really did take place among Jesuits and Moravians, and the results give a particular quality to the essays in this volume.[14]

An inquiring student must now shift focus a bit away from the broad Atlantic world to locate more precisely where the Lenape, or "Delaware," people encountered Europeans in what are today Delaware, Pennsylvania, and Ohio. This geographic context provided the stage upon which that people's religious worldviews, and that of the recently transplanted "Moravians," were acted out. The Iroquois Confederation—the Haudenosaunee—that dominated the Great Lakes region into present-day New York and into Canada was never far away, both in geographic fact and in the awareness of both Lenape and Moravian actors. This formidable group had provided both Dutch and English arrivals in New Netherlands and New England with a critical alliance in the seventeenth century, and most of us have at least some impression of their importance. But the Iroquois's badgered southern neighbors, the Lenape, have never enjoyed quite such an outstanding profile. This may explain why it does not automatically occur

---

13. Richard White, *The Middle Ground: Indians, Empires, and Republics in the Great Lakes Region, 1650–1815* (New York: Cambridge University Press, 1991), x.

14. Ibid., 33; on Native American–European religious exchanges, see 327–32. For a reflection on the meaning of White's provocative title, see Phlip J. Deloria, "What Is the Middle Ground, Anyway?" *William and Mary Quarterly*, 3d ser., 63 (January 2006): 15–22.

to us to compare the middle Atlantic area to the northeastern Atlantic. But in doing so, we are following the lead of colleagues across several disciplines whose work in disparate geographic areas has provided us with important new insights.

A recent example of this kind of effort—one that focuses on notions of saints and the idea of the "holy" in the Americas—points out that notions about gender, about the enslavement of the body, about the creation of new identities, tended to emerge within the complex region of religious belief systems. Europeans may have regarded the exchanges as part of a "spiritual conquest of the Americas to be sure, but [it was] also the American 'conquest' of Christianity."[15] These same comparisons about the holy in different places also serve to remind us not to be lazy and invoke easy, comprehensive terms like "Protestant" and "Catholic" if we truly seek to understand a particular European version of Christianity. To do so is to risk the same level of misunderstanding that we do if we remain satisfied with a naïve invocation of "Indian" religion.

Before moving into more detail about the unfamiliar areas of North America, it may pay dividends to step back and gain perspective on more comfortable ground. Even in more familiar places, new findings advance our understanding of texts, political organization, and religious viewpoints. Most North American students, for example, instinctively think of the "American South" as a land particularly marked by evangelical Protestant revival traditions. But in the past few years historians have uncovered a rather different past for an area we thought we knew. The pioneering work of both Christine Heyrman and Jon Sensbach— the former a scholar with familial roots in the Moravians, the latter an expert on Moravian work among African Americans—has corrected our textbook impressions. The real story of the American "South" is far more complicated than a simple, quick triumph of an evangelical "Bible Belt" Christianity among Europeans and Africans. To take but one example, dream interpretation and visions preoccupied the minds and hearts of many Native Americans. But few have recognized that the same fascination characterized the popular religion of the early nineteenth-century South. Second, peculiar mixtures of Native American, African, and various ethnic European religious convictions (including those of the Moravians) actually shaped this region—and the Caribbean before it. Both areas actually looked vastly different from what our conventional memory, shaped by an older literature, has allowed us to see.[16]

---

15. Jodi Bilinkoff, "Introduction," in *Colonial Saints: Discovering the Holy in the Americas, 1500–1800*, ed. Allan Greer and Jodi Bilinkoff (New York: Routledge, 2003), xv.

16. Christine Leigh Heyrman, *Southern Cross: The Beginnings of the Bible Belt* (Chapel Hill: University of North Carolina Press, 1997); Jon F. Sensbach, "Before the Bible Belt: Indians, Africans, and

Just so in the case of both the middle and northeastern Atlantic exchanges. If we seek to understand how Europeans described different peoples in these parts of the north Atlantic world, we need to bear in mind what one historian has called the "episodic" quality of European attempts to explain religious, political, and cultural differences among peoples. In every case, all such efforts were inherited from a much older history of Christianity. European notions of other peoples and their languages, though they began to emerge as separate and distinct areas of study by the eighteenth century, still fell largely under the assumptions inherited from ancient Western Christianity. Whether Catholic or Protestant, Europeans continued to struggle with their inherited conviction that humans, no matter their specific geographic location, language, or culture, were members of a common family. Whether Europeans were confident or pessimistic about their ability to penetrate the language, customs, and religious worldview of "others" depended upon their memory of other episodes, including sometimes fanciful notions about their own ancestors' ancient conversion to the Christian faith.[17]

If we seek to understand how the First Peoples regarded Christianity, Allan Greer reminded the conference participants that Christianity was itself but an "episode" in their long series of exposures to rituals and beliefs. Particular native tribes had sampled, accepted, or rejected specific practices and worldviews for their particular area and kinship group long before Europeans arrived. Despite the often bewildering diversity of linguistic, clan, and religious specifics, Native Americans, in distinguishing specific peoples and their deities and rituals, were exposed to many competing belief systems. They quickly concluded that these odd arrivals from across the water were humans. Despite their outlandish notions, behaviors, and sometimes impenetrably obscure language customs, Europeans were assumed to live under some sort of divine protection and judgment, even if they only rarely seemed to achieve a vague correlation between professed belief and actual behavior. Eventually, in episodic struggles and fatally weakened numbers, Native Americans challenged the

---

the New Synthesis of Eighteenth-Century Southern Religious History," in *Religion in the American South: Protestants and Others in History and Culture,* ed. Beth Barton Schweiger and Donald G. Mathews (Chapel Hill: University of North Carolina Press, 2004), 5–29; Jon F. Sensbach, *Rebecca's Revival: Creating Black Christianity in the Atlantic World* (Cambridge: Harvard University Press, 2005).

17. Charles L. Cohen, "The Colonization of British North America as an Episode in the History of Christianity," *Church History* 72 (September 2003): 553–68; on European memories of their own pre-Christian pasts, see Joseph R. Lucas, "Conquering the Passions: Indians, Europeans, and Early American Social Thought, 1580–1840" (Ph.D. diss., Pennsylvania State University, 1999).

linguistic, religious, and cultural reshaping of their lives demanded by Europeans along a shifting "frontier." It was along this borderland country that both Moravian Protestants and French Catholics lived precariously, whether they were originally European or Native American by birth.[18]

Even an "Atlantic" perspective, with smaller screens detailing the regions these essays cover, is not quite sufficient to see the broader patterns we hope students will discover and pursue. A satellite's perspective on the entire North American continent, complete with time-lapse imagery over the course of the seventeenth to the early nineteenth century, would reveal in startling relief the limited successes of linguistic, political, and religious exchanges. These were largely confined to the saltwater edges of the continent. Some of the most impressive understandings of language, religion, and sociopolitical organizations resulted in serious study and near mastery of the languages of Native American cultures by interested Europeans. The essays in this collection illustrate some of the most important that occurred among the French Jesuits and Protestant Moravians in the eastern middle Atlantic region. But far to the northwest, along the Pacific Rim, Russian Orthodox Christians in Siberia and Alaska settled in for a long and steady study and appreciation of indigenous languages and worldviews. By the nineteenth century, Moravian arrivals were also engaging these indigenous peoples and cultures. Catholic Spanish European exchanges on that Pacific front, quite serious and significant, remained distinct from the French Atlantic experiences. Students may recall the famous Pueblo Revolt of 1680, which rejected Spanish Franciscan missionary efforts in what is today New Mexico. The story of Franciscan–Native American exchanges in California, similarly, was marred by the deep association of these European Christians with the Spanish Crown. From the very outset royal authority had promoted a close and often less than gentle approach to conversion. Sometimes doubtful readings of indigenous texts imagined a closer connection between Native American religions and Christianity than was probably ever the case. Such errors may have been less common among the French Catholics. Until 1700

---

18. On the shifting border between European and "Indian" country, see James H. Merrell, "'The Customes of Our Countrey': Indians and Colonists in Early America," in *Strangers Within the Realm: Cultural Margins of the First British Empire*, ed. Bernard Bailyn and Philip D. Morgan (Chapel Hill: University of North Carolina Press, 1991), 117–56; on the middle Atlantic area, see Daniel K. Richter and James H. Merrell, eds., *Beyond the Covenant Chain: The Iroquois and Their Neighbors in Indian North America, 1600–1800* (Syracuse: Syracuse University Press, 1987); on the resistance patterns, see Gregory Evans Dowd, *A Spirited Resistance: The North American Indian Struggle for Unity, 1745–1815* (Baltimore: Johns Hopkins University Press, 1992).

little evidence survives to suggest that either the French monarchy or, for that matter, the Holy See in Rome paid much attention to French Catholic–Native American exchanges in the north Atlantic.[19]

Precisely because there was no close political oversight by which to control French Catholic clerics, their relationship to various Native American peoples provides some suggestive points of comparison with the Moravians. These Protestants, too, never quite "fit" into any colonial political agenda in the Americas. By contrast, the Church of England, and even its self-proclaimed "reformed" (detractors said "puritan") version in New England, never engaged Native American cultures to quite the same extent that Moravians and French Jesuits did. French Catholic activities among both Native American and African American populations, by contrast, shaped the contours of settlements from the Caribbean to the St. Lawrence River, despite a declining level of interest in these ventures on the part of Rome itself. Moreover, those activities implicated both Algonquian and Iroquoian speakers in the written and translated confessional anxieties and polemics of European Christians.[20]

Our time-lapse view also compels us to notice that among continental European Protestants of the state churches, the Swedish Lutherans did try to engage the Lenape of the Delaware River valley. A century before the German-speaking Moravians arrived, Swedish settlers grappled with the language sufficiently to produce a rudimentary speech suitable for trade but little else. This

---

19. On the Franciscan areas in California, see Steven W. Hackel, *Children of Coyote, Missionaries of St. Francis: Indian-Spanish Relations in Colonial California, 1769–1850* (Chapel Hill: University of North Carolina Press, 2004), 127–81. On the deep levels of "misreadings" between Spanish and Nahua, see Matthew Restall, *Seven Myths of the Spanish Conquest* (New York: Oxford University Press, 2003), chapter 5, "The Lost Words of La Malinche: the Myth of (Mis)Communication," 77–99.

20. For a balanced assessment of New England Puritan–Indian conversion issues, see Charles L. Cohen, "Conversion Among Puritans and Amerindians: A Theological and Cultural Perspective," in *Puritanism: Transatlantic Perspectives on a Seventeenth-Century Anglo-American Faith,* ed. Francis J. Bremer (Boston: Northeastern University Press, 1993), 235–63. On the Jesuits and the worries their activities among the Iroquoians sparked in New England's translation and publication history, see Evan Haefeli and Owen Stanwood, "Jesuits, Huguenots, and the Apocalypse: The Origins of America's First French Book," *Proceedings of the American Antiquarian Society* 116, no. 1 (2006): 59–119. The Moravian efforts are documented in the essays in this volume; on the Orthodox–Native American exchanges, see especially Andrei Znamenski, *Native Encounters with Russian Orthodox Missions in Siberia and Alaska, 1820–1917* (Westport, Conn.: Greenwood Press, 1999); Andrei Znamenski, *Shamanism in Siberia: Russian Records of Indigenous Spirituality* (Dordrecht: Kluwer Academic Publishers, 2003); Sergei Kan, "Recording Native Cultures and Christianizing the Natives: Russian Orthodox Missionaries in Southeastern Alaska," in *Russia in North America,* ed. Richard R. Pierce (Kingston, Ontario: Linestone Press, 1990), 298–313; on Aleut and Eskimo religious life, see N. M. Dauenhauer and Richard Dauenhauer, "Spiritual Aspects of Tlingit Oratory," in *Northern Religions and Shamanism,* ed. Mihály Hoppál and Juha Pentikäinen (Helsinki: Finnish Literature Society, 1992), 90–99.

limited level of interest expressed by Swedes and Finns on the far western Atlantic remained modest, mostly because Swedish authorities did not want to upset the Delaware and give the neighboring Dutch a trade advantage.

Swedish missionary work in the early decades of the seventeenth century among the Saami people of Lappland, by contrast, quickly targeted the shamanistic religion of that people for conversion. Close royal supervision and criminal penalties aimed at adultery or sorcery nonetheless were pronounced a failure by 1685. Compulsory church attendance had neither stopped Saami invocation of Sarakka, a female god, nor persuaded them to forswear reliance upon herbalists and shamans who mediated the conflict between the twin gods, the "Creator" and the "Devious One."[21]

Governor Johan Printz, the Swedish commander on the Delaware, remained cynical about any possibility of changing the non-Christians among whom he had settled—people he and his compatriots characterized as *vildar*—"wild men." He regarded them as impervious to the allure of the Swedish Lutheran liturgy, despite urgings from Sweden that such ritual approaches and study of their language might produce real understanding. Not long after the 1638 founding of New Sweden, the Swedish priest Johan Campanius embarked on his effort to translate Martin Luther's small catechism, probably finishing the task by around 1643. But Campanius's glossary of terms did not actually show a mastery of Unami-Unalachtigo use. Instead, it replicated the "trade jargon" that had been created in the first decade or so of contact. In 1690, however, his effort received a European printing, subsidized by a Swedish monarchy intent perhaps on promoting the Christianization of Americans now that the efforts in Lappland had been declared bankrupt. Much of Delaware religious life remained intact, since only in these last decades of the century did interest in the Christianization of this people intensify. Printz's construction of a Lutheran church at New Gothenburg on Tinicum Island may have persuaded Europeans to stay Lutheran. But the Lenape felt no urge to subscribe to the Augsburg Confession. Real understanding of their language would not occur until the Moravians arrived in the 1740s.[22]

These early Swedish–Native American contacts, on both a linguistic and a religious front of mutual exchanges, were never one-sided. Early accounts of

---

21. Gunlög Fur, "Cultural Confrontation on Two Fronts: Swedes Meet Lenapes and Saamis in the Seventeenth Century" (Ph.D. diss., University of Oklahoma, 1993), 18–19, 45–85; Gunlög Fur, "Saami and Lenapes Meet Swedish Colonizers in the Seventeenth Century," in *Readings in Saami History, Culture and Language III*, ed. Roger Kvist (Umeå, Sweden: University of Umeå Center for Arctic Cultural Research, 1992), 41–62.

22. Fur, "Cultural Confrontation on Two Fronts," 170–86, 193–94, 197.

the struggling European arrivals suggest that the challenge of remaining pious European Lutherans in the midst of "Indian country" proved too daunting for many. To the consternation of European authorities—and almost certainly one of the motivations for the later publication of Campanius's work—some of the early transplants opted not for the role of "settlers" but instead adopted the Lenape language and cultural ways. European authorities here, as elsewhere, awakened repeatedly to the need to pay more attention to the allure of Native American language, political and social relationships, and religious worldviews.[23]

Religious myths and ways of life did not encompass the entire spectrum of cultural exchanges, though they provided the most encompassing backdrop against which political, gender, and linguistic adjustments played out within European and Native American areas. Those adjustments, especially how they were shaped in the middle and north Atlantic world, are approached in various ways by the contributors to this volume.

Few scholars today care to spend much time trying to judge the "authenticity" of Native American conversions to Christianity. They also caution us to avoid the "golden age" myth of religious, social, political, and gender interactions within Native American groups, in which "authentic" or "pure" forms are imagined to have existed before the "negative" impact of European "impositions." Several of the essays show both prior cross-fertilizations and tensions among First Peoples, and illustrate also why even now, after such prodigious labors, we are less than certain whether we understand the terminology and the implications of some Native American terms for kinship or social and political leadership roles.

The essays are divided into three sections. The first section investigates the issue of language as it occurs in texts and problems of interpretation. The second set of essays explores the complex nature of missions and the exchanges they gave rise to. The third group attempts to recapture the voices and visions of the First Peoples. Finally, the translator of David Zeisberger's diaries provides us with a

---

23. Campanius's work is *Lutheri catechismus, Ofwersatt på American-Virginiske Språket*, ed. Thomas Campanius Holm (Stockholm: J. J. Genath, 1696). The volume contains not only the text of Luther's work but a glossary of Delaware "trade jargon" as well. On the early Swedish-Delaware contacts, see Robert S. Grumet, *Historic Contact: Indian People and Colonists in Today's Northeastern United States in the Sixteenth Through Eighteenth Centuries* (Norman: University of Oklahoma Press, 1995), 234, 237, 318–19. On the early Lutheran church and Swedish-Lenape exchanges and disagreements, see Michael Dean Mackintosh, "New Sweden, Natives, and Nature," in Pencak and Richter, *Friends and Enemies in Penn's Woods*, 13. On the spectrum of early European attempts to master Native American language, see Daniel J. Slive, "A New World of Words: Amerindian Languages in the Colonial World," essay accompanying the exhibit under the same title prepared for the John Carter Brown Library, Providence, Rhode Island, February 14–May 1, 1997, now available at www.library.upenn.edu/exhibits/rbm/kislak/index/slive.html. Cited by permission.

long meditation on the challenges of translation and the fragile nature of our probings of unfamiliar languages and peoples.

To illustrate how alert we must be to hear or read correctly what a person on the frontier between languages, political organizations, and religious beliefs "meant" by a certain action, David Edmunds uses the example of Isaac Glikhikan. His assessments of the "much admired man" provide a concrete and accessible point of entry into many of the issues that are treated in more detail in the subsequent essays.

The first essays focus on the difficult problem of surviving texts and how their interpreters continue to shape our own efforts to see through these artifacts into the complexities of the observed peoples and cultures. Christian Feest reviews for us both the traditions of ethnography the Moravians inherited and the particular contributions they made to this discipline. By surveying a number of efforts, and then focusing particularly upon David Zeisberger's work, Feest also reminds us that the purpose of Moravian missionaries was not to be professional ethnographers. That simple fact again alerts us to the difficulty of sorting out what a particular account included, left out, or perhaps unknowingly misrepresented. Hermann Wellenreuther examines the same kind of problem, but from a different perspective. By teasing out the implications of the succession of the head chiefs of the Delaware Nation, he shows us how complicated (and still debated) are our understandings of such key terms as "nation," "friendship," and "consent" within Delaware political culture. Wellenreuther approaches this task from a historian's perspective and as one of the two editors of Zeisberger's diaries. Robert Grumet, trained as an anthropologist-archaeologist, assesses the organization of Delaware life from a different angle. By examining descent notions, lineages, and social control, Grumet also shows us how such ideas and practices evolved over time, perhaps taking on new and different meanings during the turbulent decades of contact with arriving Europeans.

The sharp-eyed reader will notice that the contributors do not always agree with one another in their interpretations of the evidence. Grumet's analysis, for example, is very much at odds with Siegrun Kaiser's assessment of the meaning of words like "Munsee," "Delaware," "Unami," "Wolf," "Turkey," and "Turtle." Wellenreuther explains why he disagrees with ethnologists about the issue of internal identity and lineages within the "Delaware Nation." Exchanges at this level of technical expertise that try to explain what group identities consisted of are crucial for specialists in the field. This fact alone demanded that such disagreements be made available for the scrutiny of the scholarly community. Even those who do not care to follow all of the nuances of the argument can, we think, still benefit from observing why such disagreements continue to make issues of ethnographies and exchanges lively and important.

Whatever their particular perspective or argument, all of the contributors would concur that European exchanges with the First Peoples had already been shaped by the work of French Jesuits long before the German-speaking Moravians arrived in the north Atlantic world. The second group of essays focuses on "missions" and their critical role. For the French Catholic context, Dominique Deslandres reminds us of the importance of attempting to penetrate the mentality of the missionaries themselves—who in many respects are as foreign, as "other," to us as readers today as the First Peoples were to these Catholic Europeans. Her extended meditation on the impossibility of "acculturation" provides a background against which to understand why the Jesuit missionaries were not, perhaps, all that different from their Moravian counterparts in their struggle to master the languages and mentality of the First Peoples, despite profoundly different theological assumptions about the internal dynamics of the Christian faith. Luca Codignola pushes the story of Catholic engagement with North America into the period when Moravians and other Protestants had become genuine competitors in North America. If relatively little interest or investment by Rome had characterized the Holy See's relationship to French Catholic efforts in the previous century, this now changed. Yet, paradoxically, while Rome expressed concern for the success of Catholic efforts in the New World, Codignola concludes that the distance between the assumptions of Catholics in Rome and their counterparts in the New World may have been even greater than the cultural and linguistic differences that continued to challenge Europeans and First Peoples in mid-eighteenth-century North America. Christopher Bilodeau provides us with a close analysis of how liturgical rituals, developed in a medieval European context, served as a bridge between the French Catholics and the Wabanaki in the Maine region of the late seventeenth and early eighteenth centuries. At this local level as well, however, rituals and symbols succeeded only sometimes in connecting Native American and European understandings of the world.

This paradox can be followed in the second set of essays by expanding our perspective on the Moravians to include their work among the Cherokee. Rowena McClinton details not only misunderstandings between the Cherokee and the Gambold missionaries but the unintended consequences of Cherokee acceptance of some European ways, which further challenged the missionaries' own vision of their purpose among this people. Walter Woodward's essay is unique insofar as it singles out for extensive reflection what all historians of the Moravians have always known: that their hymnography played a key role in their communal life, and indeed in their success among both European and non-European converts. In this instance, as in the context sketched by McClinton, unintended consequences and the complexities of "reading" or "hearing" Moravian Indian use of hymns bring the issue of texts and religious and political meaning home in a particularly memorable fashion.

The third group of essays concentrates on probing the internal dynamics of specific Native American groups. Siegrun Kaiser offers an extensive examination of how the Munsee neighbors of the Mahican and Delaware resisted and rejected Moravian missionary efforts. Instead, they effectively learned to use the Moravians to political advantage, though in the end their strategies failed to save them from exile. Jane Merritt's examination of "gender frontiers" returns us very specifically to David Zeisberger and the women of the Mahican and Delaware peoples. She alerts us to the problems of possible gender bias in Zeisberger's own recording of incidents and to issues among convert wives in particular. Their mixture of genuine religious conviction and canny pragmatism allowed these women an agency probably not quite in line with what the Moravian missionaries had envisioned, one that wove together both inherited and new religious visions and political and family arrangements. Finally, Alyssa Mt. Pleasant provides an important contrast to the Moravian-Delaware exchanges by examining the Seneca responses to Presbyterian missionary exchanges in the Buffalo Creek area of New York in the crucial years of the early nineteenth century, which created a "Christian-Pagan" schism among the Haudenosaunee. If Delaware and Mahican women adapted Zeisberger's goals to their own ends, the Haudenosaunee likewise managed to use the possibility of missionary schooling to preserve aspects of their traditional life and defend their lands. They came to this position, in part, by observing what had befallen the Delaware, who had not sufficiently studied the Europeans and their objectives.

The concluding essay, by Julie Tomberlin Weber, the translator of the Zeisberger diaries, caps the volume. Her presentation at the conference provoked lively, intense, and sustained responses from the participating scholars and their audience. Weber's primary question—what does a translation do?—gives her a platform for exploring the mysterious ways in which a translation creates a new cultural entity—something not "indigenous" to either its originating culture or the one for which it is intended. Her ruminations about the complexities of the translator's task stand as a fitting summary of the challenges that face every student who seeks to puzzle out the levels of meaning texts contain for any exploration of religious meaning, social and political organization, and language itself.

From seasoned veterans to those just beginning their careers, the contributors have displayed remarkable tolerance for editorial interference. Several papers could not be included in the final volume, nor could the insightful suggestions and observations offered by session chairs and commentators. To William Joyce, Frauke Geyken, Mark Louden, Dean Snow, William Starna, Renate Wilson, Linda Sabathy-Judd, Corinna Dally-Starna, Daniel Richter, Brian Hosmer, Axel Utz, Jean O'Brien-Kehoe, Karen Kupperman, Allan Greer, Gregory Dowd, and Paul Peucker, I can only express on behalf of the Kade Institute our profound gratitude for their participation. In every instance, their presence at the conference helped to shape this volume. I hope that all who now have the benefit of reading the results of the conference will be as pleased by, and benefit as much from, these essays as have the Max Kade German-American Research Institute and those who attended. My thanks as well to Peter Potter for his interest in the project, and to Sandy Thatcher, Jennifer Norton, Laura Reed-Morrisson, Suzanne Wolk, and the staff at Penn State Press for their superb and timely attention to the book's final form.

A. G. Roeber
Penn State University, January 2008

"This Much Admired Man":

Isaac Glikhikan, Moravian Delaware

DAVID EDMUNDS

Things did not go as David Zeisberger had envisioned.[1] On June 8, 1769, the missionary was working in the fields near the new Moravian mission at Lawunakhannek, on the Allegheny River, in northwestern Pennsylvania, when a messenger informed him that Glikhikan, the famous Munsee (Delaware) war chief, foremost counselor to the Delaware village chief Packanke and a renowned orator, had arrived at the mission to speak to Zeisberger and his converts. Laying aside his hoe, Zeisberger hurried to the mission's meetinghouse, where he found Glikhikan listening to Anthony, a Delaware convert, who was regaling Glikhikan and his comrades with both the wonders of the Christian faith and the virtues of the Moravian lifestyle. Anthony's sermon seemed to mesmerize Glikhikan, and when Anthony finished, Zeisberger "briefly corroborated his (Anthony's) words, and exhorted Glikhikan to lay them to heart."[2]

Zeisberger was surprised by Glikhikan's response. He had expected the Munsee to refute the Christian doctrines, but Glikhikan listened attentively, then rose and stated, "I have nothing to say. I believe your words." Thanking the missionaries, Glikhikan left the mission and returned to Goschgoschunk, the neighboring Delaware village, where he first pondered the Moravian doctrines, then met with the assembled villagers and admonished them to treat the

---

1. The title of this essay comes from John Heckewelder, *A Narrative of the Mission of the United Brethren Among the Delaware and Mohegan Indians, from its Commencement, in the Year 1740, to the Close in the Year, 1808* (Philadelphia: McCarthy and Davis, 1820; reprint, Arno Press and New York Times, 1971), 109.

2. Edmund De Schweinitz, *The Life and Times of David Zeisberger, the Western Pioneer and Apostle of the Indians* (Philadelphia: J. B. Lippincott and Co., 1870; reprint, New York: Arno Press, 1971), 355–56. Also see Earl P. Olmstead, *David Zeisberger: A Life Among the Indians* (Kent: Kent State University Press, 1997), 160–61.

missionaries well. According to Glikhikan, "that which we heard in Lawunakhannek today is the truth.... The brethren have the right doctrine and preach the right way to happiness.... Go out of your way to hear them.... If I lived here I would go and live with them at once."[3]

The Delawares at Goschgoschunk were amazed. This was Glikhikan (the Gunsight), a war chief who had led the Delawares in intertribal warfare, and who had fought with the French against the Redcoats. This was Glikhikan, who had risen during Pontiac's Rebellion to ravage the frontier in western Pennsylvania, who in 1763 had participated in the siege of Fort Pitt, and who had staunchly opposed the entrance of the British into western Pennsylvania.[4] This was Glikhikan, previously a staunch opponent of the Christian faith, a Munsee warrior who boasted of his adherence to the old ways, a man who by his own account had prayed to whip-poor-wills and who was much persuaded by "signs," dreams, and visions.[5] At Fort Venango he had denounced and argued with the Jesuits (no mean feat in itself), and in 1762 he and other Delaware leaders had warned Christopher Frederick Post, another Moravian missionary, to leave his new station on the Tuscarawas River, in northeastern Ohio.[6] Indeed, Glikhikan's very appearance at Lawunakhannek had been in response to a request by Wangomen, a shaman at Goschgoschunk, who opposed the Moravians as a threat to his own influence. Although early historians have described Wangomen and Glikhikan as "brothers," they probably were "cousins" within the Delawares' extended matrilineal kinship system, but regardless of their specific relationship, Wangomen obviously had expected his kinsman to mount a verbal attack against Zeisberger and his converts. Wangomen was sorely disappointed. Not only did Glikhikan advise the Delawares at Goschgoschunk

---

3. De Schweinitz, *Life and Times of Zeisberger*, 356–57; Olmstead, *David Zeisberger*, 161.

4. John Heckewelder, *History, Manners, and Customs of the Indian Nations Who Once Inhabited Pennsylvania and the Neighboring States* (Philadelphia: Pennsylvania State Historical Society, 1876; reprint, New York: Arno Press, 1971), 341–42 (revised from the original in 1819 by William C. Reichel); John Gottlieb Ernestus Heckewelder, *Thirty Thousand Miles with John Heckewelder*, ed. Paul A. W. Wallace (Pittsburgh: University of Pittsburgh Press, 1958), 94. Also see Gregory Evans Dowd, *War Under Heaven: Pontiac, the Indian Nations, and the British Empire* (Baltimore: Johns Hopkins University Press, 2002), 128–31; and Francis Parkman, *The Conspiracy of Pontiac* (New York: Collier Books, 1962), 272–89.

5. "Brother Ettwein's Account of His Visit in Lagunto-utenunk, on the Beaver Creek, and Welhik-Tuppek, on the Muskingum River, August 12–September 15, 1772," in Kenneth Gardiner Hamilton, *John Ettwein and the Moravian Church During the Revolutionary Period* (Bethlehem, Pa.: Times Publishing Company, 1940), 264–65.

6. Heckewelder, *Narrative of the Mission*, 60–64. Also see Elma E. Gray, *Wilderness Christians: The Moravian Mission to the Delaware Indians* (Ithaca: Cornell University Press, 1956), 46; and Olmstead, *David Zeisberger*, 107–9.

to listen to the Moravians, within months he would renounce his traditional religious beliefs and join the Moravian community.[7]

Who was this Delaware war chief who would play such an important role in the Moravian Delaware villages for the next thirteen years? Accounts of his life prior to his conversion are sketchy at best. A member of the Wolf phratry, he was born into the Munsee band of the Delaware tribe, probably about 1730. His father remains unknown, but since he traced his descent matrilineally, he would have been raised within a closely knit but extended network of his mother's relatives. Obviously Wagomen was a brother (or cousin), and he had at least one younger sister who, like his mother, also converted to the Moravian faith. His sister's name remains unknown, but his mother, given the Christian name "Cornelia," was converted by the Moravians in 1771. She died on June 20, 1773. At the time of his conversion, Glikhikan was married to a Mingo woman, given the Christian name "Agnes" after her baptism in 1771. Glikhikan may have been previously married, since at the time of his conversion he had at least two adult sons, Gutgigamen and Gulpiken, or Ludwig, who evidently had wives and children of their own. Yet Glikhikan also had stepchildren, and a son, Jonathan, who was born in January 1771. Agnes died on August 15, 1778, and nine months later Glikhikan married Anna Beninga, a Moravian Delaware widow who had children of her own. They produced one son, Martinus, born late the following December.[8]

Prior to his conversion, Glikhikan had achieved considerable status within the Delaware tribe. In 1769 he was serving as the primary advisor to Packanke, the village chief of Kaskaskakunk, a Munsee town at the junction of the Shenango and Mahoning rivers. Glikhikan served as the speaker in the village council at Kaskaskakunk and was well known throughout the Delaware Nation for his oratory. He also was known for his skill as a war chief. Although he became a pacifist following his conversion, before 1769 he had led Delaware war parties in raids against both tribal enemies and the British. Within this

---

7. Heckwelder, *Narrative of the Mission*, 104–10; De Schweinitz, *Life and Times of Zeisberger*, 354–56. Also see C. A. Weslager, *The Delaware Indians: A History* (New Brunswick: Rutgers University Press, 1972), 65–72; and Ives Goddard, "Delaware," in *Handbook of North American Indians*, ed. William C. Sturtevant, vol. 15, *Northeast*, ed. Bruce G. Trigger (Washington, D.C.: Smithsonian Institution, 1978), 225–26.

8. David Zeisberger, *The Moravian Mission Diaries of David Zeisberger, 1772–1781*, ed. Hermann Wellenreuther and Carola Wessel, trans. Julie Tomberlin Weber (University Park: Pennsylvania State University Press, 2005), 98 (June 27, 1772). See also ibid., 142 n. 201; 148 (June 30, 1773); 153 (August 20, 1773); 261 (March 13, 1775); 462 (August 16, 1778); 490 (January 23, 1779). See also "Agnes," "Anna Beninga," and "Isaac, alias Glikhikan," in "Register of Persons," ibid., 574, 575, 583.

venue, his reputation transcended tribal boundaries, for neighboring communities of Wyandots, Mingos, and Shawnees also were aware of his prowess, and even after his conversion many were reluctant to risk provoking his anger. Indeed, among the tribes of the upper Ohio Valley, Glikhikan was esteemed as one of the most formidable war chiefs of the Delaware Nation.[9]

Yet Glikhikan's exposure to Anthony, Zeisberger, and the Moravian community at Lawunakhannek dramatically changed his life. After urging the Delawares at Goschgoschunk to accept the Moravians, Glikhikan returned to his lodge at Kaskaskakunk, pondered the Moravian doctrines, and then met with Packanke and informed him that he planned to become a Christian. He also urged the chief to invite the Moravians to establish a mission near Kaskaskakunk. Packanke eventually agreed, and in August Glikhikan returned to Lawunakhannek, inviting Zeisberger to establish new missions, not only near Kaskaskakunk but also on the Tuscarawas River in eastern Ohio. He also informed Zeisberger, "I, for my part, intend to live with you and have already informed my friends that I want to hear the Gospel and to be converted."[10]

In April 1770 Zeisberger moved his mission from Lawunakhannek to a new site near Kaskaskakunk, on the Beaver River, and Glikhikan brought his family to reside in the Moravian settlement. Packanke at first welcomed the newcomers, but as the weeks passed he became alarmed as the Moravian influence among his followers seemed to increase. He blamed Glikhikan, and on June 19, 1770, his resentment boiled over. He complained to his council that although he had asked the Moravian Delawares to settle near his village, he had never invited Zeisberger or other white missionaries; they had been invited only by one of his "young and imprudent people." He then turned to Glikhikan and proclaimed, "You left our council and have gone to theirs. Are you hoping by any chance to get white skin there? Not even one of your feet will turn white.... Were you not a brave and honored man when you sat beside me in council? You despise all that now and think you have found something better, but as time goes on you will find you were deceived." Chagrined, Glikhikan rose and replied, "I have gone to them, and where they are I will stay.[11]

---

9. De Schweinitz, *Life and Times of Zeisberger*, 355; Heckewelder, *History, Manners, and Customs*, 341–42; Heckewelder, *Narrative of the Mission*, 186–91, 204–5; Consul Wilshire Butterfield, *History of the Girtys* (Cincinnati: Robert Clarke and Co., 1890), 102–4.

10. Reverend William H. Rice, D.D., *David Zeisberger and His Brown Brethren* (Bethlehem, Pa.: Moravian Publication Concern, 1908), 33–34; Olmstead, *David Zeisberger*, 162–63.

11. Olmstead, *David Zeisberger*, 168–72.

And stay he did. Glikhikan and ten members of his family remained within the Moravian camp, and six months later, on Christmas Eve 1770, Glikhikan, given the Christian name Isaac, was baptized into the Church of the United Brethren.[12]

Zeisberger soon put him to work. Zeisberger had been informed that several small villages of Moravian Delawares and Mahicans still residing on the Susquehanna River in eastern Pennsylvania wished to join with his converts, but he was reluctant to bring them to the Beaver River valley because Packanke's village seemed much addicted to alcohol. Glikhikan earlier had informed Zeisberger that Netawatwees, a powerful Delaware chief residing in Ohio, was willing to provide the Moravians with a site for new villages on the Tuscarawas River near his village. In March 1771 Glikhikan accompanied Zeisberger to Netawatwees's village and asked the chief for permission to resettle in Ohio. Netawatwees could offer no formal invitation without consulting other Delaware leaders, so the Moravians returned to Pennsylvania to await his reply.[13]

They found that the drinking in Packanke's village had increased. In response, early in 1772 Glikhikan informed Packanke that the Moravians wished to move, and to Glikhikan's surprise, Packanke produced a string of wampum and a message from Netawatwees inviting them (and the Moravian Delawares still living on the Susquehanna) to move to the Tuscarawas Valley. In March 1772 Glikhikan and Zeisberger returned to Ohio, where they selected a village site that they called Schönbrunn, on the Tuscarawas River, near modern Philadelphia. One month later, in mid-April, Glikhikan, Zeisberger, and most of the other Moravians on the Beaver River set out for the West. They arrived at Schönbrunn on May 3, 1772.[14]

Glikhikan and the other Moravians spent the summer clearing fields and erecting cabins. In August they were joined by part of the Moravian Delawares from the Susquehanna, and in September about forty Moravian Mahicans also arrived, but they formed a separate village, Gnadenhütten, about ten miles downstream from Schönbrunn. In August 1772 Glikhikan escorted John Ettwein, a Moravian missionary from Bethlehem, Pennsylvania, who was visiting Schönbrunn, to Netawatwees's village, and in October he accompanied Zeisberger to the Shawnee villages near modern Dresden, Ohio, where Glikhikan, fluent in

---

12. Ibid., 173; "Isaac," "Register of Persons," in Zeisberger, *Moravian Mission Diaries*, 583.
13. Olmstead, *David Zeisberger*, 172–77.
14. De Schweinitz, *Life and Times of Zeisberger*, 371–77; Zeisberger, *Moravian Mission Diaries*, 91–94 (April 14–May 3, 1772). See also Olmstead, *David Zeisberger*, 178–89.

Shawnee, joined with Zeisberger to preach the gospel. The Shawnees treated them amicably but rejected the Moravians' proselytism.[15]

During the following year Glikhikan assumed a major role as intermediary between the Moravian Delawares at Schönbrunn and Netawatwees's council. His outspoken support of the Moravians engendered resentment from some of Netawatwees's advisors, who accused him of now having "the heart and brain of a white man." In September 1773 he accompanied Zeisberger on another visit to the Shawnees, but this time they encountered Kishentsi, or Hardman, an outspoken opponent of Christianity, who readily admitted his animosity toward the British and who warned Zeisberger that if he proceeded on to the Shawnee villages along the Scioto River, warriors residing there would "knock out his brains." Again Glikhikan interceded for the missionary, and both Glikhikan and Zeisberger wisely returned to Schönbrunn.[16]

During the next year, Shawnee hostility toward the Americans boiled over. In 1774, as Pennsylvania and Virginia contested for hegemony over the region, Scots-Irish frontiersmen spilled into the upper Ohio Valley. The Shawnees struck back, triggering Dunmore's War. Glikhikan's role in this conflict was limited, although he did assist White Eyes, who served as Netawawees's primary counselor, in working to keep the non-Christian Delawares and Wyandots neutral in the conflict. He also used his influence to protect traders from Pennsylvania caught in the Indian country while the conflict raged.[17]

In 1775 Netawatwees decided to move his village to the juncture of the Tuscarawas and Walhonding rivers (the "forks of the Muskingum"), and Glikhikan assisted Netawatwees in laying out the new Delaware town, named Goschachgünk. In October he also accompanied White Eyes and other Delaware leaders to Pittsburgh, where they and other tribesmen met with colonial officials who attempted to persuade the Indians to remain neutral, should any armed

15. "Brother Ettwein's Account," 258–73; Zeisberger, *Moravian Mission Diaries*, 108–14 (October 12–15, 1772).

16. Zeisberger, *Moravian Mission Diaries*, 131 (February 23, 1773); 142–44 (June 1, 1773); 144–45 (June 7, 1773); 158 (September 8, 1773); 164–73 (*"Brief Report on Brother David Zeisberger's Journey to the Shawnee with the Indian Brothers Isaac and Wilhelm"*). See also John Sugden, *Blue Jacket: Warrior of the Shawnees* (Lincoln: University of Nebraska Press, 2000), 33, 39.

17. Lord Dunmore to the Earl of Dartmouth, December 24, 1774, in Reuben Gold Thwaites and Louise P. Kellogg, eds., *Documentary History of Dunmore's War* (Madison: State Historical Society of Wisconsin, 1905), 384; Paul A. W. Wallace, *Indians in Pennsylvania* (Harrisburg: Pennsylvania Historical and Museum Commission, 1961), 180. See also Zeisberger, *Moravian Mission Diaries*, 192 (May 10, 1774); 195–96 (May 20, 1774); 197 (May 23, 1774); 217–18 (July 17, 1774); 236–42 (November 5, 1774).

conflict erupt between the colonists and Britain. Glikhikan's role in these proceedings remains unknown, but as a Moravian pacifist he undoubtedly supported the American request. Most of the Delawares hoped to remain neutral, but the Shawnees, Mingos, and Wyandots gave only lip service to the American requests. The Shawnees and Mingos still smoldered over the loss of lives during Dunmore's War, while the Wyandots maintained close ties with British agents at Detroit. Their professions of neutrality were much more tenuous.[18]

In April 1776 Glikhikan, Zeisberger, John Heckewelder, and other Moravian Delawares, at Netawawees's request, established an additional mission station, Lichtenau, ("Pasture of Light"), just downstream from Goschachgünk, Netawatwees's new town, at the forks of the Muskingum. Glikhikan also served as an intermediary between the Moravians and White Eyes, a Delaware chief whose growing attachment to the Americans angered many Delawares and even seemed to annoy Zeisberger, since White Eyes had met with American officials and had requested that they send farmers, teachers, and other agents of acculturation (but not Moravian missionaries) into the Delaware villages. In the fall, Glikhikan and other Delawares, accompanied by some eastern Shawnees and Senecas, met again with the Americans at Pittsburgh, attempting to maintain the precarious peace in the upper Ohio Valley. Ominously, neither the Mingos nor the Wyandots attended the conference.[19]

The peace initiative failed. Throughout the autumn of 1776 war parties of Mingos, western Shawnees, and Wyandots passed through the Moravian towns en route to the American frontier, and although Glikhikan and other Delawares urged them to turn back, most of the parties continued. In November one war party of Mingos publicly denounced Glikhikan as "seduced by the Virginians," and during the early months of 1777 anti-American sentiment spread among the Shawnees and part of the Delawares, particularly among the Munsees, Glikhikan's old band. In response, during April and May 1777, Glikhikan and Thomas, another Moravian Delaware, journeyed first to the Wyandot villages at Sandusky, then on to Detroit, where they met with Lieutenant Governor Henry Hamilton, the British commander in the West. Glikhikan informed Hamilton that rumors of an impending Virginian expedition against Detroit were false and assured him that the Moravians wished only to remain neutral. Hamilton seemed to accept

18. Zeisberger, *Moravian Mission Diaries,* 264–66 (April 7, 1775); De Schweinitz, *Life and Times of Zeisberger,* 429–30; Olmstead, *David Zeisberger,* 236–44.
19. Zeisberger, *Moravian Mission Diaries,* 308–26 ("*Diary of the Construction and Progress in* Lichtenau *on the* Muskingum *from April 12th until* July 1776"); Olmstead, *David Zeisberger,* 247–57.

Glikhikan's explanation and treated the Moravians with kindness. Temporarily encouraged, Glikhikan returned to the Muskingum.[20]

But conditions continued to deteriorate. Rumors of a Mingo conspiracy to either capture or kill Zeisberger permeated the Indian camps, and many of the Munsees who had been living at Schönbrunn seemed to be implicated. The non-Christian Delaware suggested that most of the missionaries should return to Pennsylvania and that the Moravian Delawares should abandon their villages at Schönbrunn and Gnadenhütten and consolidate their communities at Lichtenau, the new village near the forks of the Muskingum. Most of the missionaries remained in Ohio, but the Moravian Delawares at Schönbrunn moved to Lichtenau. In contrast, the Mahican converts at Gnadenhütten remained in their village.[21]

During the late summer and fall of 1777, Lichtenau and the neighboring village of Goschachgünk were inundated with war parties en route to the American frontier. Glikhikan and other Moravian spokesmen again attempted to dissuade the warriors, but to no avail. Many of the pro-British Indians pressured the non-Moravian Delawares to also take up the hatchet, and advised the Moravians to relocate nearer to either Sandusky or Detroit. On August 8, 1777, Pomoacan, or the Half-King, the leading war chief of the Wyandots at Sandusky, arrived at Goschachgünk with a party of more than a hundred warriors, en route to attack American posts in modern-day West Virginia. The Half-King remained at the forks of the Muskingum for two weeks, while his war party was augmented by additional warriors from Detroit. Glikhikan met with the Wyandot and asked that his warriors not harm the missionaries, whom Glikhikan described as "not only our friends; we consider them our own flesh and blood." In response, the Half-King promised that the missionaries would be safe but requested provisions for his followers. The wary Moravians provided food for the huge war party (they had little choice), but Glikhikan remained apprehensive, particularly after some of the warriors swaggered and war-danced through the streets of the mission village.[22]

As 1777 drew to a close, political pressure on the Delawares increased. From Detroit, Lieutenant Governor Hamilton issued another "invitation" to the Moravians to relocate to Sandusky, while growing numbers of non-Moravian

---

20. Zeisberger, *Moravian Mission Diaries*, 341–43 (November 12, 1776); 363–65 (March 11–16, 1777); 370–71 (April 5, 1777); 374–78 (May 1–19, 1777).
21. Olmstead, *David Zeisberger*, 258–65.
22. De Schweinitz, *Life and Times of Zeisberger*, 455–57; Zeisberger, *Moravian Mission Diaries*, 395–404 (August 8–23, 1777).

Delawares edged toward a British alliance. In November, Cornstalk, a Shawnee chief still friendly to the Americans, was murdered by frontier riffraff on the Kanawha River. His death pushed most of the remaining Shawnees into the British camp. Three months later an American expedition from Pittsburgh in search of hostile supply camps attacked some isolated, and mostly abandoned, Delaware villages in the Cuyahoga Valley. They found neither supplies nor many warriors but killed one man and a handful of women and children. The Delaware warrior slain in this infamous "Squaw Campaign" was the brother of Captain Pipe, a Delaware chief who still supported peace, but who now also questioned his commitment to neutrality.[23]

In April 1778 Simon Girty, Matthew Elliott, and Alexander McKee, three influential Indian agents previously employed by the Americans, deserted to the Crown. En route to Detroit they passed through the forks of the Muskingum, where they falsely informed both the Moravian and non-Christian Delawares that the Americans were preparing to attack all their settlements. In response, Glikhikan and White Eyes hurried to Pittsburgh, while the Moravian Mahicans at Gnadenhütten temporarily abandoned their village and moved to Lichtenau. At Pittsburgh American officials assured Glikhikan and White Eyes that the deserters had lied and that the Delaware villages were safe from any incursions. Yet conditions continued to deteriorate. Additional pro-British war parties from Sandusky and Detroit continued to pass through the Moravian camps, and during the summer of 1778 they were joined by Munsee warriors, now led, ironically, by apostate Moravians such as Newallike and Gendaskund.[24]

In August 1778 White Eyes, Captain Pipe, and Gelelemind journeyed to Pittsburgh and were either convinced or tricked into signing a questionable treaty with the Americans. In the treaty, the Delaware chiefs supposedly pledged that their tribe would relinquish neutrality and form a military alliance with the Americans. Historians still argue over whether the treaty was altered after the Delaware chiefs made their marks on it, but the agreement also stipulated that the Americans would build a new fort within the Delaware lands to protect Delaware women and children while "their warriors are engaged against a

---

23. Zeisberger, *Moravian Mission Diaries*, 411–12 (September 24, 1777); 416–17 (October 13, 1777); 422 (December 3, 1777); George Morgan to the Board of War, July 17, 1778, in Louise Phelps Kellogg, ed., *Frontier Advance on the Upper Ohio, 1778–1779*, vol. 23 of *Collections of the State Historical Society of Wisconsin* (Madison: The Society, 1916), 112–13. Also see Jack M. Sosin, *The Revolutionary Frontier, 1763–1783* (New York: Holt, Rinehart and Winston, 1967), 111.

24. Zeisberger, *Moravian Mission Diaries*, 440–42 (April 1–6, 1778); 445–48 (April 21–May 2, 1778); 451 (June 4, 1778); 454–55 (July 2, 1788). See also Reginald Horsman, *Matthew Elliott, British Indian Agent* (Detroit: Wayne State University Press, 1964), 18–24.

common enemy." In response, in November 1778 the Americans erected Fort Laurens, a small post on the Tuscarawas, but they had neither the men nor the logistical support to maintain the post, and it was abandoned nine months later.[25]

The Delawares' tenuous ties to the Americans continued to unravel. After defecting to the British, Girty, Elliott, and McKee confirmed that indeed the Moravians were passing intelligence of approaching war parties along to the Americans. In response, Hamilton increased his demands that the Moravians withdraw toward Detroit. In addition, in November 1778 White Eyes died, ostensibly from smallpox, although there is some evidence to suggest that he may have been murdered by an American militiaman. With his passing, the foremost champion of Delaware cooperation with the Americans was gone. And finally, since the Americans were so desperately short of supplies and could not furnish the Delawares, the latter grew more dependent on British traders from Detroit and Sandusky.[26]

Glikhikan took little part in these events, but he participated in the aftermath. In February the Wyandots surrounded Fort Laurens and Glikhikan risked his life to gather information about the siege. Meanwhile, hostility against the Moravian missionaries had so increased at Goschachgünk that Zeisberger felt his life was threatened. In April 1779 he led part of the Delaware and Mahican converts back to their former villages at Schönbrunn and Gnadenhütten. Although Glikhikan was now a pacifist, his former reputation as a warrior still garnered considerable respect, so he remained behind to protect and intercede for Heckewelder and those Moravians still residing at Lichtenau. He also escorted Zeisberger and other missionaries as they journeyed between the missions.[27]

In April 1780, however, Glikhikan, Heckewelder, and the Moravians remaining at Lichtenau abandoned the mission and moved to Salem, a new village/mission about five miles downstream from Gnadenhütten. The move was overdue. The Moravians had become convinced that Goschachgünk, the neighboring Delaware village, would soon be attacked, either by the Wyandots at Sandusky,

---

25. "Negotiations with the Delawares, September 12–19, 1778," in Kellogg, *Frontier Advance on the Upper Ohio*, 138–45; "Recollections of Stephen Burkam," ibid., 157; "Recollections of John Cuppy," ibid., 158–61; "Speech by Lachlan McIntosh," November 22, 1778, ibid., 178–80.

26. Heckewelder to John Gibson, March 19, 1779, ibid., 258–260; Heckewelder to Daniel Broadhead, April 9, 1779, ibid., 282–83; Heckewelder to Broadhead, June 30, 1779, in *Pennsylvania Archives, First Series*, 12 vols. (Philadelphia: Joseph Severns and Co., 1853), 7:524–26. See also Zeisberger, *Moravian Mission Diaries*, 481 (November 20, 1778); and Olmstead, *David Zeisberger*, 289–93.

27. Zeisberger, *Moravian Mission Diaries*, 497–98 (February 22–March 1, 1779); 503 (April 6, 1779); 506–7 (June 6, 1779). See also Butterfield, *History of the Girtys*, 98–104, and Heckewelder, *Narrative of the Mission*, 204–6.

who believed that Indians in the village were assisting the Americans, or by the Americans themselves, who now suspected that the town had become a new staging point for raids against the frontier. With the exception of the Moravians, any pretense of Delaware neutrality, long a precarious policy, had ended.[28]

The Moravian withdrawal from Lichtenau came none too soon. Convinced that the forks of the Muskingum had become a hotbed of pro-British intrigue, Colonel Daniel Broadhead and an expedition of 150 men attacked and destroyed Goschachgünk on April 20, 1781. They also burned the abandoned Moravian village at Lichtenau. Before retreating back to Pittsburgh, Broadhead met with Zeisberger and tried to persuade the missionary to move his missions closer to Pittsburgh, but Zeisberger, justifiably wary of American militiamen in the region, wisely refused.[29]

Glikhikan and the Moravians were soon visited by emissaries from the opposite camp. In May 1781 Pachgantshihlas, a prominent Delaware war chief from a village on the Sandusky, visited the Moravian settlements and asked the converts to resettle near his village "to live in peace and safety; where no Long Knife shall ever molest you." Glikhikan, an old friend of Pachgantshihlas, escorted him through the Moravian villages, but the missionaries and converts, still advocating neutrality, declined his offer.[30]

Pachgantshihlas was soon followed by more persuasive guests. At four in the afternoon on August 10, 1781, Matthew Elliott, the Half-King, Captain Pipe (now gone over to the British), and about 150 Indians arrived at Salem and informed the Moravians that they had something important to tell them. Formal speeches began on August 13, at Gnadenhütten, and it soon became apparent that the British Indians would first request, then force (if necessary) the Moravians to abandon their homes on the Tuscarawas and move to the Sandusky River. Both Zeisberger and Heckewelder stalled for time, asking if the Moravians might wait until the following spring, since they had planted extensive fields of corn that they wished to harvest before leaving. The missionaries' procrastination angered some of the British Indians, and on September 3 they began to

---

28. Zeisberger, *Moravian Mission Diaries*, 524 (March 29, 1780); 525 (April 18, 1780); 529 (June 17, 1780); 538 (September 8, 1780). See also Daniel Broadhead to George Washington, March 18, 1780, 150–51; Broadhead to Zeisberger, March 22, 1780, 156; Killbuck to Broadhead, July 19, 1780, 217–20; Broadhead to David Shepherd, September 17, 1780, 275–76, all in Louise Phelps Kellogg, ed., *Frontier Retreat on the Upper Ohio, 1779–1781*, vol. 24 of *Collections of the State Historical Society of Wisconsin* (Madison: The Society, 1917).

29. Heckewelder, *Thirty Thousand Miles*, 163–64; Olmstead, *David Zeisberger*, 308. Also see Broadhead to Joseph Reed, May 22, 1781, in Kellogg, *Frontier Retreat on the Upper Ohio*, 399.

30. Heckewelder, *Narrative of the Mission*, 216–24; Heckewelder, *Thirty Thousand Miles*, 165–67.

loot the missionaries' homes and kill their livestock. During the afternoon, Wyandot warriors seized and stripped Heckewelder, Zeisberger, and two other missionaries, before turning them over to Matthew Elliott.[31]

On the following day a Delaware woman stole Captain Pipe's horse and fled toward Pittsburgh, ostensibly to seek assistance from the Americans. Since the woman was a relative of Glikhikan, Delawares loyal to Captain Pipe blamed Glikhikan for the escape, "sent a war party to Salem, brought him bound to Gnadenhütten, yelled out over him the Death Hallow," and threatened to put him to death. True to his Moravian precepts, Glikhikan refused to defend himself physically. Fortunately, however, the Half-King interceded, and Glikhikan was found to have no part in the woman's flight. Yet the die was cast. On September 11 the missionaries, their families, Glikhikan, and the Moravian Delawares were forced to abandon their village and trek westward toward Sandusky.[32]

They arrived at Sandusky on October 1, 1781. They were desperately short of food. Although they had driven some of their cattle to Sandusky with them, the British Indians had slaughtered most of their swine and poultry, and their corn crop still stood in the fields along the Tuscarawas. The Half-King had promised them assistance at Salem, but on October 10 the Wyandot chief learned that two of his sons had been killed fighting the Americans near Pittsburgh, and he blamed the Moravians. Late in October, Zeisberger, Heckewelder, and several other missionaries and Moravian Delawares were summoned to Detroit, where they were questioned and found innocent of treason by Major Arent De Peyster, Hamilton's successor. Glikhikan did not accompany the delegation. Now considered Zeisberger's "most trusted lieutenant," Glikhikan remained behind to help the other missionaries "guard the mission."[33]

During the winter of 1781–82, the Moravians' food shortage worsened. In late November a small party of Moravian Delawares returned to their old fields along the Tuscarawas and harvested some of the corn, but they could not carry a sufficient amount to feed the three hundred inhabitants of Captivetown, their new settlement on the Sandusky. In mid-December Glikhikan led a small

---

31. Heckewelder, *Thirty Thousand Miles*, 170–76; Horsman, *Matthew Elliott*, 31–34.
32. David Zeisberger, *The Diary of David Zeisberger, a Moravian Missionary Among the Indians of Ohio, 1781–1791*, ed. and trans. Eugene F. Bliss, 2 vols. (Cincinnati: Robert Clarke and Co., 1885), 1:14–15 (September 4, 1781); De Schweinitz, *Life and Times of Zeisberger*, 510–11; Olmstead, *David Zeisberger*, 314–16.
33. Zeisberger, *Diary of Zeisberger*, 1:29 (October 1, 1781); 1:22 (October 10, 1781); 1:29 (October 25, 1781). See also "Minutes of an Indian Council at Detroit, November 9, 1781," and "Minutes of an Indian Council at Detroit, December 11, 1781," both in *Collections of the Michigan Pioneer and Historical Society*, 40 vols. (Lansing: Thorp and Godfrey, 1874–1929), 10:538–41 and 10:544–46, respectively.

party to the Shawnee villages on the upper Scioto, where additional corn was purchased, but food supplies remained inadequate. Other parties returned to old corn fields along the Tuscarawas, but after one of these groups was captured by American militiamen who carried them to Pittsburgh, these foraging parties were discontinued. By late January many of their cattle had died, and Glikhikan and other Moravians were forced to forage in the surrounding forests for roots and dried berries.[34]

On February 2, 1782, several Moravian Delawares taken captive by the militia in November, and then released from Pittsburgh, arrived at Captivetown. Eager to learn of events at Pittsburgh, the Half-King hurried to the Moravian settlement, where tribal protocol demanded that he and his followers be fed. But when he arrived, Glikhikan, frustrated over the Moravians' food shortage, lashed out at the Wyandot, reminding him of how hospitable the Moravians had always been to the Wyandots and other Indians who had visited their villages on the Tuscarawas, and reminding him of his promises to feed the Moravians if they relocated to Sandusky. "You have brought us to another, but not a better land," Glikhikan told him. "It is a miserable country: and you have not offered us one single grain of corn. We suffer; you rejoice. We are perishing because you have triumphed over us." Taken aback, the Half-King returned to his village.[35]

Yet the Indians who arrived from Pittsburgh also carried what seemed to be good news. They reported that animosity toward the Moravian Delawares appeared to have diminished, and that the refugees at Captivetown could now safely return to the Tuscarawas to harvest the remainder of the corn still standing in the fields. Facing starvation, the Moravians had little choice. In mid-March several parties left for the Tuscarawas, while others journeyed to the Shawnee villages, seeking additional foodstuffs.[36]

Late in February Glikhikan led a small party of converts, including many of his family, back to their old homes, where they joined with other small groups to harvest the corn standing near Salem, Gnadenhütten, and New Schönbrunn. By the first week in March the converts had divided into three parties of about fifty persons each, with Glikhikan and his family laboring in the fields near Salem. On March 4 a party of British Indians passed through Salem and warned the Moravians that they had killed and mutilated several settlers in Virginia and that they

---

34. Zeisberger, *Diary of Zeisberger*, 46–47 (November 22, 1781); 51–53 (December 23, 1781); 60–61 (January 10, 1782); 62–63 (January 23, 1782); 63 (January 30, 1782).
35. Ibid., 64 (February 2, 1782), and 64–65 (February 4, 1782); De Schweinitz, *Life and Times of Zeisberger*, 531–32.
36. Zeisberger, *Diary of Zeisberger*, 66 (February 9 and February 13, 1782); 69–70 (March 3, 1782).

feared that were being followed by militia units, but the Moravians believed that they were exempt from any blame and continued with their harvest.[37]

They should have heeded the warnings. In February several war parties from the Sandusky region had struck the Pittsburgh frontier, and settlers wanted revenge. Many settlers believed that the war parties continually passed through the old Moravian towns, and they decided to destroy the villages. On March 7 about 160 militiamen commanded by Lieutenant Colonel David Williamson descended upon Gnadenhütten, where they first killed three Indians in the forest, then surprised Indians working in the village. The Americans deceptively assured them that they meant no harm and only intended to escort them safely to Pittsburgh. John Martin, a Delaware convert, then rode to Salem, informing Glikhikan and the Moravians there of the Americans' arrival. He was followed by a small party of militiamen who assured Glikhikan and his companions that if they would join their fellow Moravians at Gnadenhütten, they also would be taken to Pittsburgh and provided with food. The Indians at Salem agreed, and as they were escorted to Gnadenhütten, Glikhikan and Israel, another convert, amicably discussed politics and religion with the militiamen.[38]

Upon their arrival in Gnadenhütten, the nature of the conversation changed. Glikhikan and the other converts were disarmed, and along with the other assembled Moravians were accused of attacking the frontiers and providing military assistance to the British Indians. The Americans also seized all of the Indians' property, which they accused them of stealing from the settlements. After some deliberation, the militiamen condemned the Moravians to death, then debated among themselves over the proper method of execution. Glikhikan and other Moravian leaders pleaded for justice, but their requests were ignored. Finally they asked for several hours to compose themselves before their death, and to this "last request" the militiamen agreed. The Indians spent the night in prayers and hymns, but at dawn on March 8, 1782, they were separated into two groups, men and older boys in one, women and children in another. They then were conducted, two by two, into two separate houses (one for the men, the other for the women), where their brains were beaten out by two militiamen wielding a heavy cooper's mallet.[39]

---

37. Heckewelder, *Thirty Thousand Miles*, 189–93; *True History of the Massacre of Ninety-Six Christian Indians at Gnadenhutten, Ohio, March 8th, 1782* (New Philadelphia, Ohio: Ohio Democrat, 1870), 6.
38. Heckewelder, *Thirty Thousand Miles*, 191–93; Olmstead, *David Zeisberger*, 330–33; *True History of the Massacre*, 6–8; Heckewelder, *Narrative of the Mission*, 312–17.
39. Heckewelder, *Thirty Thousand Miles*, 193–95; *True History of the Massacre*, 9–10.

When the slaughter ended, Isaac Glikhikan, his wife Anna Begnina, and several of Glikhikan's family members lay massacred among the ninety dead Moravian Delawares and six non-Moravian Delawares murdered by the Pennsylvanians. Two teenage boys also were beaten and scalped but somehow survived, feigned death, then crawled away after the slaughter ended. They later made their way back to Captivetown and related news of these gruesome events to Zeisberger. Fortunately, the Indians who had been gathering corn at New Schönbrunn also escaped the slaughter, since they learned of the attack and retreated back toward Captivetown before the militia arrived at that location.[40]

Thus fell Glikhikan, former war chief and champion of the Delawares, "National Helper" and "Native Elder" of the Moravian faith, and, in the words of John Heckewelder, "this much admired man . . . ready and fearless in time of danger . . . faithful to his teachers," and, perhaps most important, "a true Christian."[41]

Heckewelder's characterization may be the most significant. During the past three decades, historians of the Native American experience have argued repeatedly about the validity of Native American conversions. Some scholars, such as James Axtell, have asserted that the conversions were real, that they "bought the entire package." Axtell argues that Native Americans who accepted Christianity "were receptive to the solutions offered by the new religion and were capable of taking the decisive step away from their old religions to the new, without deceiving themselves, the missionaries, or us." According to Axtell, Christianity "satisfied new emotional needs and hunger" in a world grown increasingly chaotic to them.[42]

By contrast, Francis Jennings, Neal Salisbury, and others have questioned both the success and the sincerity of the conversions. Salisbury has argued that Native American converts to Protestant Christianity rarely accepted all the tenets of the Protestant sects and sought "to invest the imposed religion with traditional meaning." David Blanchard claims that Mohawk converts of the Jesuits were more interested in trade than in religion, and that in accepting Catholicism they simply "modified their religious practices and developed a

---

40. Zeisberger, *Diary of Zeisberger*, 73 (March 14, 1782), and 78–82 (March 23, 1782); *True History of the Massacre*, 10–12; Heckewelder, *Narrative of the Mission*, 320–26; Olmstead, *David Zeisberger*, 333–34.
41. Heckewelder, *Narrative of the Mission*, 109, 321.
42. James Axtell, "Were Indian Conversions Bona Fide?" in *After Columbus: Essays in the Ethnohistory of Colonial North America*, ed. James Axtell (New York: Oxford University Press, 1988), 100, 120, and passim.

syncretistic system of ritual that yielded the desired effect," while Nancy Shoemaker asserts that if the Jesuits attempted to "recast Indian societies in their own image, . . . it was the Indians themselves who selected which aspects of Christianity and European society they would accept."[43]

There is considerable evidence to support the last two arguments summarized in the preceding two paragraphs, and I generally agree with scholars who argue that Native Americans usually interpreted Christianity within the parameters of their own cultures rather than those of Euro-Americans. But in the case of Isaac Glikhikan, the opposite interpretation seems more valid. Glikhikan's acceptance of Moravian Christianity offers an excellent case study of what seems to have been a true conversion. For a war chief of Glikhikan's stature to renounce his former way of life completely and embrace the Moravians is reminiscent of Paul's conversion on the road to Damascus. The final decade of Glikhikan's life, his devotion and service to the Moravian cause, and his adherence to pacifism even in the face of death, bears vivid testimony to his sincerity. Glikhikan's conversion was indisputably real. John Heckewelder's telling epitaph hits the mark: Isaac Glikhikan was indeed a much-admired man, a stalwart member of the Moravian faith, and "a true Christian."[44]

---

43. Francis Jennings, *The Invasion of America: Indians, Colonialism and the Cant of Conquest* (Chapel Hill: University of North Carolina Press, 1975), 228–53; Neal Salisbury, "Red Puritans: The Praying Indians of Massachusetts Bay and John Elliot," *William and Mary Quarterly*, 3d ser., 31 (1974): 27–54; David Blanchard ". . . To the Other Side of the Sky: Catholicism at Kahnawahke, 1667–1700," *Anthropoligica* 24 (1982): 77–102; Nancy Shoemaker, "Kateri Tekakwitha: Servant of God, Seeker of Orenda," in *True Stories from the American Past*, vol. 1, ed. Altina Waller and William Graebner (Boston: McGraw Hill, 2003), 18.

44. Heckewelder, *Narrative of the Mission*, 109, 321.

I.

Texts and Interpretive Perspectives

Moravians and the Development of the Genre of Ethnography

CHRISTIAN F. FEEST

The voluminous histories of the missionary efforts of the United Brethren in Greenland, the Caribbean islands of St. Thomas, St. Croix, and St. Jan, and among the Indians of northeastern North America, written by David Cranz, Christian Georg Andreas Oldendorp, and Georg Heinrich Loskiel and published between 1765 and 1789, also constitute an important body of ethnographic writing during the same period that saw the emergence of ethnography and ethnology as a distinctive and named field of discourse. David Zeisberger's untitled manuscript, published 130 years after its original composition in what in hindsight must be regarded as an unsatisfactory translation under the title *History of the Northern American Indians*,[1] represents a major contribution to this effort inasmuch as it formed the basis for the ethnographic first part of Loskiel's *Geschichte*, a book itself widely distributed in a contemporary English translation.[2] In this chapter I attempt to place these Moravian writings in the context of the history of ethnographic writing, and specifically to look at David Zeisberger as an ethnographer.

Early modern ethnographic writing emerged in the context of the Renaissance distinction between the genres of *historia*, encompassing not only historiography but also the recording of empirical facts in general, and *scientia* as systematically delineated knowledge, at a time when the primarily spiritual goals of traveling (such as the pilgrimage) of the Middle Ages gave way to secular concerns (such as the collection and compilation of data for a better understanding of the world). The diary, combining the purposes of bookkeeping and self-observation,

---

1. Archer Butler Hulbert and William Nathaniel Schwarze, eds., *David Zeisberger's History of the Northern American Indians* (Columbus, Ohio: F. J. Heer, 1910).
2. Georg Heinrich Loskiel, *Geschichte der Mission der evangelischen Brüder unter den Indianern in Nordamerika* (Barby: Brüdergemeine, 1789), reprinted in *Nikolaus Ludwig von Zinzendorf, Materialien und Dokumente*, ed. Erich Beyreuther, series 2, 32 vols. (Hildesheim: Georg Olms Verlag, 1971–2002), vol. 21.

provided a chronological order of the observational data, which for the traveler also recorded his progress through space. The rise of the printing press promoted the new goals of socialization and integration of knowledge.

For the development of ethnographic writing, the rediscovery of ancient authors, notably of Herodot and Tacitus (but also of Arab scholars), supplied models for the systematic descriptions of cultural otherness. Cosmographies and statistical works reflecting the theory of states and government in the Aristotelian sense described the world according to kingdoms and republics. Such attempts were promoted by the humanists' project to systematize and generalize the previously private, oral advice to travelers in public, written form, which reached its first culmination in what became known as apodemic literature (dealing with the art of traveling). Written by Ramist authors of the second half of the sixteenth century, this literature set the stage for the publication until the late eighteenth century of hundreds of books advising travelers on how to derive the greatest profit from their experiences. In addition to practical advice for travelers, these works contained numerous methodological suggestions on note taking as a means of replacing orality and memory with literacy and method, such as copying from written sources, making drawings, and collecting artificial and natural curiosities. Perhaps the most important advice to travelers was to sit down at the end of the day and copy data taken from the chronological observational record into a commonplace book, in which the data were rearranged under categorical headings ("loci communes") to establish an order independent of the haphazard nature of observation. This method, which Justin Stagl in his *History of Curiosity* has suggestively linked to the rise of double-entry bookkeeping in Venice in the late fifteenth century, created a distinction between narration and description, between the chronological diary and a detemporalized synchronistic summary, and in a way prefigured the distinction between agency and structure.[3]

The early travel literature on the Americas, which played an important role in the practical application of these models, clearly reflects these trends. By the seventeenth century the distinction between what Gordon Sayre refers to as the "exploration narrative" and the "ethnography" was fully developed.[4] "Exploration narratives" or "historical narratives" (including other event-driven writings, such as the Jesuit relations, and often taking the form of diaries or of a series of

---

3. Justin Stagl, *A History of Curiosity: The Theory of Travel, 1550–1800* (Chur: Harwood Academic Publishers, 1995).

4. Gordon M. Sayre, *Les Sauvages Americans: Representations of Native Americans in French and English Colonial Literature* (Chapel Hill: University of North Carolina Press, 1997).

letters) stressed the exemplary, particular nature of the subjective experience under the continuous conditions of linear time and space, which also served to authenticate the contents of the narration; "ethnographies" (an anachronistic term for a genre that made its appearance long before the invention of the term) were based on the discontinuity of categorical order with its attendant decontextualization and dehistorization. The problem with categorical generalization is obviously that the categories chosen may not really be adequate to describe cultural otherness, but rather tend to assimilate the Other to or contrast it with the Self. This problem, however, also affects the exploration narrative, which equally has to make use of culturally constituted concepts for merely descriptive purposes. Thus the distinction between the empirical and generalization should not be seen as reflecting the difference between facts and assumptions, because the description of "facts" is equally based upon concepts existing prior to observation.

Some of the most successful travel writings combine the two genres. Captain John Smith's classificatory *Map of Virginia, With a Description of the Countrey, the Commodities, People, Government and Religion* was published together with the chronological narrative of the *Proceedings of the English Colony*.[5] As a systematic representation of both natural history and ethnography, the first part follows the precedent set by the Jesuit José de Acosta in his *Historia natural y moral de las Indias*,[6] perhaps the single most influential work of the late sixteenth century for the development of ethnographic writing.[7] Nearly a hundred years later, Baron de Lahontan's *Nouveaux Voyages*[8] featured in its first volume, written as a series of letters, "the several Attempts of the English and French to dispossess one another; with the Reasons of the Miscarriage of the former; and the various Adventures between the French, and the Iroquese Confederates of England, from 1683 to 1694," whereas the second volume, subdivided by categorical headings, presented "a full Account of the Customs, Commerce, Religion, and strange Opinions of the Savages of that Country," and included such broadly generalizing statements

---

5. John Smith, *A Map of Virginia, with a Description of the Countrey, the Commodities, People, Government and Religion* (Oxford: Joseph Barnes, 1612). A modern critical edition is in *The Complete Works of Captain John Smith*, ed. P. L. Barbour, 3 vols. (Chapel Hill: University of North Carolina Press, 1986), 1:121–289.

6. José de Acosta, *Historia natural y moral de las Indias, en que se tratan las cosas notables del cielo, y elementos, metales, plantas, y animales delias; y los ritos, y ceremonias, leyes, y govierno, y guerras de los Indios* (Seville, 1590).

7. See Anthony Pagden, *The Fall of Natural Man: The American Indian and the Origins of Comparative Ethnology* (Cambridge: Cambridge University Press, 1982).

8. Louis Armand de Lom d'Arce, Baron de Lahontan, *Nouveaux Voyages de Mr. le Baron de Lahontan dans l'Amerique Septentrionale* (La Haye: Les Frères Honore, 1703).

as: "All the Savages are of a Sanguine Constitution, inclining to an Olive Colour, and generally speaking they have good Faces and proper Persons."[9] That neither Smith nor Lahontan found it necessary to explain the need for or usefulness of generalized descriptions illustrates the extent to which the genre of ethnographic writing had already been established.

While "pure" travel narratives continued to be written throughout the seventeenth century, "pure" ethnographies were the exception. This is one reason why Roger Williams's *Key into the Language of America* is of such outstanding importance in the history of the genre. In his introduction, Williams refers both to the process of writing the book and to its purpose, and in both cases his statements illustrate the method of generalization from personal observation and the goal of socializing knowledge: "I drew the Materialls in a rude lumpe at Sea, as a private helpe to my owne memory, that I might by my present absence lightly lose what I had so dearely bought in some yeares hardship, and charges among the Barbarians; yet being reminded by some, what pitie it were to bury those Materialls in my Grave at land or Sea; and withal, remembering how oft I have been importun'd by worthy friends, of all sorts, to afford them some helps this way."[10] Besides his heavy reliance on native language and dialogue, another distinctive feature of Williams's ethnography is his meticulous subdivision into thirty-two chapters, from "Of Salutation" to "Of their Death and Buriall." By contrast, Smith uses just six subheadings following a general topographic description: "Of such things which are naturall in Virginia and how they use them," "The Planted fruits in Virginia and how they use them," "The commodities in Virginia or that may be had by industrie," "Of the naturall Inhabitants of Virginia," "Of their Religion," and "Of the manner of the Virginians government." Lahontan has ten "discourses," some of them as broadly conceived as "Of the Habit, Houses, Complexion and Temperament of the Savages of North America," and some as specific as "A View of the Heraldry, or the Coast of Arms of the Savages" and "An Explication of the Savage Hieroglyphicks."

As important in the first half of the eighteenth century as Williams was in the seventeenth was the Jesuit father Joseph François Lafitau, whose *Mœurs des sauvages ameriquains, comparées aux moeurs des premiers temps* is not so much

---

9. Louis Armand de Lom d'Arce, Baron de Lahontan, *New Voyages to North-America*, ed. Reuben Gold Thwaites, 2 vols. (Chicago: A. C. McClurg, 1905), 2:415.

10. Roger Williams, *A Key into the Language of America, Or, an Help to the Language of the Natives in that part of America, called New-England* (London: Gregory Dexter, 1643), 83. Modern edition edited by J. J. Teunissen and E. J. Hinz (Detroit: Wayne State University Press, 1973).

an ethnography as a work of comparative ethnology.[11] He uses the "ethnographic" mode of representation for compiling data relating to broad cultural categories, such as "Religion," "Political Government," "Marriage and Education," and "Warfare," in order to compare and mutually interpret the customs of American Indians and the peoples of European antiquity. Although Lafitau had spent several years as a missionary among the Mohawk of Kahnawake near Montreal, he generalizes information on many different indigenous peoples of the New World, on the assumption that "it can be said nevertheless, that the customs of the Indians in general are rather similar to theirs [i.e., those of the Iroquois]."[12] By drawing upon a multitude of sources, especially of the seventeenth century, Lafitau constructs "Indians" who are both generic and untainted by European influences such as his own missionary labors.[13]

Another development of the eighteenth century was the increasing use of questionnaires for eliciting standardized ethnographic information, mostly in connection with systematic exploration. While the Royal Society of London had already prepared such a questionnaire in the 1680s, the practice found its earliest culmination in the instructions for the second Kamchatka expedition of the 1730s and 1740s, compiled for the Academy of Sciences in St. Petersburg by Gerhard Friedrich Müller.[14] Beginning with a ten-item checklist written in 1732 and entitled "De historia gentium," Müller gradually enlarged his checklist to an instruction consisting of six parts, the last of which related to the "Description of peoples," which was made up of no fewer than 923 items to be investigated. It is obvious that such instructions—precursors of those designed by Lewis Cass and improved by Henry Rowe Schoolcraft in the first half of the nineteenth century to collect data on American Indian history and traditions—were designed to improve not only the quality of ethnographic descriptions but also that of the comparative approach pioneered by Lafitau. Although his Russian employers kept a lid on these instructions (as well as on the results of the expedition), they not only

---

11. Joseph François Lafitau, *Mœurs des sauvages ameriquains, comparées aux moeurs des premiers temps,* 2 vols. (Paris: Saugrain l'ainé, 1724).

12. Joseph François Lafitau, *Customs of the American Indians Compared with the Customs of Primitive Times,* ed. and trans. W. N. Fenton and E. L. Moore, 2 vols. (Toronto: Champlain Society, 1974–77), 1:41.

13. See Christian F. Feest, "Father Lafitau as Ethnographer of the Iroquois," *European Review of Native American Studies* 15, no. 2 (2001): 19–25.

14. Gudrun Bucher, *"Von Beschreibung der Sitten und Gebrauche der Völcker": Die Instruktionen Gerhard Friedrich Müllers und ihre Bedeutung für die Geschichte der Ethnologie und der Geschichtswissenschaft* (Stuttgart: F. Steiner, 2002).

preceded and paralleled similar efforts undertaken in the course of the Enlightenment in western Europe but also, unexpectedly, had a direct impact on the German discourse about cultural otherness, particularly in Göttingen.

It has been known for some time that the words "Ethnographie" (ethnography) and "Völkerkunde" (ethnology) made their first appearance shortly after 1770 in Göttingen in the writings of such historians as August Ludwig Schlözer and Johann Christoph Gatterer.[15] It can now be shown that Schlözer brought the ideas underlying these terms from St. Petersburg, where he had served as educator of Müller's children.[16]

The terms "ethnography" and "ethnology" clearly demarcated a previously unnamed subject matter, although the lack of formal training in this field prevented the formulation of clearly defined methodologies. The active participation of naturalists in the voyages of the Enlightenment and in the creation of ethnographic collections within natural history cabinets, however, increased an already existing influence of natural history and in particular of its dominant Linnean taxonomic paradigm, through which specific peoples (also called "nations" or "races") became the taxa to be described and classified on the basis of written and visual records as well as of artifacts representing their specific character.

This is the context in which we have to look at the achievements of the Moravian authors of the late eighteenth century, in particular David Zeisberger.

David Cranz's *Historie von Grönland* was the first of a series of books detailing the missionary labors of the Brethren, all of which followed the now classic division of the text into "ethnography" and "historical narrative." Cranz had been closely associated with Count Zinzendorf from the age of eighteen until the latter's death in 1760, and Zinzendorf had himself requested that Cranz should go to Greenland in preparation of the proposed book. Cranz spent a full year, from August 1761 to September 1762, visiting the Moravian mission stations in Greenland and associating with their Inuit converts.[17] Of the 1,312 pages of the volume published in 1765, 304 are devoted to a topographic and ethnographic account divided into three books, the first two of which describe the country and its natural resources, whereas the third, numbering 127 pages,

---

15. Han F. Vermeulen, "Frühe Geschichte der Völkerkunde oder Ethnographie in Deutschland, 1771–1791," in *Völkerkunde-Tagung 1991*, ed. M. S. Laubscher and Bertram Turner, 2 vols. (Munich: Akademie-Verlag, 1991), 1:329–44; Han F. Vermeulen, "Origins and Institutionalization of Ethnography and Ethnology in Europe and the USA, 1771–1845," in *Fieldwork and Footnotes: Studies in the History of European Anthropology*, ed. George Stocking (London: Routledge, 1995).

16. Stagl, *History of Curiosity*; Bucher, "Von Beschreibung der Sitten und Gebrauche der Völcker."

17. Erich Beyreuther, "Einführung," in Beyreuther, *Nikolaus Ludwig von Zinzendorf, Materialen und Dokumente*, series 2, 25:1–2 (Hildesheim: Georg Olms Verlag, 1995), 7*–41*.

is devoted to an ethnography entitled "Of the Greenlandic Nation" and is subdivided into six chapters: "Of their figure and way of life," "Of the behavior of the Greenlanders in their domestic affairs," "Of the behavior of the Greenlanders in society," "Of the moral behavior of the Greenlanders," "Of the religion or rather superstition of the Greenlanders," and "Of the sciences of the Greenlanders" (including an account of their language). The ethnographic section is illustrated with engravings depicting both artifacts and activities of the Inuit. Just before Cranz's book was published, Hans Egede's *Beschreibung und Naturgeschichte von Grönland* was issued in a German translation, providing the general account supplementing his earlier book about the history of the Danish mission in Greenland. While the translation of Egede's book suddenly called into question the usefulness of Cranz's own account, which had drawn heavily on Egede's original volume,[18] the first part was nevertheless published as a necessary introduction to the history of the Moravian missions, and it is still useful for the additional observations it contains. The success of the book may also be measured by the number of its German editions as well as its translations into Dutch, English, and Swedish.

Christian Georg Andreas Oldendorp's equally voluminous *Geschichte der Mission der evangelischen Brüder auf den caraibischen Inseln S. Thomas, S. Croix und S. Jan*[19] was edited and—much to the dismay of the author—pared down for publication by Johann Jakob Bossart, the curator of the Moravian natural history (and ethnography) collection in Barby, who had published an instruction on how to collect natural history (and ethnographic) specimens.[20] The original text has only recently been published in its entirety.[21] The author had spent much of 1767 and 1768 in the Virgin Islands, and his ethnographic account especially is based on his own experiences. In general outline, Oldendorp follows the example set by Cranz. Following accounts of the topography and natural history, book 3 is devoted to a description of the manners and customs first of the white and

---

18. David Cranz, *Historie von Grönland enthaltend die Beschreibung des Landes und der Einwohner &c* (Barby: Heinrich Detlef Ebers, 1765).

19. Christian Georg Andreas Oldendorp, *Geschichte der Mission der evangelischen Brüder auf den caraibischen Inseln S. Thomas, S. Croix und S. Jan* (Barby: Brüdergemeine, 1777), reprinted in Beyreuther, *Nikolaus Ludwig von Zinzendorf, Materialen und Dokumente*, series 2, 27:1–2.

20. Johann Jakob Bossart, *Kurze Anweisung Naturalien zu samlen* (Barby: Druckerei der Brüder-Unität, 1774). See also Petra Martin and Stephan Augustin, eds., *Ethographie und Herrnhuter Mission* (Dresden: Staatliches Museum für Völkerkunde Dresden, 2003), 16–17.

21. Christian Georg Andres Oldendorp, *Historie der caribischen Inseln Sanct Thomas, Sanct Crux und Sanct Jan, insbesondere der dasigen Neger und der Mission der evangelischen Brüder unter denselben*, ed. Gudrun Meier, Stephan Palmie, Peter Stein, and Horst Ulbricht, 4 vols. (Berlin: Verlag für Wissenschaft und Bildung, 2000–2002).

subsequently of the black inhabitants of the islands (and their African background). The structure of the ethnography differs from Cranz's, although it also begins with their "formation and stature" and includes a detailed description of the Creole language but arranges the data to focus on their vices and virtues.

The third volume of Moravian mission history and ethnography, published in 1789, was Georg Heinrich Loskiel's *Geschichte der Mission der evangelischen Brüder unter den Indianern in Nordamerika*. Loskiel was the only one of the three authors who had not visited the region prior to the publication of his book. Hulbert has thus suggested that Zeisberger's manuscript ethnography "was evidently written for the Rev. Henry Loskiel to aid him in the preparation of his most valuable *History of the Mission of the United Brethren among the Indians of North America*," but the documentary evidence clearly speaks against such an assumption. The manuscript itself is undated, but internal evidence indicates that it was written in New Schönbrunn in the second half of 1780 and perhaps into 1781.[22] Zeisberger's diary and letters are silent about his work on the manuscript, but it is likely that it was finished before March 23, 1781, when Zeisberger left New Schönbrunn for Bethlehem to attend the synod called by Bishop Johann Friedrich Reichel,[23] who must have taken a copy of the manuscript back to Germany.[24] The references to Loskiel's *History*, culled from the records of the Unity's Elders' Conference by Matthias Meyer,[25] reveal that Loskiel had been commissioned to write the book by September 1781, but that at this point it was thought best to "mention the condition and state of the country, of the various nations etc. in the history of the mission only occasionally to the extent necessary for the understanding of the history." Loskiel specifically complained about the lack of adequate information about the natural and political history of the country. By November 1781, however, Loskiel felt it necessary to preface the history of the mission with an account "of the country and the nations residing there." A draft of this section was finished in February 1782

---

22. Hulbert's introduction to *Zeisberger's History of the Northern American Indians*, 7. On p. 55, the manuscript says that "last winter between 1779 and 1780" the snow "here at the Muskingum" had been two feet deep (versus Hulbert and Schwarze's edition, 44); on p. 49, 1779 is referred to as "last year" (ibid., 40); on p. 170, reference is made to the destruction of the Shawnee settlements on the Scioto and their expulsion by the Americans in 1780 (date missing in translation).

23. Earl P. Olmstead, *Blackcoats Among the Delaware: David Zeisberger on the Ohio Frontier* (Kent: Kent State University Press, 1991), 33.

24. The question remains whether the manuscript now in Bethlehem is the one taken to Germany and used by Loskiel or a copy retained by Zeisberger himself.

25. Matthias Meyer, "Georg Heinrich Loskiels Lebenswerk: Die Indianermissionsgeschichte," in Loskiel, *Geschichte der Mission der evangelischen Brüder*, reprinted in Beyreuther, *Nikolaus Ludwig von Zinzendorf, Materialen und Dokumente*, series 2, 21:29*–47*.

and was found inadequate by Bishop Spangenberg in March. On April 9 the Elders' Conference suggested that Brother Zeisberger's account should be the primary basis for the introductory part dealing with the Indians, "firstly of the condition of their country and secondly of their way of life and customs." By April 27, 1782, Loskiel had finally been given access to Zeisberger's manuscript and was able to rewrite the first section, which was finished by June 1783.

It thus appears that Zeisberger's text was finished before Loskiel was commissioned to write the *History,* and that it was written independently of it. This leaves us with the question why Zeisberger wrote the book-length manuscript in the first place. After thirty-five years of intimate acquaintance with the Iroquois, Delaware, and their neighbors, he was clearly in a position to provide a summary account, and he was obviously inspired by the earlier attempts of Cranz and Oldendorp—but this does not answer the question why he did it at that particular time. One possibility is that he was prompted to do so by Bishop Reichel, who had arrived in North America in April 1779, although there is no evidence that Zeisberger met the bishop before March 1781.

Other than the English translation, the German manuscript of Zeisberger's text is divided into six chapters with underlined headings, and subdivided into more or less clearly marked sections. "Of the Indians' figure and way of life" (1–27) begins with an account of their physical characteristics, hairstyles, and ornaments, and proceeds to a discussion (unmarked) of their subsistence; marked sections deal with clothing, "domestic life and economy," character (entitled simply "North American Indians"), "travel," and "sicknesses." The second chapter, "Of the condition of the land, where the Indians have lived, but primarily where the Delawares are nowadays living" (28–108), deals with the Delaware and their relationship to the Cherokee, Six Nations, and Mahican; the rivers of their country, the climate, and the trees (with a special section on the "sugar tree"), the oil wells, stones, medicinal plants, quadrupeds, fowl, snakes, and fish (including reptiles, mollusks, and vermin)—very much in the tradition of earlier natural history accounts focused on native resource use as a source of information.

The third chapter details the "Manners and customs of the Indians" (108–36) and starts out with an account of "How a boy shoots his first deer" (with notes on their respect for the elders); this is followed by sections on menstrual customs, courtship and marriage, childbirth and various aspects of domestic life, including a long digression on love and hunting medicines, clothing, habitations, death and burial. Chapter 4 is about "The Indians' political institution and constitution" (136–207) and discusses modes of government, warfare, and trade, but also games and amusements, external affairs, and sorcery. "Of their service to god and superstition" (207–28) summarizes beliefs and ceremonies but also includes a long section on prophetism. The sixth and final chapter, "Of their sciences" (229–49), is concerned with languages, oratory, mathematics, divisions of time, genealogy, history, geography and cosmology, medicine, death, and burial customs, but also includes additions on peace pipes and on animals and plants. Obviously, Zeisberger's rather rambling account—with additions simply inserted whenever he became aware of his oversight—should not be regarded as more than a rough draft, perhaps finished in haste so as to be ready for Bishop Reichel before his departure.

In basic outline, the structure of Zeisberger's text thus follows book 3 of Cranz's *History of Greenland*, but Zeisberger also includes information on the country, climate, minerals, plants, and animals, which Cranz had discussed much more systematically in the first two books. Even some of the sections within the chapters follow the sequence suggested by Cranz. Thus Cranz had also opened his chapter on "sciences" with a discussion of language and oratory, followed by genealogy, mathematics, divisions of time, cosmology, medicine, and death and burial.

What is striking about Zeisberger's text, in view of what has been said above about the relationship between the specific observational record and the generalized ethnographic summary, is its apparent independence of the diaries.[26] While the diaries contain information that is of ethnographic interest, it is hard to imagine the author transferring empirical data from his chronological account into his classified generalizations. Most probably the lack of much correspondence between the two bodies of information may be found in the specific community-related purpose for which the diaries were kept; they differed in scope and direction from the day-to-day observations of a traveler. There is, of course, some overlap in subject matter, but the two texts are complementary rather than corresponding. Most of the information in the ethnography is not supported by the diary, and some of the rather cryptic ethnographic references in the diary are not contextualized and explained in his "systematic" statement.[27] Another basic difference between the two texts is that the diary focuses on the present, whereas the ethnography (as in the case of Lafitau) is primarily concerned with the ways of life of the community in its unconverted state.

---

26. David Zeisberger, *Herrnhuter Indianermission in der Amerikanischen Revolution: Die Tagebücher von David Zeisberger, 1772 bis 1781*, ed. Hermann Wellenreuther and Carola Wessel (Berlin: Akademie Verlag, 1995).

27. Readers of the ethnography will look in vain, for example, for an explanation of the poisons or medicines *wapachsigan* and *machtapassican* (ibid., 122, 130, 144, 146, 147, 161, 243).

This raises the question whether Zeisberger could have derived some of his information from published sources. A search of the most likely literature (including the German translation of Lafitau published in a Pietist volume in Halle),[28] however, reveals no indication of plagiarism. It is indeed rather unlikely that Zeisberger had much of a library of travel accounts available in New Schönbrunn, and the hasty manner in which the text appears to have been written also supports the view that it was largely or completely based on the recollections (rather than records) of half a lifetime among native peoples of the region. The structure of the text supplied by Cranz's volume cannot, however, completely make up for the lack of a systematic method of collecting data (such as by means of questionnaires or checklists).

Although Zeisberger clearly states that most of his information applied to the Delaware, among whom he had lived for such a long period of time, data applying to the Iroquois (as well as the Munsee, Mahican, Shawnee, Nanticoke, and others) are apparently included, sometimes (but not always) marked as such. In much the same way that Lafitau's generic Indians have a recognizable Iroquois background, Zeisberger's Indians are based largely upon Delaware data, but in both cases one can never be completely certain. In terms of the new ethnographic paradigm of the Enlightenment, with its focus on specific peoples, Zeisberger's generalization may be regarded as old-fashioned or as the result of an assumption about "Indianness" as a meaningful subject.

While there is no evidence that Zeisberger used published sources, Loskiel, by contrast, supplemented his reorganized version of the Zeisberger text with additions from Jonathan Carver's *Travels Through the Interior Parts of North America*,[29] whose own slender ethnographic account had itself been blown up to giant proportions by his British publisher, as well as from oral and perhaps written Moravian sources. While Loskiel's approach is more systematic than Zeisberger's as far as the presentation of the data is concerned, his lack of personal experience made him mix up data relating to the cultural practices of different tribes even more than his predecessor had done.[30]

---

28. Siegmund Jacob Baumgarten, ed., *Algemeine Geschichte der Länder und Völker von America*, 2 vols. (Halle: Johann Justinus Gebauer, 1752), vol. 1.

29. Jonathan Carver, *Travels Through the Interior Parts of North America in the Years 1766, 1767, and 1768* (London, 1778).

30. For example, in drawing together the information on burial and mourning customs from different sections of Zeisberger's manuscript, Loskiel created a paragraph that starts out with information on the Nanticoke but continues without any indication of a change of focus to data that may rather apply to the Iroquois. Loskiel, *Geschichte der Mission der evangelischen Brüder*, 156–57.

Although based on sometimes extensive empirical evidence, the Moravian ethnographies of Cranz, Oldendorp, and Zeisberger conform to an already established pattern of ethnography. Based on the circumstances of their composition, they vary in importance and usefulness for modern ethnohistorical and historical ethnographic research. If Zeisberger's text presents problems due to its level of generalization, this is not so much a shortcoming of the author as a problem inherent in any ethnography with ill-defined subject matter.

In other respects, the ethnographic practices of the Brethren were certainly more up to date. As Augustin has recently pointed out, Herrnhut (and more especially Barby) maintained a more than passing relationship with Göttingen.[31] The natural history cabinet established in Barby, which like Göttingen also featured an ethnographic collection assembled on James Cook's third voyage (and which also included some specimens perhaps collected by Zeisberger), was established well ahead of such institutions elsewhere. Moravian writings were read with interest and mined for data in Göttingen as important ethnographic sources for a comparative ethnology. If the missionaries in the field, whose primary duties obviously lay elsewhere, were not pofessional scholars following the latest research practices, they should not be blamed for not being something they never aspired to be. While ethnohistorians might wish for fewer problems with the sources they have to rely upon, such problems are part of our daily fare.

---

31. Stefan Augustin, "Herrnhut und Göttingen im 18. Jahrhundert—wissenschaftsgeschichtliche Aspekte der Beziehungen zwischen Mission und Universität," *Abhandlungen und Berichte des Staatlichen Museums für Volkerkunde Dresden* 49 (1996): 159–180.

The Succession of Head Chiefs and the Delaware Culture of Consent:

The Delaware Nation, David Zeisberger, and Modern Ethnography

HERMANN WELLENREUTHER

∼

No Euro-American colonist of the eighteenth century offered a detailed and thoughtful description and analysis of the succession problem within Native American societies. American thought on this subject was dominated by European concepts of white male rule and domination. Instead of thinking about the succession issue, colonial politicians and superintendents for Indian affairs searched for ways to increase their influence on the choice of successors to this office.[1] The only person after Joseph François Lafitau who was interested in the succession issue was David Zeisberger. Zeisberger's *Diaries,* his letters, and his account in his *History of the Northern American Indians* provide the basis for an argument I follow into the nineteenth century. Zeisberger's views do not always square with twentieth-century ethnohistorical scholarship. I argue, however, that from a historian's perspective Delaware life and political culture, as described by Zeisberger, mark in their contextualized form a distinct and specific phase that is valid only for the second half of the eighteenth century. For that period, the method of selecting the successor to the head chief was based on a culture of consent that embodied, defined, and united the Delaware Nation. The person

---

I am particularly grateful to Professor Christian Feest for his critical reading of an earlier draft of this essay and for his many helpful and insightful suggestions. If I have not accepted all of those suggestions, the resulting errors are purely my responsibility. I likewise acknowledge his kindness in supplying me with a copy of David Zeisberger's original German version of his *History of the Northern American Indians.* Both Professor Claudia Schnurmann and Dr. Frauke Geyken read and discussed aspects of the essay. I am grateful to both of them.

1. Colin G. Calloway, *The American Revolution in Indian Country: Crisis and Diversity in Native American Communities* (Cambridge: Cambridge University Press, 1995), 7–8; on the changing role of chiefs within Native American societies, cf. the perceptive remarks by Daniel K. Richter, *Facing East from Indian Country. A Native History of Early America* (Cambridge: Harvard University Press, 2001), 147–48.

whose succession was debated is Netawatwees, the head chief of the Delaware, who died on October 31, 1776.

The Succession Issue in Its Historical Context

Efforts to regulate Netawatwees's succession probably began at the conference in Pittsburgh in October 1773. According to the report to Sir William Johnson, George Croghan and the Seneca representatives jointly informed "the Nations then present that the Delaware Chief Custalogo was superannuated. . . . In like manner the Delawares of Newcommer's Town below Tuscarawas had appointed Captain Grey Eyes al. Sir William [i.e., White Eyes], to be their Chief in the place of their former Chief Newcommer who they thought unfit for the charge."[2]

This report has a number of interesting features. It demonstrates first Sir William Johnson's and his agents' efforts to support the Six Indian Nations' claim of overlordship over the Delawares. Second, with respect to Netawatwees's successor, Croghan had obviously misunderstood events. After Echpalawehund joined the Moravian mission congregation in late summer 1773, White Eyes had become his successor as speaker of the Delaware Head Council.[3] There is no evidence that prior to 1777 White Eyes had been designated chief or acted as chief.

David Zeisberger mentions the succession issue for the first time on February 12, 1776, in connection with his discussions with the Delaware Council about the transfer of the mission congregation from Schönbrunn to Lichtenau. One of the councilors, who is identified as "Killbuck's son," pressed Zeisberger for a quick decision. He wanted to build a house in the new mission congregation.

---

2. James Sullivan and Milton W. Hamilton, eds., *The Papers of Sir William Johnson*, 14 vols. (Albany: State University of New York Press, 1921–65), 12:1047–48. Captain "Grey Eyes al. Sir William" was identical with Captain White Eyes, Indian name Quequedegatha, at that time the speaker of the Delaware Head Council and without doubt one of the most influential councilors and captains of the Delaware. "Captain Pipe" referred to the council member and war captain of the Wolf tribe, Indian name Hopocan, later successor of Packanke, whom Croghan and others called Custaloga. This chief died sometime after 1775; Netawatwees, whom the English called "Newcomer," died on October 31, 1776.

3. David Zeisberger, *Herrnhuter Indianermission in der Amerikanischen Revolution: Die Tagebücher von David Zeisberger, 1772 bis 1781*, ed. Hermann Wellenreuther and Carola Wessel (Berlin: Akademie Verlag, 1995), 104 (August 7, 1772), 127 (February 7, 1773), 138 (April 5, 1773) and passim (hereafter cited parenthetically in the text by page number). My translation. The exact date of White Eyes' promotion is not clear. By May 1774, however, White Eyes was clearly the speaker of the council (cf. ibid., 193–94 [May 9–10, 1774]). Both Croghan and Sir William Johnson overlooked the fact that White Eyes belonged to the Turkey tribe, while the new chief had to belong to the Turtle tribe, as did Netawatwees.

Zeisberger adds: "who was named in *Pittsburgh* to be *Chief* after *Netawatwees*" (303).[4] In the years before, Benimo or John Killbuck Sr., son of Netawatwees, father of "Killbuck's son," and a chief of the Wolf tribe, had played a large role in Zeisberger's diary as one of the determined opponents of the Moravian missionaries (161, 283). The missionary returned to the subject after the mission congregation had moved from Schönbrunn to Lichtenau. On April 21, 1776, Netawatwees, along with many others, attended the religious services at Lichtenau. Among these was again "Gelelemind or John Killbuck, who was designated to be chief after Netawatwees" (311–12). Zeisberger added that Gelelemind asked him "to what extent a believer or person who wants to become a believer could be concerned with *Chief Affairs?*" (312–13). Before this entry the reader had already learned that Gelelemind was chief of Goschachgünk, the head settlement of the Delaware on the Muskingum River and center of the Turtle tribe.

From this point forward Gelelemind played a popular role in the diary. Surprisingly, though, the designated chief did not become the actual chief after Netawatwees died on October 31, 1776, during a conference at Fort Pitt (340).[5] This, however, Zeisberger had assumed. When, on November 26, 1776, Gelelemind asked Zeisberger about the proper time for formally transferring his home from Goschachgünk to Lichtenau, Zeisberger replied that in these dangerous and unstable times his presence at Goschachünk was needed more than ever because "if there was no sovereign among them," the danger of the Delaware being dragged into the war would be much greater (345).[6] A few days later, Zeisberger had to realize that the issue of Netawatwees's succession was still wide open; under his diary entry for December 9, 1776, he noted that "a certain Indian" was trying "to reintroduce heathen ways, sacrificing and preaching among the Indians" in Goschachgünk. Zeisberger was concerned because this Indian preacher not only maintained "that the Brothers' teaching is not for the Indians, but for the White people," but planned to collect his followers in a new town and was "working on getting the office of *Chief* to another line and of putting in someone who is an enemy of the Brothers" (347).

The close union between the leading family of the Turtle tribe and the mission congregation, coupled with the danger that the new chief would possibly soon become a converted Christian, had rekindled a nativist reaction within the

---

4. This was obviously incorrect.
5. On October 3, 1776, Netawatwees had informed the mission congregation that he would personally attend the conference at Fort Pitt; he asked the congregation to look after his blind daughter during his absence. Ibid., 338.
6. In the original German, Zeisberger's phrase was "wenn kein Regente unter ihnen wäre."

settlements. The succession issue and the position of the mission within the Delaware Nation were for the first time linked. That linkage threatened the culture of consent within the Delaware Nation. In the coming months, affairs were dealt with by "the chiefs"—which meant White Eyes as war captain and Gelelemind as chief of Goschachgünk. Disagreements continued to prevent the election of the head chief. According to Zeisberger, White Eyes at least on one occasion chaired a council meeting that discussed nonmilitary matters, although as war captain he clearly acted outside his competence (360). On the council's agenda was a discussion of the future relationship between the mission congregation and the Delaware Nation. After the eloquent plea of White Eyes for their closer union, the council agreed to circulate a formal message about such a union to all the neighboring nations (361–62). That resolution sharpened the cleavages between the Wolf and the Turtle and Turkey tribes.

The succession of Netawatwees remained unsolved as long as White Eyes lived. Once he was dead—he was murdered by an American militia officer on November 5, 1778 (478)—the succession problem was settled remarkably quickly outside the culture of consent. In the absence of the chiefs of the Wolf tribe,[7] and with the Turkey tribe (to which White Eyes had belonged) unable to compete for the chieftainship, Gelelemind was the only surviving chief who met the criteria. He moved quickly to establish his position as head chief of the nation. Four days after the news of the death of White Eyes arrived, Gelelemind appointed Welapachtschiechen, chief of the Turkey tribe, his closest and most trusted head councilor (479). The announcement pleased Zeisberger but certainly not those who believed in the old Indian ways, for Welapachtschiechen, together with a large following, had joined the mission congregation in September 1776 and was baptized on December 25, 1777; his new name was Israel (337, 423).

The succession issue was, if we follow Zeisberger, determined by a number of factors, among which Euro-American interference was probably less prominent than colonists believed. The linkage between the succession issue and the relationship between the Moravian mission and the Delaware Nation was more important. It is evident that after the death of the incumbent, succession was not an automatic process but was linked to the level of consent within the Delaware. The scant remarks suggest that the succession issue became the concern of interest groups that tried to shape the discussion according to their

---

7. They had, with most of their members, left the region and council immediately after the conclusion of a treaty with the American army toward the end of October 1778. Ibid., 478 (November 24, 1778).

concepts and needs. Whether this story reflected the normal peacetime process is difficult to say. It is even more problematic to generalize from the long time span in which the issue of Netawatwees's succession remained open. This may have been partly due to the stalemate between the tribes. While the majority of the Wolf tribe rejected the Moravian mission, the Turkey and Turtle tribes supported it. Thus only one thing is clear: succession was not an automatic process but a concern that could become enmeshed in tribal politics; it could be solved satisfactorily only in an environment marked by a culture of consent.

Date, Concepts, and Theories

This conclusion is only partly supported by David Zeisberger's discussion of the succession issue in his *History of the Northern American Indians*, a treatise he wrote two years after the succession issue had been solved. Surprisingly, Zeisberger offers here not one but three versions that are not in all respects compatible. He distinguishes between the actual mechanics of settling the succession and its preconditions. Of these he lists three: First, the chief must always "be a member of that tribe in which he presides." Second, "the sons of a chief cannot inherit their father's dignity," because sons belong to the mother's lineage, which is different. Marriage partners never belong to the same lineage; thus succession within the same lineage is limited to brothers,[8] nephews, and grandsons.[9] Third, the chiefs of the tribe from which the head chief is to be elected have no voice in the election of the chief; only the chiefs of the other two tribes have a say in the decision, a precondition that requires a consensual relationship between the tribes.[10]

---

8. A case in point would be the Shawnee chiefs Cornstalk and Nimho.
9. Archer Butler Hulbert and William Nathaniel Schwarze, eds., *David Zeisberger's History of the Northern American Indians* (Columbus, Ohio: F. J. Heer, 1910), 98–99. Zeisberger does not name brothers, although he must have been aware that Cornstalk and Nimho were brothers. I add Zeisberger's original German version: "Es kann kein anderer zum Chief gewählt werden, als einer aus demselben Stamm . . . [wenn ein Chief stirbt] so kann keiner von seinen Söhnen Chief werden." David Zeisberger, "Von der Indianer Gestalt und Lebensart," Archives of the Moravian Church, Bethlehem, Pennsylvania, Indian Mission Records, box 2291, Personalia, Zeisberger III, folder 1, no. G 1 (hereafter Zeisberger, "Von der Indianer Gestalt"), fols. 150–51.
10. Hulbert and Schwarze, *Zeisberger's History of the Northern American Indians*, 112. The German version reads: "Ist ein Haupt Chief zu wählen, näml. vom Turtle Tribe, so kann der Stamm selber keinen Chief machen, sondern die andern zwey Chiefs vom Turkey und Wolf Tribe müssen ihn dazu machen, und wiederum so, wenn von diesen 2 Stämmen eine Chief Stelle leer ist." Zeisberger, "Von der Indianer Gestalt," fol. 175. It is not absolutely clear whether the passage cited refers to the head chief. I base my assumption on Zeisberger's remark that "the successor of Netawatwes, who was

Within these preconditions Zeisberger then lists three distinct ways of choosing a successor: "The principal captain may choose a chief and inaugurate him." He adds that "the captains, who have always the people on their side, may thus forsake a chief."[11] Zeisberger's second method is that, "in general, some person who lived in intimacy with the deceased chief, and is well acquainted with the affairs of state is chosen to be his successor. . . . If he is discreet and wins the favor of the captains and the people, the former in particular, will support him in every possible way."[12]

Both methods assign the captains a key role in securing a consensus of the "captains" and the "people" in support of the new head chief. What could possibly be interpreted as his third method contains elements of the first two but differs significantly in its ritual contents: "The election is conducted in the following manner. As each tribe lives in a town of its own, the two chiefs, upon whom the election devolves, meet with their councilors and people at an appointed place, and after all necessary preparations have been made . . . they move in a procession toward the town where the election is to take place." Once they have entered the town and are seated in the council house, "one of the two chiefs, in a singing tone, opens the proceedings by explaining the object of the meeting, condoling with the chief elect. . . . Next he declares him to be chief and formally fills the office made vacant by the death of the former chief."[13]

---

chosen by Europeans prominent in Pittsburg . . . is not respected" (113). This remark can only refer to the office of the head chief and to Gelelemind. If this is true, then Welapachtchiechen, in the absence of the chiefs from the Wolf tribe, would have had the right to elect Gelelemind.

11. Hulbert and Schwarze, *Zeisberger's History of the Northern American Indians*, 98. The German version reads: "Der oberste Capitain kann einen Chief wählen und einsetzen und es steht auch in seiner Macht, ihn wieder abzusetzen wenn er will und der Chief kein guter Regente ist oder handelt gegen ihre Gebräuche, oder will zu eigenmächtig seyn und nach seinem eigenen Gutdüncken handeln, keinen Rat annehmen; so können ihn die captains, die das Volck immer auf ihrer Seite haben und lenken können, wie sie wollen, sitzen lassen, ihn nicht allein nicht unterstützen, sondern es wohl merken lassen und an den Tag geben, daß sie nicht mit ihm harmoniren, und damit ist der Chief eine Null, er hat kein Volk, ist alleine für sich Chief und hat nichts zu thun und kann auch nichts thun." Zeisberger, "Von der Indianer Gestalt," fol. 150.

12. Hulbert and Schwarze, *Zeisberger's History of the Northern American Indians*, 100. "Ein solcher ist auch bey des Chiefs Lebzeiten immer um ihn gewesen, und hat Unterricht von ihm in allen Sachen bekommen, ist daher nicht fremd und jedermann weiß und sieht, daß er dazu destiniret ist und nach den Rechten es seyn muß. Hat er Verstand und weiß sich bey den Captains und dem Volck zu insinuieren, daß er deren Gunst hat, so helfen ihm die Captains und unterstützen ihn, gehen ihm mit Rath und That an die Hand, und darin besteht seine Macht und Gewalt." Zeisberger, "Von der Indianer Gestalt," fols. 153–54.

13. Hulbert and Schwarze, *Zeisberger's History of the Northern American Indians*, 112. The German version reads: "Das geht so zu: Jeder Stamm wohnt gemeiniglich in einem Town mit seinem Chief. Diese 2 Chiefs, die einen vom 3ten Stamm creieren sollen, versammeln sich mit ihren Counsellors und ihrem Volck, und nachdem sie sich dazu präpariert haben (denn es werden ein Stück oder 30 und

There are two ways to interpret these passages: First, it is possible to understand the three passages as one process.[14] Second, the three descriptions represent three different election procedures. In this case, the second probably comes closest to what happened in Goschachgünk, for Gelelemind had been described as "chief designate" as early as February 12, 1776. The absence of the ritual Zeisberger mentions could be explained by the simple fact that aside from Gelelemind no two chiefs were available to chair the proper ritual of inauguration. That was the result of the fundamental disagreements between the Wolf tribe and the two other tribes.

Zeisberger's narrative in his diary differs from his remarks in his *History of the Northern American Indians*. The one embeds the story of Netawatwees's succession within the events of the mission congregation. The other lifts the succession problem to a level in which ethnographic factors hold center stage but historical contexts are largely ignored. Zeisberger's asides make it clear that while formulating the general rules for electing a chief, he had Netawatwees's succession in mind. These rules were formulated on such a high level of abstraction that they lost much of their specificity. Only by linking them to the story related in the diary do they receive their time-specific meaning. The first represents an ethnological, the second a historical, perception.

---

mehr Belte of Wampum dazu erfordert) und alle ihre Speeches dazu in gehöriger Ordnung haben, so ziehen sie alle zusammen aus ihrem Town aus in Procession und die zwei Chiefs gehen voran, und einer davon sagt den ganzen Weg die Speeches, die sie an den zu machenden Chief zu thun haben in dem Ton, der allein bey einer solchen Gelegenheit und bey keiner anderen gewöhnlich ist. So kommen sie in das Town singend eingezogen, wo der Chief soll gewählt werden. Diese haben dazu schon alles praepariert, was erforderlich ist. Sie ziehen also singend auf die Ost-Seite des Council Haus ein, die beiden Chiefs voran, gehen auf eine Seite um die zwey oder drey Feuer herum, die schon gemacht und das Haus zurecht gemacht ist und setzen sich auf die andere Seite nieder. Darauf kommen die aus dem Town hinein, gehen herum und bewillkommen sie, geben ihnen die Hand und setzen sich auf die andere Seite gegen über. Einer von den beiden Chiefs fängt gleich seinen Spruch an, singt aber alles, meldet den Zweck ihrer Zusammenkunft und condoliert dem neuen Chief, wischt ihm die Thränen von seinen Augen, reinigt ihm seine Ohren, und die Kehle, nimmt alle Betrübniß über den Tod des verstorbenen Chiefs von seinem Herzen hinweg und tröstet ihn über alles [Leid?] das er darüber gehabt. Wenn das geschehen, declariert er ihn zum Chief und ersetzt durch ihn die Stelle des Verstorbenen." Zeisberger, "Von der Indianer Gestalt," fols. 175–76. I have transcribed the German passage in its entirety.

14. This possibility is indicated by the sentence with which Zeisberger introduces the third election mode: "Von ihren Gebräuchen und Ceremonien bey der Wahl eines Chiefs hätte melden sollen, da von den Chiefs gehandelt worden, und da ich nun wieder in die materie hinein komme, so will es hier thun. Wer aus der Freundschaft dazu kann gewehlt werden, davon ist schon gemeldet worden. Ist ein Haupt-Chief zu wehlen neml. vom Turtle Tribe, so kann der Stamm selber keinen Chief machen, sondern die anderen zwey Chiefs vom Turkey und Wolf Tribe müssen ihn dazu machen und wiederum so, wenn von diesen 2 Stämmen eine Chief Stelle leer ist, so können und müssen die anderen 2 Chiefs einen neuen machen. Das geht so zu." Zeisberger, "Von der Indianer Gestalt," fol. 175.

To complicate matters, Zeisberger adds in his *History* a remark to his third description of succession that casts doubts on his diary narrative. After stating expressly that "the new chief enters upon his office by consent of the tribe and whole nation" and that "whoever obtains the office of chief in any other way is not respected"—remarks clearly intended to underline the importance of the procedures he had outlined—Zeisberger adds, "This is the case with the successor of Netawatwes, who was chosen by Europeans prominent in Pittsburg. Such a one amounts to nothing. . . . Thus the Delawares at present have no real ruler, to whom they are devoted and from whom they are willing to take counsel."[15]

In light of the diary, Zeisberger's denigration of Gelelemind as head chief is puzzling. Until November 1778 the missionary had only good things to say about the grandson of Netawatwees. In the following weeks, the military situation in the region deteriorated dramatically. The first signs that these developments began to affect the relationships between the mission congregation and the Delaware appeared in February 1779. In the following months Gelelemind repeatedly asked the Christian Indians to bring their missionaries to Fort Pitt or Fort Laurens, because he was, so he claimed, unable to guarantee their safety. Zeisberger interpreted these demands as renewed efforts "to get rid of us in this way. Then when we are finally gone, the *Chiefs* will make themselves masters of our people and do what they want with our Indians."[16] Relationships did not improve when, in early March 1779, Zeisberger realized that the treaty concluded between the Delaware Nation and American commissioners in October 1778, in which the Delawares had promised warriors for American military expeditions, could be interpreted to encompass the Christian Indians, too.[17]

That is exactly what happened in late 1779. Gelelemind and the council demanded in a formal message, "once again explicitly . . . that our Indians arise immediately and go with him; if they refused they would suffer the consequences with the rest of the *Nations*."[18] The Christian Indians refused. At the same time it became clear that relations between the mission congregation and the non-Christian Delawares in Goschachgünk were almost irreparably damaged. On March 5, 1781, finally, the mission congregation formally notified the people of Goschachgünk that "we do not want to have anything to do with them, and

---

15. Hulbert and Schwarze, *Zeisberger's History of the Northern American Indians*, 113.
16. David Zeisberger, *The Moravian Mission Diaries of David Zeisberger, 1772–1781*, ed. Hermann Wellenreuther and Carola Wessel, trans. Julie Tomberlin Weber (University Park.: Pennsylvania State University Press, 2005), entry for February 22, 1779.
17. Ibid., entry for March 7, 1779.
18. Ibid., entry for August 20, 1779.

they should leave us in peace and stay where they are, because we do not desire their company."[19]

The diary offers an explanation for Zeisberger's disparaging remarks about Gelelemind's status as head chief of the Delaware. Before late November 1778 Zeisberger gave not a single indication that he harbored any doubts about the rightful succession of Gelelemind to Netawatwees. The missionary's perception of the succession issue was largely based on *his* self-imagined culture of consent between the "good people" who hungered after salvation in the Delaware Nation and the mission congregation. This consent marginalized the Wolf tribe as the unrelenting sons of Satan.

The two sources offer different modes of reasoning. The *History of the Northern American Indians* suggests that the succession of chiefs was a process shaped exclusively by factors within the Delaware Nation on the basis of "the consent of the tribe and the whole nation." The diary, by contrast, diffuses the hermetic concept of the *History*, links it to the outside world—in this case the Moravian mission and the War of Independence—historicizes it, and thus dissolves Zeisberger's categorical statements in the *History*.

The events associated with the election of a successor to Netawatwees as head chief of the Delaware Nation point to the importance of the cultural context within which Delaware politics functioned: Concerns that touched the nerve of the nation could be satisfactorily solved only in a cultural environment, a culture of consent, that was marked by fundamental agreement on these issues between the three major components of the nation: the captains and chiefs of the great council and the members of the individual tribes. Disagreement in any one of these vital areas affected negatively the ability to solve other important problems. This culture of consent required a harmony on the issues of the nation, and if that did not exist, the nation had to continue searching for a new harmony or risk the danger of breaking into its discrete parts.[20] The nation had no conflict-solving strategy but searching for consensus through discussion.

Captain Pipe's View According to Lewis Cass

The only other sources that contain descriptions of the Delaware mode of selecting or electing their chiefs are the manuscripts produced in the early

---

19. Ibid., entry for March 5, 1781.
20. On the difficult issue of the extent to which the Delaware tribes formed one whole, see below.

1820s under the supervision of the Michigan territorial governor, Lewis Cass.[21] The two relevant manuscripts report interviews with Captain Pipe and the Indian trader William Conner.[22] Their discussion of the succession of Delaware chiefs differs remarkably from Zeisberger's. The first manuscript offers the following description:

> When a Chief dies, his brother or son succeed as a council may determine. No female chiefs. The principal Chief always from the Wolf tribe, but was selected by the other tribes. . . . All the tribes elect the Chief for the others excluding from the election the tribe for whom the elections is held. The Chief is named as a successor, previous to the death of the incumbent and is always related to him. . . . This person is always chosen, and never objected to. All signify their assent. . . . The brother, if he behaves well must be named Chief in preference to the son. The sister's son succeeds also in preference to his own son.[23]

The style of this first manuscript suggests that these are rough notes rather than a polished protocol of the interviews with Conner and Pipe. The second manuscript is probably based on these notes. Both differ in some respects: According to

---

21. These were published by C. A. Weslager, *The Delaware Indians: A History*, (New Brunswick: Rutgers University Press, 1972), 473–98, and C. A. Weslager, *The Delaware Indian Westward Migration, with the Texts of Two Manuscripts (1821–22) Responding to General Lewis Cass's Inquiries About Lenape Culture and Language* (Wallingford, Pa.: Middle Atlantic Press, 1978), 165–205. The relationships between these manuscripts are not clear. Weslager dates the manuscript "Account of some of the Traditions, Manners, and Customs of the Lenee Lenaupaa or Delaware Indians" (Weslager, *Delaware Indians*, 473–98) in the handwriting of C. C. Trowbridge as winter 1823–24; according to Weslager, this manuscript is based largely on interviews with Captain Pipe, who at that time still lived at Sandusky, where he had moved around 1780. The other manuscript, "Delaware Traditions and Language," preserved mostly, too, in the handwriting of Trowbridge, was, according to Weslager, composed at the same time and during the same visit (Weslager, *Delaware Indian Westward Migration*, 160–61), and was also based largely on interviews with Captain Pipe. In addition, William Conner was interviewed. Conner was the son of Richard Conner and his wife, Peggy Conner, who had been accepted into the Moravian Mission congregation of Schönbrunn on May 8, 1775; their son William was born on December 21, 1777 (Zeisberger, *Herrnhuter Indianermission*, 606); for the next twenty years William lived with the Moravian missionaries. This background indicates that Conner must certainly have been familiar with many Delaware customs. On Lewis Cass, see Willard Carl Klunder, *Lewis Cass and the Politics of Moderation* (Kent: Kent State University Press, 1996); Robert William Unger, *Lewis Cass: Indian Superintendent of the Michigan Territory, 1813–183; A Survey of Public Opinion as Reported in the Newspapers of the Old Northwest Territory* (Ph.D. diss., Ball State University, Muncie, Indiana, 1967).
22. Cf. John L. Larson and David G. Vanderstel, "Agent of Empire: William Conner on the Indiana Frontier, 1800–1855," *Indiana Magazine of History* 80 (1984): 301–28.
23. Weslager, *Delaware Indian Westward Migration*, 172–73.

the latter, not the "council" but "a body of men called Lupwaaeenōāwuk or Wise Men" assemble "when the office of chief becomes vacant and in the presence of the people they consult together upon the qualifications of the aspirants and having decided [on a successor] they appoint another meeting for his inauguration, to which, as to the first, they invite the nation generally." At that second meeting the wise men solemnly introduce the new chief to his office by "placing a belt around his neck telling him, now you have the speech, see that you keep it, and adhere to the advice contained in it."

This polished protocol differs in three points from the rough notes. First, it does not mention the right of the old chief to nominate his successor to the council. Instead the whole process is transferred to a group of "wise men" who derive their authority from the "Great spirit"; this council is identical with the "Great Council" repeatedly mentioned by Zeisberger.[24] This great council was the embodiment and forum of the culture of consent. Second, while Zeisberger stresses matrilineal authority as an important factor in selecting the successor, the rough notes on the interviews with Captain Pipe and Conner indicate this only as a possibility; indeed, the polished reports omit completely matrilineal relations as a factor. These variations boil down to two significant differences between Zeisberger's descriptions and those of the early 1820s: While Zeisberger assigns matrilineal ties an important role in the selection process, the Cass/Trowbridge reports downplay this factor. Yet sources from as late as the 1870s indicate that "children followed their mother's lineage."[25] This may be the result of a slow process of acculturation to Euro-American concepts of heredity. Third, Captain Pipe asserted that the "principal Chief [is] always from the Wolf tribe," as the rough notes phrased it. This was most probably the result of the events between 1777 and 1779.

Zeisberger's *History* and the interviews with Captain Pipe and William Conner both categorically define rules, behavioral patterns, and procedures as if they had existed from time out of mind. Only the comparison reveals the time-bound nature of both documents. One important difference distinguishes Zeisberger's reports from those of Captain Pipe and William Conner: While Zeisberger defined the culture of consent as harmony within and between tribes, Pipe and Conner restricted it to the level of the council. "The people"

---

24. Cf. Zeisberger, *Herrnhuter Indianermission*, entry for June 23, 1774. Weslager, *Delaware Indians*, 288–90, does not mention here or elsewhere the existence of such a great council before Zeisberger's time.

25. Weslager, *Delaware Indians*, 391, quoting from an interview of Lewis Henry Morgan with Delaware head chief Charles Journeycake's mother, who was then approximately seventy-six years old.

have disappeared. Other sources, however, indicate that general acceptance by the tribal institutions and by members of the tribe was essential for the functioning of a head chief.[26]

The Historicity of the Mode of Electing Chiefs Among the Delaware

Rough notes and polished protocols of Cass and Trowbridge make it clear that as far as the Moravian influence on Delaware ethnography is concerned, the nineteenth century was the century not of David Zeisberger but of his assistant in the Ohio mission field, Johann Gottlieb Ernestus Heckewelder (1743–1823). For it was to Heckewelder's writings that Conner and Pipe frequently responded in these interviews. Heckewelder had published in the last fifteen years of his life three substantial books on the Delaware. Most of Zeisberger's writings still remained at that time in manuscript. His publications were of a strictly religious nature.[27] From today's perspective, Zeisberger's most important work (aside from his *Diaries*), his description of the Delaware, remained unpublished until 1910, when Archer Butler Hulbert and William Nathaniel Schwarze published an English translation under the somewhat misleading title *History of the Northern American Indians*.[28] Zeisberger's reputation has rested principally on this slim but important volume.

Has the publication of the *History of the Northern American Indians* had any impact on the ethnography of the decades after 1910? Obviously, ethnologists like Anthony F. C. Wallace, Clinton Alfred Weslager, and Herbert C. Kraft used both Zeisberger's and Heckewelder's works in their histories of the Lenni Lenape.[29] All authors restrict their use of the two Moravian missionaries' writings

26. Ibid., 389–91 and passim.
27. *A Collection of Hymns for the use of the Christian Indians, of the Missions of the United Brethren in North America*, first published in 1803, or his *Essay of a Delaware Indian and English Spelling Book for the Use of Schools of the Christian Indians on Muskingum River* (Philadelphia, 1776; 2d printing, 1806). Probably his most influential piece for Delaware ethnography of the first part of the nineteenth century was published posthumously in 1827 in the prestigious *Transactions of the American Philosophical Society*, n.s., 3 (1827) by that society's secretary and former correspondent of Heckewelder, Peter Stephan du Ponceau, under the title *Grammar of the Language of the Lenni Lenape or Delaware Indians*.
28. Hulbert and Schwarze, *Zeisberger's History of the Northern American Indians*. For the German version see note 9, above.
29. Anthony F. C. Wallace, *King of the Delawares: Teedyuscung, 1700–1763* (Syracuse: Syracuse University Press, 1990), and Anthony F. C. Wallace, "Women, Land, and Society: Three Aspects of Aboriginal Delaware Life," *Pennsylvania Archaeologist* 17 (1947): 1–35; Weslager, *Delaware Indians* and *Delaware Indian Westward Migration*. See also Herbert C. Kraft, ed., *A Delaware Indian Symposium*,

to English texts.[30] Only Kraft and Weslager used Zeisberger's *History of the Northern American Indians* as evidence for Delaware patterns of living, belief systems, and social structures.[31] Weslager seems to have trusted Zeisberger more than he did Heckewelder.[32]

One illustration will return us to my general theme. Kraft has this to say about the position and selection of chiefs among the Delaware:

> It has also been said that the sachem or "chief" who was to represent the interests of a particular phratry was selected by the older women of his phratry, sometimes referred to as "chiefmakers." There is no evidence that the Lenape or Munsee had permanent chiefs before the

---

Anthropological Series no. 4 (Harrisburg, Pa.: Pennsylvania Historical and Museum Commission, 1974); Herbert C. Kraft, *The Lenape: Archaeology, History, and Ethnography*, Collections of the New Jersey Historical Society, vol. 21 (Newark: New Jersey Historical Society, 1986).

30. This is the case with all of the contributions to the volume of essays edited by Kraft with the exception of William A. Hunter, "A Note on the Unalachtigo," in Kraft, *Delaware Indian Symposium*, 147–52.

31. Kraft, *Lenape*, 122, 126, 133–34, 141, 155, 158, 169–70, 177–79, 181–82, 185–86, 189, 191; Weslager, *Delaware Indians*, 43–47, 80, 392–93, 441.

32. Weslager, *Delaware Indians*, 43–44. The reasons Weslager gives for trusting Zeisberger more than Heckewelder apply to both, namely, each "was a conscientious, thorough, and reliable observer, fluent in the Delaware tongue, and a confidant of the Indian leaders." There were differences in attitude and temperament between the two: Zeisberger always retained some distance from his "Indian Brethren," while Heckewelder considered himself something of an advocate for the Delaware. While Zeisberger was more concerned with hard ethnographic facts, Heckewelder was more interested in the "soft side" of Delaware traditions, customs, and beliefs, which make up the largest part of his *History, Manners, and Customs of the Indian Nations*. Any discussion of Delaware ethnography and modern scholarship on the Delaware faces a number of difficult and controversial issues. Partly these are the result of different approaches of historians and ethnologists. There is general agreement that the Delaware only gradually evolved into something akin to an ethnically unified body. Little or no consensus has been reached as to *when* this happened. Some argue that it never happened and that therefore the Delaware Nation did not exist and could not have separated into its three tribes. I concur with Jane T. Merritt, *At the Crossroads: Indians and Empires on a Mid-Atlantic Frontier, 1700–1763* (Chapel Hill: University of North Carolina Press, 2003), 31–33, and Weslager, *Delaware Indians*, 140ff., that the three tribes, partly in response to Euro-American pressures, joined sometime well before the 1720s. Ethnologists appear to agree about the internal structure of the Delaware Nation. Originally the Delaware Nation consisted of three separate entities called Unami, Munsee, and Unalachtigo (Wallace, *Teedyuscung*, 9–11; Weslager, *Delaware Indians*, 43–47; Kraft, *Lenape*, xv–xviii). These three retained their identities; internally, each of them was divided into the three lineages Turtle, Turkey, and Wolf. Each had its own chiefs and individual councils. On the contrary, I maintain on the basis of Zeisberger's writings that in the second half of the eighteenth century lineages and tribes merged into one and became the Turtle, the Wolf, and the Turkey tribes united by a common language (or three dialects closely related), customs, rituals, a head chief, and a head council. Still, it remains difficult to say whether lineages extended beyond the tribes into other tribes. Zeisberger calls lineages "friendships" (*Freundschaften*). All of these tribes retained their individual chiefs and councils. The following section attempts to describe some of the consequences of this view.

European-contact period; and even in historic times it is not clear that the Delaware matrons did in fact select a chief, although Iroquois matrons did have this privilege. Instead, it appears more likely that when an aged Delaware chief was nearing death he nominated a successor from among those whose lineage qualified them to take his place.[33]

The author cites as proof an article by Anthony F. C. Wallace from 1947, and then adds that the "statement that successors were nominated by dying chiefs is found" in Weslager's *Delaware Indians: A History*.[34] Weslager cites documentary evidence from the late seventeenth and early eighteenth centuries. But neither ethnologist uses the more elaborate and ethnographically explicit discussion reported above in Zeisberger's *History of the Northern American Indians*.

A second example is related to a still controversial issue: the problem of subdivision within the Lenni Lenape. Kraft states categorically that the notion that the "Delaware Nation was originally divided into three 'tribes' . . . resulted from a misinterpretation and misunderstanding of a carefully worded German manuscript written by a Moravian missionary, David Zeisberger, who did not employ the term 'tribe,' but spoke instead of *Hauptstämme* (principal branches)."[35] Kraft cites as proof two passages in Zeisberger's text: The first is at the beginning of the second chapter: "Die Delaware Nation, die aus drei Nationen nemlich Unamis, Wunalachtico und Monsys besteht, haben ehedem in der Gegend von Philadelphia gewohnt."[36] Zeisberger does not speak of "Stamm," or "tribe," or "Hauptstamm" in this passage but of "drei Nationen," three nations, certainly terms different from those suggested by Kraft. That author's second citation from Zeisberger's text raises the question what the missionary meant by the term "nation."

The most important differences between the German original and the translation are that Zeisberger speaks of "als eine Nation," the translators of "each nation, considering itself a unit"; that Zeisberger writes "ein Regiment unter sich, so unvollkommen und mangelhaft es auch ist," which the translators render as "has a kind of government of its own choosing, imperfect as it may be." Kraft's remarks refer to the second part of the two texts: The German text speaks of

33. Kraft, *Lenape*, 134.
34. To be precise, in Weslager, *Delaware Indians*, 63.
35. Kraft, *Lenape*, xv.
36. Zeisberger, "Von der Indianer Gestalt," fol. 28. The English version reads: "The Delaware Nation, consisting of three tribes, the Unamis, Wunalachticos and Monsys, formerly lived in the region about Philadelphia." Hulbert and Schwarze, *Zeisberger's History of the Northern American Indians*, 27.

"one nation" consisting of "three main tribes" (*Hauptstämme*)—a word identical in its meaning with the word "tribe"; and indeed, in the next sentence he uses the term "tribe" in exactly the same meaning and context as he used the term "Hauptstamm." Kraft equally errs in his statement that "neither did Zeisberger identify and associate these Indian groups with animal totems"[37]—for that is exactly what Zeisberger did. In the diary Zeisberger too speaks of the "Wolf tribe."[38] At the same time, Zeisberger did not use the term "tribe" as a synonym for phratry; for in Zeisberger's terminology the phratry is a "Freundschaft," a friendship.[39]

The textual comparison suggests a problem: The modern consensus among ethnologists holds that the internal structure of the Delaware is not characterized by the division into three tribes.[40] Zeisberger would probably agree to such a statement as far as its application was restricted to prehistoric times. But on the testimony of contemporaries he definitely would disagree with respect to his own lifetime or the time of Euro-American settlement. For at the beginning of his second chapter and shortly after describing the "Delaware Nation" as consisting of three "Nationen," he pointedly noted that within the "Moravian congregation on the Muskingum River there are some old people, who were in Philadelphia when the first houses were built there. They are able to relate how peaceably and agreeably the whites and Indians dwelt together. . . . Even among the savages there are old people, who tell the following, as I have heard it from various individuals."[41]

These reports form the basis for Zeisberger's description of Delaware life *before* the arrival of Europeans.[42] Since all North American Native American culture depended on the formulation and continuation of their historical identities not through the written but through the memorized word, I see no reason why the

---

37. Kraft, *Lenape*, xv.
38. Cf. Zeisberger, *Herrnhuter Indianermission*, 283 (August 12, 1775).
39. Cf. ibid., 129 (January 14, 1773). In the English translation the text reads: "It is customary among the Indians for the eldest in the friendship to perform the annual sacrifice to keep illnesses away and so things will go well for them. Three or four or more deer or bears are required for this. If this is not observed, but is neglected, and one of them becomes ill, then it is surely because the sacrifice was not made. *Echpalawehund* is the eldest in the family and has performed the sacrifice each time. His friends now see that he is abandoning his old customs and traditions and wants to become a believer. Therefore they have already said that they would have to follow him if he did this. Otherwise things would not go well for them."
40. Kraft, *Lenape*, xvi. He writes: "Names such as Delaware, Lenape, Munsee, Unami, and Unalachtigo are all historic seventeenth- and eighteenth-century names. But they did not exist in prehistoric times or at the time of European contact; nor did the Lenape Indians constitute a tribe or group of tribes in any political sense"—which is precisely what Zeisberger maintained.
41. Hulbert and Schwarze, *Zeisberger's History of the Northern American Indians*, 27.
42. Ibid., 27–32.

descriptions of these old Delawares, recorded by Zeisberger, should be discounted.

Zeisberger insisted repeatedly that the Delaware consisted of three political units he called either "nation" or "tribe"—indeed, the interchangeable use of both terms may suggest a basic insecurity or fluidity within the internal structure that was caused by contact with Euro-American culture. I have no doubt that Zeisberger meant what he said. The Delaware he perceived as a *confederation* of three tribes, and each tribe was subdivided into what Zeisberger called "friendships." These were the basic components that constituted the culture of consent. This general political and social structure assigns the problem of the succession of chieftains a vital importance for eighteenth-century Lenni Lenape history. For the confederation was held together first through the head chief, second through the great council, and third through the cooperation of the tribal chiefs with the head chief in the great council. In Zeisberger's times the satisfactory solution of the succession issue represented the vital point at which the fragile structure of the Lenni Lenape confederation could survive or break. Disagreement on a head chief who was acceptable to all Delawares cut the only functional link between the three tribes. The successful solution of the succession issue required a culture of consent.

According to Zeisberger, the "Delaware Nation" consisted of "three *nations*." This raises a final point. Today we associate the term "nation" with a sovereign state whose inhabitants live within fixed borders and are governed according to a particular political constitution. What does Zeisberger mean by the term "nation"? The term had been discussed within the Moravian Church in the late 1750s and early 1760s. After an acrimonious debate, the General Synod had concluded that for Moravians something like a "national consciousness" had no meaning, because they were focused exclusively on their Elder, Jesus Christ.[43] Zeisberger shared this concept, refused to admit that something like a "special consciousness" of the Munsees or the Mahicans existed, and rejected the Munsees' pleas for a separate Munsee settlement.[44]

The implication of this particular conception of "nation" for Zeisberger's understanding of the Lenni Lenape as a political entity is clear: According to him the Lenni Lenape were defined by a sense of cultural, linguistic, and religious togetherness, but not by a sense of political unity. It was a loosely defined

---

43. Cf. Hermann Wellenreuther, "Bekehrung und Bekehrte: Herrnhuter Mission unter den Delaware, 1772–1781," *Pietismus und Neuzeit* 23 (1997): 152–74, especially 172.

44. Zeisberger, *Herrnhuter Indianermission*, 363 (March 11, 1777); 366–67 (March 23, 1777); for the Mahicans, see 209–11 and passim.

confederation held together principally by a head chief. On his skill and intelligence depended the survival of the Lenni Lenape in general and, according to Zeisberger, of the Christianization of the Delaware in particular. This means, too, that any understanding of Zeisberger's terminology must start with the special meanings he gave these terms—and these meanings are embedded in a German political, linguistic, and cultural tradition. For Zeisberger, the political constitution of the Lenni Lenape was composed of three tribes, each of which had its own political structure and religiously defined substructure he called "Freundschaft." These three were held together by a Head Council and a head chief. Mutual concerns of the three tribes had to be debated and decided unanimously in this highest council. The head chief was expected to lead and guide these deliberations. Within the historical development of the Delaware, Zeisberger's description represents, I argue, one distinct stage in an open-ended developmental process.

The Zeisberger diaries suggest not only a somewhat different internal structure of the Lenni Lenape from that advocated by modern ethnologists and ethnohistorians. More important, in the second half of the eighteenth century the fragility of the Delaware Nation, largely held together by the skill and experience of the head chief and his most trusted advisor, confirms the centrality of a culture of consent within the Lenni Lenape. Once the head chief Netawatwees had died, the new directorate of White Eyes, as captain and speaker of council, and Gelelemind, as head chief designate, was able to maintain harmony within this culture of consent. When the directorate broke down with the murder of White Eyes, nativist tendencies[45] and factionalism resulting from British and American pressures, coupled with divergent attitudes about the Moravian mission, led to the collapse of that culture of consent. The Delaware Nation evolved into something new, glimpses of which can be seen in the interviews with Captain Pipe and William Conner.

The importance of Zeisberger's *Diaries* is clear: They force us to historicize the Delaware Nation. By offering us a rich and exciting picture of what the Delawares were like in the second half of the eighteenth century, they force us to acknowledge that, like any other social entity, the Delawares were and are subject to change, were indeed defined by changing times. Not only did the mode of selecting head chiefs change, but so did the meaning of key terms such

---

45. Well described by Gregory Evans Dowd, *A Spirited Resistance: The North American Indian Struggle for Unity, 1745–1815* (Baltimore: Johns Hopkins University Press, 1992), chapter 3.

as "tribe," "nation" and "phratry." These insights were gained not on the basis of sources produced by the Delawares but by Euro-Americans who couched their observations in time-specific terms. Their cultural implications, their historicity and specific meanings, incorporate the history of the Delaware Nation into the larger history of the Atlantic world.

Zeisberger's *Diaries* as a Source for Studying Delaware Sociopolitical Organization

ROBERT S. GRUMET

∽

Few repositories contain more sizable or substantive documentation of greater value to ethnohistorical research than the Moravian Archives. As the editors of David Zeisberger's *Diaries* note, relatively few ethnohistorians have drawn deeply from this valuable resource. Among those who have, William A. Hunter employed these materials extensively in his "Documented Subdivisions of the Delaware Indians," published more than twenty-five years ago in the *Bulletin of the Archaeological Society of New Jersey*.[1] This article included data drawn from the newly microfilmed German-language manuscript of Zeisberger's *History*, whose title Hunter translated more aptly as *Condition or Mode of Life*.[2] Hunter was among the first to call attention to the problems caused by the translators'[3] conflation of Zeisberger's terms for nation (*Nationen*), tribe, and principal lineage (*Haupt-stamme*) in the original manuscript.[4]

This problem is known today among scholars as Heckewelder error,[5] in reference to Zeisberger's colleague's equation of the three Delaware nations (i.e., Munsee, Unami, and Unilachtego) with the Wolf, Turtle, and Turkey phratries in his "History, Manners, and Customs of the Indian Nations," published in 1819.[6]

---

1. William A. Hunter, "Documented Subdivisions of the Delaware Indians," *Bulletin of the Archaeological Society of New Jersey* 35 (1978): 37–38.

2. David Zeisberger, *Von der Indianer Gestalt und Lebensart* (1780), Archives of the Moravian Church, Bethlehem, Pennsylvania, Indian Mission Records, box 2291, Personalia, Zeisberger III, folder 1, no. G 1.

3. Archer Butler Hulbert and William Nathaniel Schwarze, eds., *David Zeisberger's History of the Northern American Indians* (Columbus, Ohio: F. J. Heer, 1910), 27.

4. Zeisberger, *Von der Indianer Gestalt*, 28.

5. Ives Goddard, "Delaware," in *Handbook of North American Indians*, ed. William C. Sturtevant, vol. 15, *Northeast*, ed. Bruce G. Trigger (Washington, D.C.: Smithsonian Institution, 1978), 225.

6. John Heckewelder, "History, Manners, and Customs of the Indian Nations, Who Once Inhabited Pennsylvania and the Neighbouring States," *Memoirs of the Pennsylvania Historical Society* 12 (1876): 51–53 (first published in 1819).

Michigan Territorial agent Charles C. Trowbridge soon recognized, in a study written five years later, that members of each phratry could be found in each Delaware nation of the time.[7] Heckewelder's conflation of the three, however, was widely reprinted, while Trowbridge's unpublished manuscript languished in obscurity. This assured the error's widespread acceptance by both knowledgeable specialists, for more than a century and a half, and by a less critical readership down to the present day.

Keeping Trowbridge's critical insight in mind, my own research on Delaware politics and society has focused upon the ways northernmost Munsee people used their kinship systems and diplomatic skills adaptively to survive invasion, depopulation, and dispossession during the historic contact period, between 1600 and 1800. The documentary record of Munsee sociopolitical life consists primarily of many thousands of individual references, penned by colonists, to named individuals, statuses, relationships, groups, and places mentioned in deeds, treaties, legal records, and other documents. Most of these references are dated; many are fixed to particular locales, activities, or events; the majority are contained in sources preserved in repositories scattered in and around the historic Munsee homeland. That homeland stretched across the northern portions of the mid-Atlantic seaboard from the lower Hudson to the upper Delaware River valley.

A vast and confusing range of spellings and meanings of the names, categories, and titles documented in these references has led some scholars to perceive dissonance and disorganization caused by contact with ethnocentrically biased strangers uninterested in, and hostile to, the Indians they were writing about. But, as I have argued elsewhere, this wide range of variation can be viewed more usefully as evidence of a flexible and highly adaptive worldview unintentionally documented by people speaking a different language and unhampered by the need for orthographic precision. Unlike histories, petitions, promotional tracts, and other narrative accounts written for particular purposes, the more incidental nature of this documentation allows scholars to screen data tainted by personal interest or cultural myopia. Like archaeologists piecing together bits of data into meaningful reconstructions, ethnohistorians can discern social facts in the patterns formed by these written fragments.

Edward H. Spicer showed how small populations could employ open-ended, flexible forms of social organization capable of adapting to a wide variety of

---

7. See C. A. Weslager, *The Delaware Indians: A History* (New Brunswick: Rutgers University Press, 1972), 480–81.

environments. That adaptation helped them maintain a sense of identity essential for survival.[8] The particular Munsee expression of this ethos of flexibility is revealed in complex documentary patterns that suggest the existence of a dense and widespread sociopolitical network. Within this network Munsees and other Delawares organized themselves socially, politically, and ritually at appropriate tiers of what Edward E. Evans-Pritchard called "levels of socio-political integration."[9] They did this by forming task groups of varying sizes and durations. Frederick O. Gearing, in his study of Cherokee politics, from the family, lineage, phratry, village, tribe, ad hoc confederacy, to more permanent national levels, called these groups "structural poses."[10] At each level chiefs and councils who arrived at their positions by achievement rather than ascription governed by the power of persuasion rather than the persuasion of power. By doing so, they achieved the level of consensus necessary to get things done in a family-centered culture that frowned upon compulsion of kinsfolk.

As in all societies, these activities were governed by a guiding set of principles determining ancestry, descent, affiliation, and social control. Delaware interpretations of these rules favored the emergence of traditions that fostered attitudes of tolerance and flexibility. These helped the vastly outnumbered, technologically outclassed, and increasingly pressed Delaware people to take advantage of opportunities and rise to challenges that overwhelmed other groups whose responses to invasion or intrusion were limited by more rigid or coercive belief systems, social hierarchies, or political orders.

Missions and Diaries

The new edition of Zeisberger's *Diaries* contains data of high quality potentially capable of testing the validity of these propositions. As the editors point out, Moravian statutes governing conduct did not explicitly require Indians to give up many aspects of their existing way of life. This, on its face, indicates that conversion did not significantly alter the adaptive Delaware social order. Moravians, however, proscribed attendance at rituals, most of which supported traditional family life. More important, the Moravians prohibited polygyny, instead mandating residence in nuclear families. This rule had the effect of assuring

---

8. Edward H. Spicer, "Persistent Cultural Systems," *Science* 174 (1971): 795–800.
9. Edward E. Evans-Pritchard, *The Nuer* (London: Cambridge University Press, 1940).
10. Frederick O. Gearing, "Priests and Warriors: Social Structure for Cherokee Politics in the 18th Century," *Memoirs of the American Anthropological Association* 93 (1962).

that neolocality (establishment of new households following marriage) would replace the traditional Delaware matrilocal postmarital residence form, in which a husband moved in with his wife's family.

Neolocality also suppressed the avunculate, a practice widespread among matrilineal peoples (although not yet recognized in extant Delaware data samples) in which sons moved in with maternal uncles at puberty or for a short time after marriage. This custom, known among anthropologists as spouse service, compensates the matrilineage of the husband's family for the loss of its son with the temporary services of his wife. Changes wrought by Moravian community rules of conduct weakened strong bonds forged by these practices, cutting converts off from traditional family supports and, as the missionaries surely hoped, binding them more strongly to their new communities. These limitations and modifications inevitably affected the range and type of options open to Delaware converts and their pagan kinsfolk. They also present formidable challenges to researchers trying to develop models that faithfully reconstruct aboriginal Delaware sociopolitical forms and functions.

Zeisberger's *Diaries* provide a considerable body of high-quality data documenting Delaware sociopolitical life in the Ohio missions. Moravians in general sought the most accurate information for the most efficient management of mission affairs. Zeisberger was a particularly fluent speaker of the Delaware language familiar with many aspects of their traditional culture and society. The diary form places much of its data within specific times and places. Readers thus have the opportunity to contemplate data gathered by a knowledgeable speaker with a strong vested interest in accurately documenting individual names, family relations, village, tribal and national identities, and settlement and leadership patterns at a particular time and place in Delaware history.

Personal Names

Zeisberger's *Diaries* contain the personal names of 486 Indian converts and one white proselyte, a trader named Richard Conner who lived among the Indians. Nearly all are identified by Christian baptismal names. Almost half of these people were newborns or young children who died soon after baptism. Sixty-nine of the remainder, mostly first- and some second-generation converts, also are identified by their Indian names. Very few Indian names of convert children or grandchildren are recorded.

Ten Indian elders who had used Indian names as surnames prior to baptism retained those names following their baptisms.[11] Two men, evidently nicknamed Tom and James Davis in their former lives, accepted new Moravian names, Matthaus and Nathaniel. One who used a European name, Sam Evans, retained it after joining the Brethren. Neither they nor any other Indian convert passed on names from former lives to succeeding generations. Only the white trader Richard Conner and his wife, Peggy, a former white captive of the Shawnees, retained their surnames at baptism and passed them on to their posterity. Thus nearly all other converts gave up either their Indian names or surnames following acceptance into the Moravian Brethren.

Linda Sabathy-Judd referred me to an instruction on the subject issued from Bethlehem to the Fairfield Mission in Ontario on March 16, 1802.[12] The letter notes that "using Indian heathen names as surnames raises difficulties. Often these names have peculiar meanings and many would object. Perhaps it could be done gradually. Brother David [Zeisberger] could be written about it."[13] Whatever their reasons, the Moravian practice of giving Christian names to Indian converts, a practice not required of non-Indian Moravians, joined differences in language, culture, and skin color to distinguish Indian proselytes from their European coreligionists.

Kinship Terms

Numerous examples have surfaced of English translations of German kinship terms such as mother, father, son, daughter, husband, wife, brother, and sister. Kinship terminologies provide close insights into family life and structure. Although Zeisberger and Schmick recorded some basic Delaware-language kin terms in their dictionaries,[14] little else is known about the Delaware terminology system during the contact period. Most anthropologists agree that the Delaware-language kin terms collected by pioneer ethnologist Lewis Henry

---

11. These were Johannes Papunhank, Jacob Gendaskund, the brothers Job and Bill or Wilhelm Chelloway, Joseph Peepi, Joseph Schebosch, Thomas Onondaga, and Samuel, Rebecca, and Sarah Nantikok.
12. Linda Sabathy-Judd, e-mail to author, October 14, 2004.
13. Archives of the Moravian Church, Bethlehem, Pennsylvania, box 168, folder 6, item 1.
14. Carl Masthay, ed., "Schmick's Mahican Dictionary," *Memoirs of the American Philisophical Society* 197 (1991); *Zeisberger's Indian Dictionary, English, German, Iroquois—the Onondaga and Algonquian—the Delaware* (Cambridge, Mass: John Wilson and Son, 1887).

Morgan in Kansas in 1859 and in recently gathered lexicons[15] reflect a system changed by "altered rules of residence, decreased polygyny, and increased economic and political importance of men."[16]

The references documenting the 486 Indians listed by name identify kin relations. All congregation members, including the missionaries, addressed one another as brothers and sisters. Neither these nor any of the terms used to identify familial relations are presented in the Delaware language. All, however, were recorded by a fluent speaker of Delaware familiar with their kinship system and anxious to arrive at the closest approximations of the terms in German for both ministerial and managerial reasons. German Moravian meticulousness has permitted the compilation of nine genealogical charts of Munsee families of three to four generations in depth. Collectively and individually, these are useful in examining aspects of Munsee sociopolitical life in the missions.

One example of English kin term usage contained in the diaries sheds particularly revealing light on the structure of aboriginal kinship terminology. Newcomb, who had little more than Morgan's kin terms to rely upon, developed a reconstruction indicating that aboriginal Delaware kin terminology most closely resembled a matricentered version of the Hawaiian kin term system.[17] Wellenreuther and Wessel explain Gelelemind's reference to his maternal kinsman Netawatwees by the terms grandfather and uncle as expressions "of honorary titles [rather] than as reflections of kinship relations." We may, however, also be seeing here the first identifiable example of bifurcate merging kinship terminology in the Delaware record. Bifurcate merging terminologies "group together various relatives who are ordinarily distinguished (and assign) them a common kinship designation."[18]

In this case, Gelelemind's merging of the terms uncle and grandfather for Netawatwees would have been matched by a reciprocal joining of the terms grandnephew, nephew, and son by Netawatwees or those referring to Gelelemind's relationship to him. Such merging, through "which generation levels are overridden," is a classic feature of Crow kinship terminologies. Indeed, many matrilineal societies employ such terms to bind maternally related kinsfolk more closely

---

15. For example, Lucy Blalock, Bruce Pearson, and James Rementer, *The Delaware Language* (Bartlesville, Okla.: Delaware Tribe of Indians, 1994).

16. William W. Newcomb Jr., *The Culture and Acculturation of the Delaware Indians*, Anthropological Paper no. 10 (Ann Arbor: University of Michigan Museum of Anthropology, 1956), 43.

17. Ibid., 44–48.

18. George Peter Murdock, *Social Structure* (New York: Macmillan, 1949), 125.

across generational lines.[19] Crow systems further merge terms for maternal uncles (i.e., mother's brothers) with the term for father.

Descent Principles

Anthony F. C. Wallace's abundantly documented observation that "maternal lineages were the most conspicuous mechanisms of descent and family affiliation among the Delawares" still stands.[20] But these were not the only mechanisms. As early as 1735, Forks of Delaware chief Nutimus pointed out that his property rights descended not only along the female line. He told Pennsylvania's provincial secretary, James Logan, that "his mother came from this [Pennsylvania] side of the [Delaware] River & by her he had a Right here as likewise had to some Land in the Jerseys which his father left him."[21] Frank G. Speck and his student William Christie MacLeod suggested that Delaware fathers passed family hunting territories patrilineally to sons.[22] Reexamining Pennsylvania land records consulted by Speck and MacLeod, Wallace and Newcomb found that Delaware communal territories descended along the matrilineal line.[23]

More recently, Carol Barnes suggested that both camps were right. She found that the particular demands of "the sexual and seasonal division of labor inherent in the Delaware's flexible adaptation to their environment created at least two opposing tendencies in social organization. The closely-knit, matrilineal organization favored by agricultural activities was countered by the loosely-knit, patrilineal organization which went with hunting and gathering."[24] Nutimus's statement of paternal connections suggests an intriguing corroboration of a paternal principle at work in a matrilineal society.[25] This single example, in

19. Ibid., 166.
20. Anthony F. C. Wallace, *King of the Delawares: Teedyuscung, 1700–1763* (Syracuse: Syracuse University Press, 1990), 8 (first published in 1949).
21. Ibid., 21–22.
22. Frank G. Speck, "The Family Hunting Band as the Basis of Algonkian Social Organization," *American Anthropologist* 17, no. 3 (1915); William Christie MacLeod, "The Family Hunting Territory and Lenape Political Organization," *American Anthropologist* 24, no. 3 (1922): 452.
23. Anthony F. C. Wallace, "Women, Land, and Society: Three Aspects of Aboriginal Delaware Life," *Pennsylvania Archaeologist* 17, nos. 1–4 (1947): 18; Newcomb, *Culture and Acculturation of the Delaware*, 23–24.
24. Carol Barnes, "Subsistence and Social Organization of the Delaware Indians: 1600 A.D.," *Bulletin of the Philadelphia Anthropological Society* 20 (1968): 15.
25. Robert S. Grumet, "That Their Issue Be Not Spurious: An Inquiry into Munsee Matriliny," *Bulletin of the Archaeological Society of New Jersey* 45 (1990): 19–24.

which property rights were not traced beyond two generations, was not by itself strong enough to support Barnes's suggestion that the Delaware practiced double descent, a type of bilineal system rare and in decline elsewhere in the world. It is perhaps wiser to regard suggestions of Delaware property transmission from paternally related fathers to children as examples of complementary filiation, a far more common practice found in most unilineal societies. Filiation, a tool for maintaining formal bonds with paternally related fathers and their families (otherwise merely in-laws in matrilineal societies), allows the father's family to transmit affinal (i.e., in-law) rights and prerogatives to children without resorting to expensive and potentially divisive multigenerational patrilines.[26]

Zeisberger's *Diaries* also include an example of primogeniture at work. On September 11, 1774, Zeisberger baptized Gelelemind's brother Gutkigamen into the Brethren as Thomas, officiating at his marriage to Sabina the same day. Although Thomas was noted as a grandson of Netawatwees, it was his older brother who rose to become chief of the Delaware Nation following Netawatwees's death in 1776. Thomas's close relation to the Delaware succession may, however, have had some bearing on his subsequent assumption of high-profile roles as national helper, sexton, lay preacher, and key culture broker in the Moravian community.

Family Households

Societies organized along matrilineal descent principles often require families to live in matrilocal households. Few sources, however, comment on Delaware household arrangements during the historic contact period. Scholars rely primarily upon Adriaen van der Donck's description of traditional Indian household arrangements in New Netherlands for their reconstructions of aboriginal Delaware family life. Van der Donck observed that "from sixteen to eighteen families frequently dwell in one house, according to its size. The fire being kept in the middle, the people lay on one side thereof, and each family has its own place . . . a hundred, and frequently many more, dwell together in one house."[27] Labadist missionary Jasper Danckaerts was the first, and the only, colonial observer to note that the Delaware organized

---

26. Meyer Fortes, "The Structure of Unilineal Descent Groups," *American Anthropologist* 55, no. 1 (1953): 25–39.

27. Quoted in Adriaen van der Donck, *A Description of the New Netherlands* (1655), ed. Thomas F. O'Donnell (Syracuse: Syracuse University Press, 1968), 80.

household residence along unilineal lines. Describing an extended Indian family residing in a longhouse household consisting of twenty-eight people in 1679, he observed that "all who live in one house are generally of one stock, as mother and father with their offspring."[28]

All other known sources for Delaware household organization, including those inferred in the genealogies constructed from the Zeisberger diaries, date from the mid- to late eighteenth century.[29] Without exception, they describe nuclear families and neolocal residence patterns. Citing Murdock's classic formulation that "rules of residence reflect general economic, social, and cultural conditions,"[30] Newcomb noted that Delaware neolocality arose as a function of the "isolation and emphasis placed upon nuclear families, the decrease of polygyny, the scattering of kinsmen, and the individualistic emphasis placed upon economic activity."[31] All but the last condition obtained in the strictly communal Moravian towns. The prevalence of this entire suite of conditions in contemporary pagan Delaware communities presents the intriguing possibility that mission residence patterns actually encouraged the preservation of earlier forms rather than those current among their heathen kinfolk.

Lineages

Groups of matrilineally related families joined together in named lineages stood at the center of traditional Delaware social life during the historic contact period. Lineages represented the primary landholding group in all Delaware nations. Family rituals and ceremonies cemented temporal and spiritual ties between lineage members and their ancestors. Chiefs and councils holding communal territories in trust for ancestral spirits disposed of lineage land-use rights. Yet, for all their importance, the names of Delaware lineages were not preserved in colonial records. Anthropologists have shown how internal tensions inherent in lineage systems cause most to divide into segments over comparatively short periods of time. Colonists interested in clear corporate identities and hard national boundaries probably had little patience for what appeared to be vaguely defined and seemingly ephemeral mélanges of families and friendships.

---

28. Jasper Danckaerts, *Journal of Jasper Danckaerts, 1679–1680*, ed. Bartlett Burleigh James and J. Franklin Jameson (New York: Charles Scribner's Sons, 1913), 56.
29. For example, Heckewelder, "History, Manners, and Customs," 155.
30. Murdock, *Social Structure*, 17.
31. Newcomb, *Culture and Acculturation of the Delaware*, 45–46.

Zeisberger used the German terms for friendship and family interchangeably to identify Indian lineages. Unfortunately, like other colonial chroniclers, he neither named nor traced the extent of these friendships and families to any great degree in his diaries. Fortunately, another set of colonial sources may identify Delaware lineages by name. The first of these, dated April 27, 1677, listed the names of four families (Amogarickakan, Mahow, Kettyspowy, and Kakatawis) represented by four chiefs (Kaelcop, Ankerop, Kugakpo, and Wengiswars) of Esopus Indians residing in the lower Walkill and Rondout river valleys just south of New York's Catskill Mountains.[32] Each of these family names appears to have belonged to a notable Esopus elder.

Nearly seventy years later, in a document dated August 27, 1743, another Esopus chief and four of his "under sachims" (two of them descendants of one of the chiefs mentioned in 1677) identified themselves as representatives of four tribes (Mogewehogh, Kighshepaw, Mahaw, and Kaghkatewees) bearing the same family names.[33] These data suggest that particular lineages founded by eponymous forebears could persist for several generations. The more successful of these clans could, in time, become nuclei of tribal polities.

Lewis Henry Morgan collected the first unambiguously identifiable list of Delaware lineages (groups he called "sub-gentes") with the help of a knowledgeable Kansas Delaware man named William Adams in 1860.[34] The terms were organized into the classic tripartite phratry framework, twelve lineages in the Wolf and Turkey phratries and ten in the Turtle phratry. Mark Raymond Harrington found that his Canadian Delaware informants in 1907 remembered all but two of these terms, though not all were recollected as clan names. Harrington noted that "the names of clans are said to have had their origin in some traditional peculiarity of their ancestors or from some locality once frequented by them."[35]

Harrington's observation encourages speculation that members of the O-ping-ho-ki, or "Opposum Ground," clan listed among the Turkey phratry lineages in Kansas and Canada may have been descendants of Oping Turkey

---

32. Edmund Bailey O'Callaghan and Berthold Fernow, eds., *Documents Relative to the Colonial History of the State of New York*, 15 vols. (Albany: Weed, Parsons, and Co., 1853–87), 13:504–5.

33. Charles A. Philhower Collection, manuscript group on file, n.d., Special Collections, Alexander Library, Rutgers University, New Brunswick, New Jersey.

34. Lewis Henry Morgan, *Ancient Society, Or Researches in the Line of Human Progress from Savagery Through Barbarism to Civilization* (1877), ed. Eleanor Burke Leacock (Cleveland: Meridian Books, 1963), 176.

35. Mark Raymond Harrington, "A Preliminary Sketch of Lenape Culture," *American Anthropologist* 15, no. 2 (1913): 210.

tribe members mentioned in New York agent Edward De Kay's report of his visit to the Cashigtonk Indian town in the upper Delaware River valley in present-day Damascus, Pennsylvania, on December 21, 1745.[36] The Opings were also known as Pomptons, from today's Pompton, near the New York border in northern New Jersey, and better known as Wappingers, as they were called when they were living in present-day Dutchess County, New York.

At the time of De Kay's visit they were living with Esopus and Minisink people at Cochecton. According to De Kay, the Cochecton community consisted "of Two Tribes Vizt the Wolves & Turkeys."[37] The tribes had gathered together in part to select a new chief to replace their recently deceased leader. Although De Kay did not identify the constituent kin groups of either tribe, subsequent documents clearly show that they selected Oping sachem Nimham as their leader.[38]

Phratries

Acculturation pressures erased the collective memories of ever-decreasing populations forced to move far from traditional towns like Cochecton. There, ancestral graves and locales had once given substance and meaning to lineages. Memories of the totemic Wolf, Turkey, and Turtle phratries, by contrast, endure to the present day. Phratries were a pervasive presence in traditional Delaware society. The Cochecton example listing two phratries suggests that some Delaware communities organized themselves into moiety divisions through which matrilineal phratries exchanged men from one phratry to the other. Subsequent records suggest the presence of tripartite phratry systems in Delaware communities west of the Allegheny Mountains. Whatever their form, content, location, or origin, phratry systems stood at the center of traditional Delaware society, political organization, and, ultimately, spiritual life. The system fell out of use shortly after the last Big House Ceremony, whose ritual organization depended upon it, was held in Oklahoma in 1924.[39] The dramatic social and

---

36. Edward Manning Ruttenber, "Cochecton," *Historical Papers of the Historical Society of Newburgh Bay and the Highlands* 13 (1906): 182.

37. Cf. Grumet, "That Their Issue Be Not Spurious," 22.

38. Robert S. Grumet, "The Nimhams of the Colonial Hudson Valley, 1667–1783," *Hudson Valley Regional Review* 9, no. 2 (1992): 87.

39. Robert S. Grumet, ed., *Voices from the Delaware Big House Ceremony* (Norman: University of Oklahoma Press, 2002).

political changes that eroded the kinship basis of Delaware culture during the nineteenth century had destroyed its foundations.

Both modern-day Delawares and scholars agree that phratry members saw themselves as people of one blood. Following the rule of phratry exogamy, they regarded marriages between members of the same phratry, no matter how distantly related their lineages, as incestuous. This assured that members of at least two phratries could be found in every Delaware community, no matter how small. People connected to this kinship network therefore had a high expectation of finding blood relatives from whom they could expect hospitality and protection wherever they traveled in the Delaware world.

Nearly all sources agree that phratry chiefs served as key leaders in Delaware society. Hunter has shown that the Susquehanna Valley Delaware King Sassoonan and his successors in the western country, Tamaqua, Shingas, and Pisquetomen, were Turkey phratry chiefs. Custaloga (also known as Packanke) and his successor Hopocan, "the Pipe," led the Wolf phratry.[40] Hunter also describes how Turtle phratry chief Netawatwees, a Delaware leader who figures prominently in Zeisberger's *Diaries,* rose to become the most influential Delaware chief in Ohio.

It is tempting to contemplate the possibility that Netawatwees belonged to the Turtle phratry O-ka-ho-ki lineage, translated suggestively as "Ruler" by Morgan in Kansas and less compellingly from O-ke-ho-ki as "Bark Country" by Harrington in Canada. The possibility that this lineage may have originated in the lower Delaware River valley Okehocking community (in present-day Chester County, Pennsylvania), which moved among Sassoonan's people around Shamokin sometime between 1718 and 1732, is even more tantalizing.[41]

Towns, Tribes, and Nations

Okehocking was one of many towns and tribes chronicled by colonial observers[42] within what present-day Oklahoma Delaware elders call Lenapehoking, the Delaware homeland.[43] Okehocking disappeared into memory along with Cochecton,

---

40. Hunter, "Documented Subdivisions of the Delaware," 32–35.
41. Marshall J. Becker, "The Okehocking: A Remnant Band of Delaware Indians," *Pennsylvania Archaeologist* 46, no. 3 (1976): 50–51.
42. For a list, see Goddard, "Delaware," 237–38.
43. Herbert C. Kraft, *The Lenape-Delaware Indian Heritage: 10,000 B.C.–A. D. 2000* (Elizabeth, N.J.: Lenape Books, 2001).

Oping, Minisink, Esopus, and other tribal and town names when their former constituents were forced to leave Lenapehoking for new Munsee and other Delaware communities in Ohio. The new Ohio social landscape neither simply copied nor completely differed from their old cultural world. Like Lenapehoking, the Ohio land was a complex and variable milieu of communities. Zeisberger's *Diaries* indicate that Delawares built, within twenty years, seventeen towns of varying sizes and compositions (twelve Delaware, three Munsee, two shared by Munsees and Delawares, and four mission communities) at various locales along the Allegheny, Cuyahoga, Muskingkum, and Sandusky river valleys.

The names of the Munsee, Unami, and Unilachtego nationalities that came together to form the Delaware Nation in Ohio had all emerged in exile. The name Munsee, for example, first appeared in 1727 as a reference to descendants of Minisink Indians living in the Susquehanna country. The first known mention of the term Unami, for its part, occurred at a 1757 Easton treaty meeting as a name identifying Tamaqua and other descendants of Sassoonan's community at Shamokin. The name of the third Delaware nation, Unilachtego, is far more scantily documented. Zeisberger first noted that they lived somewhere west of Kittanning in far western Pennsylvania in 1769. He then located them along the Muskingum River four years later. Hunter has since suggested that Unilachtego was a Munsee word Zeisberger collected in Ohio, where it identified people tracing descent from Jersey shore ancestors.[44]

Zeisberger's *Diaries* identify the national identities of forty-two Unami and thirty-nine Munsee converts living in the Moravian towns. The ten Munsee genealogies gleaned from Zeisberger's *Diaries* indicate that people married within the same nationality. This form of national endogamy was reinforced by bilateral descent of national identities in which nearly all children of Munsee parents whose national identities Zeisberger recorded also tend to be Munsees. One genealogy, however, differs from the others. The two children of Paulus, a Munsee, and Theodora (nation unknown) both took Unami spouses. The elder child, Johann Martin, is identified as a Unami. His brother, Daniel, and Samuel, the eldest of Daniel's five children, are both identified as Munsees. These data, sparse as they are, suggest that at least some Delawares took spouses belonging to other nations. Unless all traditional rules of descent and social order had broken down by this time, it seems certain that Delawares marrying outside their nation took spouses from one of the other two Delaware phratries.

44. Hunter, "Documented Subdivisions of the Delaware," 31, 33, 36, 37.

Social Control

All Delaware polities, from the family to the national level, were governed during times of peace by facilitative civil leaders and councils, and during wartime by more authoritarian captains.[45] Civil leaders maintained the social order through consensus. Consensus in Delaware society did not mean unanimity. Instead, it conveyed (sometimes grudging) consent.[46]

Although leaders maintained their positions by demonstrating strong negotiating skills, birth played a major role in determining who could become a chief. The diaries show how succession to the paramount leadership position of the Delaware Nation in Ohio followed traditional rules of matrilineal succession closely. On April 21, 1776, Zeisberger noted that Gelelemind (also known as John Killbuck Jr.) was Netawatwees's designated successor. Netawatwees, the Turtle phratry sachem, had achieved top leadership of the Ohio Delawares in 1765. So successful had his rise to power been that he managed to convince Zeisberger that the Delawares had always chosen their leaders from the Turtle phratry,[47] despite the fact that Netawatwees's predecessor, Tamaqua, belonged to the Turkey phratry.[48]

Wellenreuther and Wessel express mystification at Netawatwees's apparent choice of Gelelemind, a close phratry kinsman, as his successor. Zeisberger had explained that only more distantly related maternal great-grandsons or nephews could succeed their fathers. Gelelemind certainly was not Netawatwees's great-grandson. That he occasionally addressed the old man as uncle as well as grandfather, however, indicates that, as his nephew, Gelelemind was firmly in the line of succession. Genealogical connections further indicate how the grandnephew, nephew, and son Gelelemind might have risen "to the dignity" of his grandfather, uncle, and putative father, Netawatwees. Netawatwees's eldest son, Bemino (also known as Killbuck Sr.), belonged to the Wolf phratry, indicating that Bemino inherited this affiliation from his mother.

Helena, Bemino's wife and Gelelemind's mother, for her part, almost certainly belonged to a highly influential Turtle phratry lineage. Perhaps she was an actual

---

45. See Robert S. Grumet, "Sunksquaws, Shamans, and Tradeswomen: Middle Atlantic Coastal Algonkian Women During the Seventeenth and Eighteenth Centuries," in *Women and Colonization: Anthropological Perspectives*, ed. Mona Etienne and Eleanor Burke Leacock (New York: Bergin-Praeger Scientific, 1980), 47–49, for a detailed discussion of traditional leadership patterns.

46. George Silberbauer, "Political Process in G/wi Bands," in *Politics and History in Band Societies*, ed. Eleanor Burke Leacock and Richard B. Lee (Cambridge: Cambridge University Press, 1982), 23–35.

47. Zeisberger, *Von der Indianer Gestalt*.

48. Hunter, "Documented Subdivisions of the Delaware," 35.

or classificatory sister of the Turtle phratry chief Welapachtschiechen (also known as Captain Johnny and baptized as Israel). If Gelelemind employed a variant of the Crow system, merging Delaware terms for maternal grandfather and uncle, he would also have regarded Netawatwees as a father. Netawatwees, in return, would have reciprocated with a similar term, merging the terms grandnephew and nephew with son. In this way users of the Crow system could symbolically reduce generational distance separating maternally related kin to produce a matrilineal version of the father-son relationship.

Whatever his position in the Delaware succession, Gelelemind did not remain long in the position of Delaware national chief following the death of Netawatwees in 1776. Instead, he evidently followed his desire to convert and joined the Moravian Brethren in 1789. Subsequent records note that his kinsman Tetapachksit rose to the position of paramount Delaware chief.[49]

These connections were probably encouraged by cross-cousin marriages. Considered incestuous in many societies, marriages between first cousins, children of brothers and sisters, who after all belonged to completely different phratries, were favored in societies employing the Crow kinship terminology system. Multiple unions of cross cousins, either through polygyny or by marrying brothers off to wives from different phratries, helped particular lineages in each phratry retain power and influence over spans of many generations.

Zeisberger's *Diaries* contain information capable of shedding new light on the structure and function of Delaware social and political organization during a particularly stressful period in their history. Analysis of Zeisberger's observations on the relationship between Netawatwees and Gelelemind suggests that Delawares employed a bifurcate merging kinship terminology characteristic of Crow kin-term systems. Other observations suggest the practice of such customs as primogeniture, preferential cross-cousin marriage, and national endogamy.

The *Diaries* also raise new questions. What, for example, was the significance of the Christian names given converts? How did they reflect Indian status, conduct, and identity in the missions? And how did residence in Moravian missions affect the social and political life of converts and members of the larger Delaware community? Future investigators will find information in Zeisberger's *Diaries* and other Moravian sources of great help in answering these and other questions relating to intercultural relations on a shifting frontier during a turbulent time in history.

---

49. John Gottlieb Ernestus Heckewelder, *Thirty Thousand Miles with John Heckewelder*, ed. Paul A. W. Wallace (Pittsburgh: Pittsburgh University Press, 1958), 419, 441.

II.

Missions and Exchanges

The Impossible Acculturation:

French Missionaries and Cultural Exchanges in the Seventeenth Century

DOMINIQUE DESLANDRES

The centrality of translation in accounting for the missionary experience of Europeans, Catholic or Protestant, requires that we devote serious attention to questioning the use of diaries and missionary narratives as serious anthropological and historical sources. The quality of conversions, the role of gender or medicine or music in attracting converts, and other questions have marked the historiography of Catholic missions and engendered much debate. To a remarkable degree, Moravian and Catholic missions shared more in common than they themselves, and perhaps even we as scholars, have been willing to concede. The aims the missionaries pursued—the Christian utopia—the methods they used, the reactions they expected, the way they expressed their thoughts and hopes, and the way they translated—yes, translated—their mystical and practical experience are remarkable in their similarities once we dig beneath the surface of differences they sometimes exaggerated.

As scholars of the religious fact, of the "lived religion," as Daniel Richter has put it, we have to withdraw from our particular studies and take a more global look at what should be called the "missionary mind," or rather the "Christian missionary mind." Some years ago the movie *Black Robe* described the culture shock that occurred between the French missionaries and the Amerindians of New France in the seventeenth century.[1] The Jesuit Laforgue, lost among the Huron tribes, is shown as doubting the validity of his mission and even as losing his own faith. The movie ends with the feeling that he will convert to the religion of the Other. But this representation is, to my mind, totally anachronistic. In

---

1. Based on *Black Robe: A Novel* (New York: Dutton, 1985) by the Canadian Bryan Moore, the movie was made in 1991 by the Australian Bruce Beresford.

effect, the French missionary of the seventeenth century is not a man of doubt. He knows. He never doubts; he is convinced that he is absolutely right.

If the Amerindian morals may sometimes interest him—he may wear snowshoes or eat native food—if the customs and languages of these French peasants who are nothing more than "pagans under a Christian cover" puzzle him, the faith of the Other remains to him impossible, unthinkable, incorrect, intolerable. Most of the time, in the mission narratives, the Other is described as being ignorant of what is necessary for redemption, that is, for the realization of the Christian utopia. In the worst case he is without religion, and in the best case he is shown as practicing a debased form of Christianity, corrupted by ignorance, superstition, or heresy.

I have begun with this excursus on modern film by way of introducing a more serious reflection on the meaning of this encounter of beliefs, an encounter that the historians have named wrongly "acculturation." I take as the basis of my reflection the French missionary context of the seventeenth century, a context that witnessed the expansion of Tridentine missions inside France (among the lukewarm Catholic and the Protestant populations) and outside France, mainly among the North American Indians.[2]

Beginning with Columbus, the interpretations of the Euro-Amerindian encounter were numerous, varied, and often conflicting, but all agreed, indeed insisted, on the inexorability of the assimilation of the Amerindians by Western civilization. We had to wait for ethnohistory, appearing in the 1950s, to explain differently the phenomenon of acculturation and to admit different perspectives.[3] One of the merits of this new field of history is to have exhumed one of the actors of the encounter, the Amerindian, that historiography had almost totally erased from the collective subconsciousness.[4]

For a long time, in effect, the Amerindians have been seen as peoples without history, without written trace or real impact on these lands that the Europeans considered virgin. Without a past and thus without a future, they had only the

---

2. This has been the main topic of my book *Croire et faire croire: Les missions françaises au XVIIe siècle* (Paris: Fayard, 2003).

3. James Axtell, "The Ethnohistory of Early America: A Review Essay," *William and Mary Quarterly*, 3d ser., 36 (1978): 110–44.

4. William N. Fenton, "Training of Historical Ethnologists," *American Anthropologist*, n.s., 54 (1952): 328–39; William N. Fenton, *American Indian and White Relations to 1830: Needs and Opportunities for Study* (Chapel Hill: University of North Carolina Press, 1957), 3–27; Bruce G. Trigger, *The Children of Aataentsic: A History of the Huron People to 1660*, 2 vols. (Montréal: McGill-Queen's University Press, 1976), 11–26; and Bruce G. Trigger, *Natives and Newcomers: Canada's "Heroic Age" Reconsidered* (Montréal: McGillQueen's University Press, 1985), 3–51.

choice between physical vanishing or accepting the values of a civilization that saw them as second-rank inhabitants of the continent. This image concerned not only the historiography of the United States. We know now that the way the Canadian history of the Franco-Amerindian encounter has been written explains in large part the mental apartheid that, on the one hand, erased the Amerindians from the memory and daily life of the Canadians and, on the other hand, set the Amerindians into a rigid myth, that of the "savage."[5]

But our historical perspective has, in fact, changed. During the 1960s, joining the resources of anthropology and history, several excellent studies succeeded in giving the Amerindian point of view on the culture shock their peoples lived through in North America. Think of the remarkable works of Canadian anthropologist Bruce G. Trigger, who successfully demonstrated that the Huron had not only a place in Canadian history but a history of their own.[6] Carried away with enthusiasm at having found a new field, however, research drifted off somewhat. Scholars have tended to see the encounter as idiosyncratic to the history of New France, while often neglecting to place this history in the more global context of Westernization, based on the expansion of Christianity. In this process, historians have been prone to discredit French missionaries and to see them as the primary agents of destruction of Amerindian cultures and religions. Such a view can be explained by several factors: the way one makes history, anti-clericalism, even denial.

In effect, a whole generation of scholars, trained as they were to quantify and construct "serious" sources for socioeconomic history, felt uneasy when confronted with the phenomenon of religious belief and practices. Either they did

---

5. Donald B. Smith, *Le "Sauvage" pendant la période héroïque de la Nouvelle-France d'après les historiens français du XIXe et XXe siècles* (Cahiers du Québec, Lasalle: Hurtubise, 1979); Sylvie Vincent and Bernard Arcand, *L'image de l'Amérindien dans les manuels scolaires du Québec* (Montréal: Hurtubise, 1979).

6. See, for example, André Vachon, "L'eau de vie dans la société indienne," *Canadian Historical Association Annual Report* 37 (1960): 23–32; Conrad Heidenreich, *Huronia: A History and Geography of the Huron Indians* (Toronto: McClelland & Stewart, 1971); Cornelius C. Jaenen, "Amerindian Views of French Culture in the 17th Century," *Canadian Historical Review* 55 (1974): 261–91; Cornelius C. Jaenen, *Friend and Foe: Aspects of French-Amerindian Cultural Contact in the 16th and 17th Century* (Toronto: McClelland & Stewart, 1976); Trigger, *Children of Aataentsic*; Paul Ronda, "'We Are Well as We Are': An Indian Critique of Seventeenth-Century Missions," *William and Mary Quarterly*, 3d ser., 34 (1977): 66–82. In addition, see John A. Dickinson, "Annaotaha et Dollard vus de l'autre côté de la palissade," *Revue d'Histoire de l'Amérique française* 35 (1981): 163–78; Denys Delâge, *Le pays renversé: Amérindiens et Européens en Amérique du Nord-Est, 1600–1664* (Montréal: Boreal Express, 1985); Trigger, *Natives and Newcomers*; James Axtell, *The Invasion Within: The Contest of Cultures in Colonial North America* (New York: Oxford University Press, 1985). This is not meant to be an exhaustive but merely a suggested list.

not wish to or they could not bring themselves to understand it, and they tended to discredit it as part of hagiography. Others dismissed religion as part of a subjective and qualitative way of looking at history, incompatible with a serious historical study of the beginnings of New France. Most of the time they did not know what to do with it, and in consequence they laid the entire topic aside.

But the Franco-Amerindian encounter cannot be reduced to economic exchanges, where material interest explains everything. Could materialism have been the sole motive for conversion to Catholicism? How can we know? How can we explain that these Amerindians, who subsisted primarily on meat, respected the Catholic fasts, even during their winter hunts, even though there were no Frenchmen around to impose fasting on them? Can materialism alone explain the will of these missionaries to settle in this cold and uncivilized country? No. Something happened between the missionaries and the Amerindians, something that asked for a study that is neither a critique nor an apology, that calls for neither sympathy nor derision but for an explanation free from anticlericalism or clericalism. This "something" has something to do with the alterity (otherness) and the construction of identity. It can be recognized in the remarks of an anonymous Montagnais Indian who invited the Jesuit Paul Le Jeune, the superior of the Quebec mission, to believe in Montagnais religion just as he himself believed the missionary's teachings on the Christian doctrine. This Montagnais invited Le Jeune to believe in the power of dreams: "since he was believing us when we were telling him something or showing him some image, we had to believe him when he was telling us something about his own nation."[7]

Historically, the French missionaries were the avant-garde of France's discovery of the peoples of New France; they became explorers, cartographers, ethnographers, translators; often they were authoritarian, sometimes diplomats, most of the time spoilsports, for their utopian aims clashed with the nascent capitalism of the young colony. Because they left numerous narratives about their exploits, they are our primary, and sometimes our only, witnesses of the encounter with the Amerindians. And their missions were the theater of profound epistemic shocks, which they described at length. The whole history of colonial France and New France pays tribute to these documents.[8] But they are not without problems.

---

7. "Tout ainsi qu'il nous croyoit quand nous luy disions quelque chose, ou que nous luy monstrions quelque image, de mesme que nous luy devions croire quand il nous disoit quelque chose propre de sa nation." Paul Le Jeune, *Relation de 1633*, in *Monumenta novae franciae*, ed. Lucien Campeau, 9 vols. (Québec: Presses de l'Université Laval, 1967) (hereafter *MNF*), 2:436.

8. The most famous edition of the Jesuit Relations is that by Reuben Gold Thwaites, ed., *The Jesuit Relations and Allied Documents: Travels and Explorations of the Jesuit Missionaries in New France, 1610–1791*, 73 vols. (Cleveland: Burrows Brothers, 1896–1901).

How are we to read these testimonies without taking their authors' motives into account? The terms they used in these narratives are dictated by the way they looked at life and death, at the world, at the Amerindians, and at themselves. Everything is linked. The study of representations of the Amerindians—the representations of the Others—leads to the study of representations of the self; the taking into account of alterity/otherness leads to the process of construction of identity.

The point of view of the missionized is thus not left to one side. It constantly shows up, but filtered by the way missionaries looked at the indigenous peoples. In effect, when he described the non-Christian or the almost-Christian, the missionary was talking above all about himself, about his dreams, his projects, his utopia, and in so doing he constructed himself. Inside such a system of thought, he became an ethnologist somehow, despite himself.

For these reasons, in my own writing, I have tried to reconsider the history of the Franco-Amerindian encounter while taking into account the point of view of the missionaries—my goal has been literally to write an ethnohistory of the missionaries.[9] Such an enterprise is founded on two elements: first, the encounter with otherness, and second, the construction of the self, both placed in the larger context of the French mission, itself a subject that must be integrated into a even larger movement: the Catholic Reformation of the Council of Trent, which took form in Europe and aimed at the social and religious integration of very different peoples. A movement was thereby triggered that set the stage and formulated the terms for the Westernization of the planet.

The Impossible Acculturation

The French missionaries were often the protectors of the cultures they approached. Like Franciscans in New Spain, Jesuits in China, Paraguay, Canada, and elsewhere tried to sort through the cultural elements to determine which were compatible with Christian principles. Their choice, which has been perceived as ethnological, relied on the Euro-Christian Tridentine civilization from which they came. If they sometimes tried to preserve the way of life of the missionized

---

9. Deslandres, *Croire et faire croire*. See also Dominique Deslandres, "Histoire socio-religieuse au Québec: Les derniers courants de la recherche," *Bulletin d'information du comité international des sciences historiques* (1993): 141–46; Dominique Deslandres, "À quand une ethnohistoire des missionnaires?" *Études d'histoire religieuse* 61 (1995): 115–24; and Dominique Deslandres, "Qu'est-ce qui faisait courir Marie Guyart? Essai d'ethnohistoire d'une mystique d'après sa correspondance," *Laval théologique et philosophique* 53, no. 2 (1997): 285–300.

on the basis of Christian ideals, they did not realize that this renewal was imposed by their own moral and intellectual precepts, based on their interpretation of the ancient Christian tradition of mission—that of the Apostles. The sources demonstrate that the missionaries didn't come to the mission lands to change themselves. They were, one can say, the incorruptible of the faith, the unconvertible.[10] These men and women, tough experts as they were in religious controversies, would never accept the religious ideas of these Others they had come to save. In fact, their presence in these mission territories was based on giving to, not on receiving from, the missionized. The missionaries were not prepared to receive anything that could raise questions about the validity of their mission or the legitimacy of their presence among the missionized. They were convinced that it was not only just but necessary and compulsory to propagate the Christian doctrine, and in so doing to save the world. As the Jesuit Ragueneau put it:

> There is, doubtless, much to endure among all those Missions as regards hunger, the insipidity of the food, the cold, the smoke, the fatiguing roads, and the constant danger, in which one must live, of being killed by the Hiroquois during their incursions, or of being taken captive, and enduring a thousand deaths before dying once. But, after all, it is easier to bear all these ills than to carry out the advice of the Apostle: *Omnibus omnia fieri propter Christum,* "to become all things to all men, in order to will all to Jesus Christ." It is necessary to have a tried Patience, to endure a thousand contumelies; an undaunted Courage, which will undertake everything; a Humility that contents itself doing nothing, after having done all; a Forbearance that quietly awaits the moment

---

10. The French word "inconvertible" was used in this sense during the seventeenth century, as shown by Gabriel Audisio, *Les Français d'hier: Des croyants, XVe–XIXe siècle* (Paris: A. Colin, 1996), 397. Moreover, in an exemplary way, Vincent de Paul tells how he succeeded in resisting his friends' efforts to convert him to Jansenism: "Je suis obligé tres particulierement de bénir Dieu et de le remercier, de ce qu'il a permis de ce que les premiers et les plus considérables d'entre eux qui progressent cette doctrine, que j'ai connus particulierement et qui étaient de mes amis, n'aient pu me persuader leurs sentiments. Je ne vous saurais exprimer la peine qu'ils y ont prise et les raisons qu'ils m'ont proposées pour cela, mais je leur opposais entre autres choses l'autorité du concile de Trente qui leur est manifestement contraire : et voyant qu'ils continuaient toujours, au lieu de leur répondre, je récitais tout bas mon 'Credo'; et voilà comme je suis demeuré ferme en la créance catholique; outre que de tout temps, et même dès mon bas âge, j'ai toujours eu une secrète crainte dans mon âme . . . de me trouver par malheur engagé dans le torrent de quelque hérésie qui m'emportât avec les curieux des nouveautés, et me fit faire naufrage en la foi." Vincent de Paul, *Entretiens spirituels aux missionnaires,* ed. André Dodin (Paris: Le Seuil, 1960), 996.

chosen by the Divine Providence; finally, an entire Conformity to his most holy will, which is prepared to see overturned, in one day, all the labors of ten or of twenty years. It is upon such foundations that these growing Churches must be built, and the conversion of these countries must be established; and it is this which God asks from us.[11]

These observations lead us to reject the term "acculturation," used by many scholars to describe the missionary phenomenon. This term, coined in 1880, has in fact changed in meaning over the years. In 1936 anthropologists defined it as the mechanisms by which the encounter of two or more cultures occurs. Today, however, one speaks of "acculturation of the Americas" when describing the process by which Amerindians assimilated European values. One speaks of the "acculturation of an emigrant" when describing his adaptation to the foreign culture into which he enters.

All these uses of the term "acculturation" reflect a reduction of meaning; and often they reflect a cast of mind that sees the encounter of two or more cultures in hierarchical terms, with the inevitable absorption of the "weak" or "inferior" culture by the "dominant" or "superior" one. The whole concept of exchange, of cultural interpenetration, that gave the term its richness is thus lost.

This is why we must be careful in our use of the concept of acculturation and must emphasize that "conversion" is not "acculturation," that missionaries are not "agents of acculturation," and that to try to integrate the Other into Euro-Christian civilization is not a project of acculturation. Otherwise we assume that the missionaries were ready to change the Christian message, ready to be won by the religion of the Other. This was not the case during the sixteenth and seventeenth centuries.[12]

---

11. Reuben Gold Thwaites's translation of the passage (*Jesuit Relations*, 143–45) reads: "Il y a sans doute beaucoup à souffrir dans toutes ces missions, pour la faim, pour l'insipidité des vivres, pour le froid, pour la fumée, pour la fatigue des chemins, pour le péril continuel dans lequel il faut vivre, d'estre assommé des Hiroquois marchant dans la campagne, ou d'estre pris captif et y endurer mille morts avant qu'en mourir une seule. Mais après tout, tous ces maux ensemble sont plus faciles à supporter qu'ils n'est aisé de pratiquer le conseil de l'Apostre: 'Omnibus omnia fieri propter Christum'; de se faire tout à tous pour gagner tout le monde à Jésus-Christ. Il est besoin d'une patience à l'espreuve pour endurer mille mépris, d'un courage invincible qui entreprenne tout, d'une humilité qui se contente de ne rien faire ayant tout fait, d'une longanimité qui attende avec paix les momens de la providence divine, enfin, d'une entière conformité à ses très saintes volontez, qui soit preste à voir renverser en un jour tous les travaux de dix ou vingt années. C'est sur ces fondemens qu'il faut bastir ces églises naissantes et qu'il faut establir la conversion de ces pays, et c'est ce que Dieu demande de nostre part." Paul Ragueneau, *Relation de Huronie, 1648, MNF*, 7:394–95 (see also 370).

12. On acculturation, see Robert Redfield, Ralph Linton, and Melville J. Herskovits, "Memorandum for the Study of Acculturation," *American Anthropologist*, n.s., 38 (1936): 149.

The Unthinkable Otherness

In effect, the new, the unknown, could have been constituted by the otherness idiosyncratic to the Amerindian peoples; this radical otherness, this "étrangeté," would have introduced dramatic changes into the religion lived by the French Catholics, but this did not occur. The new, the unknown, could have been introduced in the methods of conversion of very different kinds of peoples. Nor did this occur. Finally, the new, the unknown, could have been lived, analyzed, understood by the missionaries, who then would have been profoundly transformed. But this didn't happen. None of these possible outcomes were realized within the Euro-Amerindian encounter, and for many reasons—most of them linked as much to the perception of self and Other as to the "integrist" or even fundamentalist understanding of the Christian religion in the seventeenth century.

From a semantic point of view, Otherness is what is different, distinct. From a philosophical point of view, what is Other constitutes a category of being and of thought, referring to the heterogeneous, the diverse, the multiple (in opposition to the unitary, the homogenous, the analogous). For historians working in the Western tradition—that is, the Eurocentrist tradition—the Other comprises that which is not European. And what was not European captured the imagination of Europe from the sixteenth century on. Of course, the category of Other had already included Muslims—Europe's Mediterranean neighbors and its economic and military competitors—who received and read both Judaic and Christian scriptures but who, having added their own, additional revelation, were regarded by Christians as enemies of the true faith. The European imagination had even assimilated the Chinese and Indians of the Indies, the far eastern "barbarians," whose unbelievable wealth arrived in caravans and who, according to the tradition, had already been Christianized by the Apostles. With the discovery of the Americas, however, Europeans were confronted with a radical alterity; they had to understand and accept the existence of human beings who were not accounted for in Revelation.

This understanding, which today seems obvious, ran completely counter to the mentality of the time, shaped by a religious tradition that saw Adam as the "father of humanity" at the time of the world's creation. In this context, it is easy to understand why the recognition of the Other for what it was would be very long in coming. Even the most favorable spirits would resist the idea of a radically different Other, for this Other could not predate or originate outside the Bible. Thus, in its very existence, the Other was disturbing, incongruous, misplaced, mostly because it corresponded to nothing, to no known model. But, if it was really accepted as Other, the whole authority of the scriptures would be called into question, would crumble; this would be the end of the world.

Because of this anxiety, the missionaries and the theologians of the time tried by whatever means necessary to justify the existence of the Other, incarnated by the First Nations of America. Missionaries and theologians tried their best to integrate this radically different example of humanity into a familiar system of thought. They equated North American Indians with European peasants.[13] They developed the hypothesis that these people were the tribes of Israel, lost and found again, or that the Revelation of Christ's Word had spread throughout the world and then, because of a lack of pastors, was forgotten or, worse, evolved into ridiculous superstitions.[14] These strong reactions may be explained by the fact that, in the pre-Cartesian context of the early seventeenth century, respect

---

13. For example: "Pour l'esprit des sauvages, il est de bonne trempe, Je croy que les âmes sont toutes de mesme estoc et qu'elles ne diffèrent point substantiellement. C'est pourquoy ces barbares, ayans un corps bien fait et les organes bien rangez et bien disposez, leur esprit doit opérer avec facilité. La seule éducation et instruction leur manque. Leur âme est un sol très bon de sa nature, mais chargé de toutes les malices qu'une terre délaissée depuis la naissance du monde peut porter. Je compare volontiers nos sauvages avec quelques villageois, pource que les uns et les autres sont ordinairement sans instruction. Encore nos paysans sont-ils précipuez [avantagés] en ce point. Et néantmoins, je n'ay veu personne jusques icy de ceux qui sont venus en ces contrées qui ne confesse et qui n'advoue franchement que les sauvages ont plus d'esprit que nos paysans ordinaires." Paul Le Jeune, *Relation de 1634, MNF*, 2:596.

14. "Quelques-uns adoroient le Soleil, et lui offroient des Sacrifices, jettant dans le feu de la graisse d'Ours, d'Orignac, et d'autres bêtes, et faisant brûler du pétun et de la farine de bled d'Inde. Il y en avoit qui reconnoissoient un certain Messou qui a réparé le monde. Cette connoissance est belle, et a bien rapport à la venue du Messie, qui a été le Réparateur du monde. Mais l'aveuglement de l'infidélité a obscurci cette belle lumière par une Fable des plus ridicules; parce que les Hurons, qui sont ceux qui avoient cette connoissance, disoient que ce Messou avoit réparé le monde par le moien d'un Rat et d'une Rate musquez. Quelques autres avoient recours à certains génies, qu'ils disoient présider sur les eaux, dans les bois, sur les montagnes, dans les vallées et en d'autres lieux." Marie de l'Incarnation, *Correspondance*, ed. Guy-Marie Oury (Solesmes: Abbaye St-Pierre, 1971) (hereafter MI); *Lettre à son fils, 1670*, MI, 916; and *Lettre à son fils, été 1647*, MI, 335. See also *Lettre à son fils, 1643*, MI, 200, where the Ursuline reports: "Le Capitaine de cette Nation étoit un grand Sorcier, et l'homme du monde le plus superstitieux. Je lui écoutois soutenir la vertu de ses sorts et de ses superstitions, et peu après il vint trouver le Père contre qui il avoit disputé, lui apporta ses sorts et le tambour dont il se servoit dans ses enchantemens, et protesta de s'en vouloir jamais servir. Je vous envoye ce tambour afin que vous voyiez comme le Diable amuse et séduit ce pauvre peuple avec un instrument d'enfant; car vou sçaurez que cela sert à guérir les maladies, à deviner les choses à venir, et à faire de semblables choses extraordinaires." As Paul Le Jeune writes, "[Ils] reviennent facilement de ces folles superstitions quand on leur en fait voir la vanité, et qu'on les instruit des véritez de notre sainte Religion, qui portant avec elles l'onction dans le cœur, leur donne un goût bien plus doux et plus innocent que ne font tous ces vains enchantemens." Paul Le Jeune, *Relation de 1637, MNF*, 3:562–63.

for the *Auctoritates* prevailed over deductive knowledge. "I believe, therefore I am" prevailed over "I think, therefore I am."[15] Freedom in religious matters was thus obscene, unbearable. Let us remember that Pope Clement VIII, reacting to the Edict of Nantes, exclaimed: "Freedom of conscience for everyone is the worst thing in the world."[16]

15. Europeans were only just beginning to abandon analogical thinking and ordinary people were far from exploring, as Descartes would do, objective thought based on doubt. The majority of the European population went on unquestioningly judging others in relation to themselves. These American "savages," then, after being classified as human beings, had to be brought back to Christianity, which they had failed to preserve. Outside Christianity—the only true religion, the only conceivable religion—no redemption was possible.

16. Quoted in G. Audisio, *Les Français d'hier*, II, 383. See also Bernard Cottret, *L'Édit de Nantes, 1598* (Paris: Perrin, 1998); Thierry Wanegfellen, *L'Édit de Nantes: Une histoire européenne de la tolérance du XVIe siècle au XXe siècle* (Paris: Livre de Poche, 1998).

The Holy See and the Conversion of Aboriginal Peoples in North America, 1760–1830

LUCA CODIGNOLA

In 1995, in reviewing the attitude of the Holy See toward the conversion of North America's aboriginal peoples from the early days of "discovery" through the end of the Seven Years' War, I argued that by 1660 Roman Catholic missions to the aboriginal peoples of North America, until then a proclaimed object of European expansion, had lost their central relevance. Whereas in British continental colonies there had never been any real conversion "policy," because anti-Catholic penal laws and the small number of the faithful made sheer survival the only real issue at stake, in Canada by 1660 the church focused on the population of European origin and allowed missionary activity to be pursued only when it coincided with the Crown's policy. This shift, which the Holy See shared with the other European countries directly involved in the New World, was due to the difficulty of the missionary task and to the intellectual disillusionment engendered by the aboriginal societies.[1]

In this chapter I address the same issue with regard to the period immediately thereafter. What was the attitude of the Holy See toward the conversion of the aboriginal peoples of North America between the end of the Seven Years' War and the pontificate of Pius VIII (Francesco Saverio Castiglioni, 1761–1830)? This is a very long period, encompassing at least three generations. In the north Atlantic world, those who lived between 1760 and 1830 witnessed events of such magnitude that their descendants later referred to the era as the "Age of Revolutions"—the Conquest of Canada, the War of American Independence, the French Revolution, the Napoleonic Wars, and, from 1815 to 1830, the beginning of a constant and growing migration of people from Europe to British North America and the

---

1. Luca Codignola, "The Holy See and the Conversion of the Indians in French and British North America, 1486–1760," in *America in European Consciousness, 1493–1750*, ed. Karen Ordahl Kupperman (Chapel Hill: University of North Carolina Press, 1995), 195–242.

United States. Although in several western regions they still constituted the majority of the population, the aboriginal peoples of the United States were either greatly reduced in number or constantly pushed westward. This trend was less evident in British North America, where aboriginal peoples and peoples of European origin were less numerous and political alliances traditionally replaced what in the United States was outright dispossession. The history of the aboriginal missions in this period has often been told and does not need to be chronicled here, although it could be argued that renewed attention to the role of the aboriginal peoples in the early Republic has not yet focused on missionary history.[2]

In Canada, the immediate aftermath of the Seven Years' War seemed to confirm the scant interest in the aboriginal missions that had characterized the previous century. Left to its own means and unable to receive new clergy from France, the Canadian church struggled for its own survival and was entirely concerned with the needs of the population of European origin. The aboriginal peoples were indeed concentrated in the diocese of Québec, which was now even more immense, as it included most of the American West. No extra hands, however, could be spared for their salvation. Jean-Olivier Briand (1715–94), recently appointed bishop of Québec, expressed this sentiment rather clearly in 1769. Unless Jesuit missionaries were allowed to step in, he admitted, no priest would take care of the aboriginal missions, "for which Canadians have no taste, but that are my obligation nevertheless."[3] His successor, Louis-Philippe Mariauchau d'Esgly (1710–88), was hoping to use new recruits from Ireland for his aboriginal missions, for which he had no clergy to spare.[4] In fact, the end of the French regime had simply confirmed a situation that had prevailed for some decades. Work with the aboriginal peoples had long been left almost entirely to the

---

2. For the most recent literature, see Olive Patricia Dickason, *Canada's First Nations: A History of Founding Peoples from Earliest Times* (Toronto: McClelland & Stewart, 1992), 234–35, 240; Carol Devens, *Countering Colonization: Native American Women and Great Lakes Missions, 1630–1900* (Berkeley and Los Angeles: University of California Press, 1992), 45–89; Gregory Evans Dowd, *A Spirited Resistance: The North American Indian Struggle for Unity, 1745–1815* (Baltimore: Johns Hopkins University Press, 1992), 60–64; Terrence Michael Murphy and Roberto Perin, *Concise History of Christianity in Canada* (Toronto: Oxford University Press, 1996), 65–68, 154, 156, 180–82; Tanis C. Thorne, *The Many Hands of My Relations: French and Indians on the Lower Missouri* (Columbia: University of Missouri Press, 1996), 134–55; and J. R. Robert Choquette, *Canada's Religions: An Historical Introduction* (Ottawa: University of Ottawa Press, 2004), 181–224.

3. Jean-Olivier Briand to [Giuseppe Maria Castelli], Québec, October 29, 1769, Archives of the Sacred Congregation "de Propaganda Fide," Rome (hereafter APF), Udienze, vol. 11, fols. 50rv–51rv.

4. Louis-Philippe Mariauchau d'Esgly to Thomas Hussey, Québec, November 13, 1785, Archives de l'Archidiocèse de Québec (hereafter AAQ), 22A, V, no. 199.

regular orders, mainly Jesuits, Sulpicians, and Capuchins. For all practical purposes, these were independent of the bishop of Québec and were mostly active on the peripheries of the diocese—in Acadia, in the West, and in upper Louisiana and Louisiana proper.

In the British continental colonies, soon to become the United States, there was even less interest in the aboriginal mission. The papers of John Carroll (1736–1815), the bishop of Baltimore, who had headed the Catholic Church since 1784, and those of his successors in Baltimore and in the other, newly created episcopal sees, show that their main interest lay with the community of European origin and that their preoccupations were directly related to the management of their internal conflict. The aboriginal peoples were never entirely forgotten, but, just as in British North America, the insufficient clergy could hardly be spared for their special needs.[5] In 1798, for example, Carroll refused to post two Sulpicians, Jean-Louis-Anne-Madelain Lefèbvre de Cheverus (1768–1836) and François-Antoine Matignon (1753–1818), with the Penobscot and Passamaquoddy nations in the New Brunswick–New England region, where they had recently spent four months.[6] Furthermore, very few priests were linguistically qualified or manifested any wish to be posted with the aboriginal peoples. Those who did were regarded as saintly men sent by God to provide for the needs of the most destitute and unfortunate part of the flock. When he became bishop of Boston, Lefèbvre de Cheverus found only one missionary who was willing to minister to the aboriginal nations. But when, in 1818, an exhausted Jacques-René Romagné (active 1811–19) returned to France after eight years of missionary activity, the bishop was left "in a predicament and in an uncertainty with regard to the poor Passamaquoddy Indians."[7] Most often, when these missionaries died or left, there was no one to replace them.

Individual missionaries often took the initiative and only later informed their superiors. In 1789 nine chiefs of the Oneida Nation in upstate New York directly petitioned the pope, Pius VI (Giovanni Angelo Braschi, 1717–99) for the formal appointment of one Jean-Louis-Victor Le Tonnelier de Coulonge, whom they had just elected as their bishop. The following year a certain Jean de La Mahotière, self-styled "first general agent of the Oneida nation," further

---

5. See *The John Carroll Papers*, ed. Thomas O'Brien Hanley, 3 vols. (Notre Dame: University of Notre Dame Press, 1976); *John Carroll Recovered: Abstracts of Letters and Other Documents Not Found in the John Carroll Papers*, ed. Thomas W. Spalding and Paul K. Thomas (Baltimore: Cathedral Foundation Press, 2000).

6. Jean-Louis-Anne-Madelain Lefèbvre de Cheverus to John Douglas, Boston, August 31, 1798, Westminster Diocesan Archives, London, A, vol. 47, no. 221.

7. Lefèbvre de Cheverus to Joseph-Octave Plessis, Boston, May 17, 1819, AAQ, 7CM, II, no. 37.

explained that four Frenchmen were planning to civilize this aboriginal nation, that Le Tonnelier de Coulonge himself had donated 500,000 *livres* to the enterprise, and that six Capuchins were soon to join the mission. The Holy See could send its annual installment via the Spanish consulate or the French embassy of New York. The Holy See officials and Antonio Dugnani (1748–1818), archbishop of Rhodes and nuncio in France, looked favorably upon the project but wondered why it had never been reported by either Carroll or Jean-François Hubert (1739–97), then bishop of Québec, who did not seem to have been aware of the proceedings.[8] The plan may have originated in some Parisian aristocratic circles that had felt the early brunt of the French Revolution, but there is no doubt that the Oneida signatories were fully aware of the proceedings. Similarly, in 1791 Carroll was suddenly made aware of some four hundred aboriginal families, originally from Acadia, who now lived in due Catholic form in the forests close to Boston and were serviced by a French-speaking priest.[9] These might have been the same aboriginal nations visited by Lefèbvre de Cheverus and Matignon about a decade later.

If the aboriginal peoples could be somewhat ignored by the church in regions that by 1760 had long since become overwhelmingly European, that is, east of the Alleghenies and along the St. Lawrence basin, it was impossible to ignore them where they constituted the vast majority of the overall population, that is, in most of the Maritime Provinces of British North America, west of Montréal, and in the Ohio Valley, upper Louisiana, and Louisiana proper. (When Louisiana became a Spanish colony, Rome as well as Québec and Baltimore were automatically excluded from its ecclesiastical administration.) There the aboriginal peoples were to be counted in the tens of thousands and Europeans were still a small minority, as Pontiac's War showed all too clearly. During the French regime, missionaries in those regions had been comparatively numerous. There were Discalced Carmelites, Capuchins, and Jesuits in Louisiana, Capuchins and priests of the Séminaire de Québec in upper Louisiana, Jesuits in the Ohio Valley and in the West, and Jesuits and Spiritans in the Maritime Provinces. The outcome

8. Quotation in Jean de La Mahotière to Pius VI, Oneida Castle, May 17, 1790, APF, Congressi, America Centrale (hereafter C, AC), vol. 2, fols. 568rv–569rv. See also Oneida Nation to Pius VI, Oneida Castle, April 25, 1789, fols. 564rv–567rv; Oneida Nation to Pius VI, Oneida Castle, April 25, 1789, fols. 572rv–575rv; Antonio Dugnani to Leonardo Antonelli, Paris, August 2, 1790, fols. 570rv–571rv; and Propaganda to Dugnani, Rome, September 11, 1790, fols. 577v–579rv.

9. Martin Hody to Propaganda, Paris, November 7, 1791, APF, Fondo Vienna (hereafter FV), vol. 26, fols. 245rv–246rv; Propaganda to Hody, [Rome], January 14, 1792, APF, Lettere, vol. 262, fols. 6v–7rv. The original information is contained in a letter from John Carroll to Hody, dated from Baltimore on July 15, 1791, not included in Hanley, *Carroll Papers*.

of the Seven Years' War and the severance of the well-established chain of command in the Catholic hierarchy caused the almost immediate collapse of this missionary network. "The missions among the savages have greatly suffered on account of the calamities of the war," explained Christopher (Kit) Stonor (1716–95), the Roman agent of the English clergy.[10] The Holy See was indeed deluged by reports from missionaries who listed faraway western nations and recalled their former accomplishments, especially in the Maritime Provinces and Louisiana. Unfortunately, these priests were now based in France and had little hope of returning to their missions.[11] Almost three generations were to go by before these missions enjoyed a great revival, in the 1830s and 1840s, which was by no means a pale reminder of the great missionary enthusiasm of the early seventeenth century, at least in the North American West.

Signs of that revival, however, were nowhere to be seen after the Seven Years' War. The few missionaries who remained in the West, mostly French speaking, were placed in a precarious position. London had replaced Paris as the new capital of the empire, but given the fact that Great Britain was a Protestant country, who was in charge of spiritual matters? This was not simply a jurisdictional and legal issue. Priests needed faculties (i.e., spiritual powers) that could be granted only by a local bishop or by the Holy See, as everyday matters such as baptisms and marriages needed to be properly regulated and administered. Baptism was the prime sacrament to be conferred upon a person, the necessary threshold toward the full enjoyment of a Christian life and final salvation. In the early seventeenth century, Jesuit missionaries had been adamant in not administering baptism to any aboriginal person, with the exceptions of infants, people on the verge of death, and those who had been fully instructed in the tenets of their new faith. The outcome of the Seven Years' War does not seem to have affected the attitude of the missionaries toward this sacrament, although the issue of the appropriate way to translate the formula of baptism into aboriginal languages had been referred to Rome as late as the 1750s.[12]

---

10. [Christopher Stonor] to [Propaganda], [Rome], [1763 or March 1764], Westminster Diocesan Archives, London, B, vol. 137, nos. 417–23.

11. Pierre de La Rue, abbé de L'Isle-Dieu, to [Castelli], Paris, February 20, 1764, APF, Congregazioni particolari (hereafter CP), vol. 137, fols. 25rv–28rv; Jean-Louis Le Loutre and Jean Manach to [Pietro Pamphili Colonna], Paris, April 9, 1764, fols. 43rv–44rv; Hilaire de Genevaux to Propaganda, Sedan, September 24, 1764, APF, FV, vol. 37, fols. 17rv, 22rv; François-Philibert Watrin to [Pamphili Colonna], [France], [1765]; APF, C, AC, vol. 1, fols. 424rv–430rv, 433rv; Simon de Parey to Aimé de Lamballe, Sedan, April 14, 1766, fols. 451rv–452rv.

12. Propaganda's internal memorandum, [Rome], July 16, 1755, APF, FV, vol. 58, Index, fol. 32r; [Silvio Valenti Gonzaga] to Henri-Marie Dubreil de Pontbriand, Rome, July 22, 1755, APF, Lettere,

Marriage dispensations, on the contrary, were affected by the end of the French regime. In 1764 the Jesuit Sébastien-Louis Meurin (1707–77) explained to the pope, Clement XIII (Carlo Rezzonico, 1693–1769), that he did not know whether his faculties were still valid in the absence of any proper superior. Meurin was at the time the only missionary among the Illinois of upper Louisiana. These faculties, however, were "of the utmost importance for a missionary who finds himself in a very distant country, among savages and barbarians." Marriage dispensations, which included the power to allow a couple of close relatives to marry legally, were, according to Meurin, of special relevance if one wanted to avoid concubinage among aboriginal peoples.[13] The issue of proper sacramental marriages had always been a subject of debate within the Catholic Church. In principle, the church recognized only marriages between two Catholic partners performed by a Catholic priest. The cession of Canada to a Protestant Crown reopened the issue with regard to both Europeans and aboriginals: should the church recognize a marriage between a Catholic and a Protestant? Or a marriage between two Catholics if it was celebrated by a Protestant minister? After 1760 cases of this sort became daily occurrences. Should the priest ban the irregular couple from church and, de facto, consign them and their offspring to the Protestant churches? Between 1763 and 1765 the matter was debated in Québec, at the Sorbonne in Paris, and in Rome. Precedents relating to mixed marriages in Holland were recalled, but no substantial agreement was reached, although leniency seemed to be favored by most.[14] Yet the matter was of great urgency. In 1766 Briand was confronted by the case of an aboriginal couple who had been convinced by "some ignorant

---

vol. 185, fols. 114v–116r; Dubreil de Pontbriand to Giuseppe Spinelli, Québec, November 15, 1756, APF, Congressi, America Settentrionale (hereafter C, AS), vol. 1, fols. 171rv–172rv; L'Isle-Dieu to [Spinelli], Paris, March 3, 1757, fols. 173rv–174rv, 179rv–180rv; Niccolò Antonelli to the Assessor of the Holy Office [Benedetto Veterani?], Rome, September 14, 1757, APF, Lettere, vol. 191, fol. 121r; N. Antonelli to the Assessor of the Holy Office [Veterani?], Rome, April 28, 1759, vol. 195, fol. 61v.

13. Sébastien-Louis Meurin to Clement XIII, [Illinois country], [1764], APF, Udienze, vol. 10, fols. 25rv–26rv.

14. [L'Isle-Dieu] to [Propaganda], [Paris], [February 20, 1764], APF, C, AS, vol. 1, fols. 1[e]rv–6rv; L'Isle-Dieu to [Castelli], Paris, February 20, 1764, APF, CP, vol. 137, fols. 15rv–16rv; [L'Isle-Dieu] to [Castelli], [Paris], [February 20, 1764], fols. 29rv–30rv; L'Isle-Dieu to [Castelli], Paris, February 27, 1764, fols. 53rv–54rv; L'Isle-Dieu to [Castelli], Paris, April 2, 1764, fols. 33rv–38rv; Castelli to Mario Marefoschi, [Rome], May 25, 1764, APF, C, AS, vol. 1, fols. 190rv–191rv; Marefoschi to Assessor of the Holy Office [Veterani?], Rome, May 25, 1764, APF, Lettere, vol. 205, fols. 82v–83r; Propaganda's internal memorandum, [Rome], January 24, 1765, APF, FV, vol. 59, fols. 236rv–239r. See also the appropriate files in Archivio della Congregazione per la Dottrina della Fede, Rome, Archivio del Sant'Offizio, De Matrimoniis, box 6 (1761–64), folder 18, fols. 388rv–466rv; box 8, folder 17, Québec 1770 (8 folios, not paginated). To my knowledge, only Giovanni Pizzorusso has worked in these archives with an eye to North America. See his "I dubbi sui sacramenti dalle missioni *ad infideles:*

Catholics" to marry before a Protestant minister. The woman had been a concubine of both her current husband and of his father. Briand managed to persuade the couple to separate, but he needed the faculty to dispense them from Rome so that they could be married properly. Several weeks had elapsed since his request. Rome was very slow, and Briand found it "extremely difficult to keep them in their duty."[15]

In the 1770s, Meurin and Pierre Gibault (1737–1802), two missionaries active in the Michigan and the Illinois-Missouri regions, expressed their attitudes toward aboriginal marriages. In compliance with the policy of the British Crown, they invariably agreed to celebrate marriages between mixed couples of European and aboriginal origin, but did so "always reluctantly" and "only to reduce an evil that could not be avoided." In agreement with the local Crown officials, Meurin maintained that "the legitimate offspring of these bad unions are less harmful to the crown's interests than the bastards who tend to live with the savage nations and thus become even worse, due to the lack of education and of restraints."[16] Indeed, Gibault stated bluntly that it made little difference whether a child of mixed blood was born in or out of wedlock, since in both instances they were "harmful to the Crown."[17]

In spite of the Sorbonne's pronouncements and the Holy See's guidelines, the validity of mixed marriages continued to be a thorny issue. A few years later Briand expressed his opinion that no special faculties or dispensations were necessary when a European Catholic and a pagan aboriginal person wanted to marry, because that marriage was by definition null and void: "There is simply no marriage between a man in due form and a pagan and unbaptized savage woman." Such bluntness was perhaps justified by the unacceptable behavior of Gibault, then a missionary with the Illinois, who had recently absolved a man who not only had entered into such a matrimony but had also later "unjustly and inhumanly repudiated" the poor woman. For good measure, he had robbed her of 600 *livres* under the pretense of paying for an unnecessary dispensation, a sum that was to be returned forthwith, the bishop insisted.[18] About a generation later, contradictory decisions were made in Sault Ste. Marie with regard to an aboriginal woman, hastily married only half an hour after being baptized,

---

Percorsi nelle burocrazie di Curia," in *Amministrare i sacramenti tra Vecchio e Nuovo Mondo*, ed. Paolo Broggio et al. (Rome: École française de Rome, forthcoming).
    15. [Briand] to L'Isle-Dieu, [Québec], August 30, 1766, AAQ, 11CM, I, no. 29a.
    16. Meurin to [Briand], Prairie-du-Rocher, June 11, 1770, AAQ, 7CM, VI, no. 26.
    17. Pierre Gibault to [Briand], Vincennes, [November 1770], AAQ, 7CM, VI, no. 23.
    18. [Briand] to [Gibault], Québec, April 26, 1777, AAQ, 7CM, VI, no. 43.

and a *métis* woman, who was refused the same privilege in spite of being duly baptized and instructed, because she lacked her father's permission and a certificate proving that she was not already married.[19] In an effort to facilitate the entry of aboriginal persons into the Catholic Church, a bishop of Québec suggested that converted aboriginal men who had more than one wife be allowed to keep the wife they liked best, instead of the first one. The issue went all the way to the Sacred Congregation of the Holy Office in Rome, whose cardinals went to great lengths to give an impartial verdict. Anthony Kohlmann (1771–1836), a former Jesuit superior in the United States, was asked for his opinion, and a similar case regarding Polinesia submitted by Étienne Rouchouze (1798–1843), bishop of Nilopolis and vicar apostolic in Eastern Australia, was compared to the North American one. In the end, however, no firm decision was made.[20]

Marriage cases like these were so common that it is likely that most of them went unrecorded, as the local missionaries made their decisions without consulting with their superiors. This seems to confirm the pre-1760 pattern, which was marked by notable differences between missionaries in the field and faraway jurisdictional authorities or would-be missionaries. This gap became even wider after 1760. Missionaries in the field acted on the whole according to their own conscience and personal whim, their doctrinal upbringing tempered by the need to be accommodating in order to save more souls. In the Canadian and American West it would have been impossible to be more demanding, the missionaries being so few and the aboriginal peoples so numerous. Flexibility and optimism were indeed a necessity. In the 1820s, for example, the newly appointed vicar apostolic in the Northwest, Joseph-Norbert Provencher (1787–1853), reported that in his immense jurisdiction aboriginal women normally had carnal knowledge of English, Scottish, and French-Canadian men, either Catholic or Protestant. That was indeed a bad thing. The good side of it all, however, was that their offspring were almost invariably Catholic, as these women easily agreed to be baptized and to marry according to the laws of the Catholic Church.[21] Early seventeenth-century Jesuits, whom we know so well

---

19. Jean-Baptiste Marchand to Jean-François Hubert, L'Assomption-du-Détroit, July 1, 1797, AAQ, 7CM, V, no. 137.

20. [Angelo Mai] to Anthony Kohlmann, [Rome], April 9, 1836, APF, Lettere, vol. 317, fols. 356v–357r; [Mai] to Domenico Cattani, [Rome], April 15, 1836, fols. 358rv–359r; [Mai] to Joseph-Norbert Provencher, [Rome], January 14, 1837, vol. 318, fol. 80rv.

21. Provencher to Propaganda, near Saint-Boniface, July 3, 1824, Brevis relatio, APF, Scritture Originali riferite nelle Congregazioni Generali (hereafter SOCG), vol. 937, fols. 703rv–704rv; Joseph Signay to Giacomo Filippo Fransoni, Québec, November 2, 1835, vol. 951, fols. 184rv–185rv.

though their published sources, appeared to be similarly optimistic, at least until the late 1640s, but they were certainly less accommodating. In both the early seventeenth century and the post-1760 era, however, missionaries felt little sympathy for the aboriginal societies, which continued to be styled as savage and barbarian and were the source of little cultural attraction. Agape before his innumerable western flock, Provencher, for all his youthful optimism, doubted whether his aboriginal nations could really be "styled as inhabitants, being nomadic peoples."[22] An experienced missionary was similarly unimpressed and even more aware of the gap between wishful thinking and real means. North of Lake Superior, the Sulpician Jean-Baptiste Marchand (1760–1825) explained, a multitude of different aboriginal nations were "nomadic, brutish, and entirely lost. . . . Besides, how could we get there? How much would it cost to maintain a missionary there?"[23]

Individual whims also greatly influenced the missionaries' own attitude toward the aboriginal peoples. These whims are very difficult to detect in the published Jesuit relations, but they show themselves rather clearly in the later missionaries' personal correspondence. Although a sense of Christian duty and pastoral piety was certainly present, my extensive reading of such correspondence has yielded no example of personal sympathy or attraction. The "good Indians" were always those farther away or yet to be met.[24] The missionaries' primary flock, one must recall, consisted almost entirely of the population of European origin—whether French, Irish, German, or English. The aboriginal peoples were mostly regarded as a nuisance that stood in the way, and a dangerous one at that. Danger was indeed ever present and grew with distance from the more settled regions in the East or along the St. Lawrence. In the seventeenth century martyrdom was accepted, and sometimes wished for, when it was caused by those who were the target of the missionary activity itself. In the eighteenth and nineteenth centuries, however, a missionary would find little glory in being killed by a raiding party on his way from one European village to another. While reporting on the death of Pontiac (1720–69), the Ottawa leader Gibault warned that this episode "might kindle a major war among the nations."[25] In 1770 the

---

22. Provencher to Propaganda, near Saint-Boniface, July 3, 1824, Brevis relatio, APF, SOCG, vol. 937, fols. 703rv–704rv.
23. Marchand to Plessis, L'Assomption-du-Détroit, October 25, 1797, AAQ, 7CM, V, no. 138.
24. See, for example, Joseph-André-Mathurin Jacrau to Pamphili Colonna, Québec, August 20, 1766, AAQ, 1CB, IV, no. 188; Michael Ennis to Philip Crane, Philadelphia, September 4, 1795, December 8, 1795, APF, C, AC, vol. 3, fols. 62rv–63rv.
25. Gibault to [Briand], Kaskaskias, June 15, 1769, AAQ, 7CM, VI, no. 18.

journey from Prairie-du-Rocher to Vincennes, a village that had not seen a priest for six years, was deemed too dangerous to be undertaken by any missionary.[26] Gibault barely managed to slip through the lurking aborigines and save his scalp by taking all sorts of precautions,[27] which included the carrying with him of "my gun and my two pistols," as he did "whenever I leave for any journey." Feeling that some further explanation was in order, Gibault added, "I agree that if it were for religion, being a priest . . . I should not defend myself, but a miserable Indian who has no other intention but to assuage his barbarity, who only wants my scalp, and who shall also tear off my horse's mane and mine, and who shall burn me slowly on the fire if he ever takes me alive for the only pleasure to watch me suffer, who shall make me eat my own flesh after roasting some piece of my body, . . . should I suffer all this without defending myself? Should I allow a tiger to devour me, or any other animal that often attack men in these lands? In this Indian there seems not to be more intelligence than in that beast."[28] According to other missionaries, in the 1780s and 1790s massacres were a normal occurrence in the Detroit region.[29] In short, the disappearance of all aboriginal peoples from western North America would have been openly regretted by most missionaries as a wasted opportunity, but the historian gets the feeling that they would have welcomed it privately. As the famous seventeenth-century Jesuit leader, Paul Le Jeune (1592–1664), would have said, to console himself after the Jesuits' disastrous experience with the Huron, "God demolishes only to rebuild better than before."[30]

Faraway jurisdictional authorities, such as the local bishops, the European superiors, and the officials of the Holy See, expressed a markedly different attitude.[31] Rarely did these people meet a real aboriginal person, nor were they

---

26. Meurin to [Briand], Prairie-du-Rocher, June 11, 1770, AAQ, 7CM, VI, no. 26.
27. Gibault to [Briand], Kaskaskias, June 15, 1770, AAQ, 7CM, VI, no. 22.
28. Gibault to [Briand], Vincennes, [November 1770], AAQ, 7CM, VI, no. 23.
29. Louis Payet to Hubert, Detroit, February 20, 1786, AAQ, 7 CM, V, 45; no. 80, François-Xavier Dufaux to [Hubert], [Detroit], October 26, 1790; no. 82, Dufaux to Hubert, Detroit, February 1, 1791; no. 96, Pierre Fréchette to [Hubert], Detroit, May 20, 1793.
30. Paul Le Jeune, *Relation de ce qvi s'est passé en la Novvelle France en l'Année 1639* (Paris: Chez Sebastien Cramoisy, 1640), 89, now published in Lucien Campeau, ed., *Monumenta Novae Franciae*, vol. 4, *Les grandes épreuves (1638–1640)* (Rome: Institutum Historicum Societatis Iesu, and Montréal: Les Éditions Bellarmin, 1989), 312.
31. The myth of the noble savage, an overstated category in so-called Indian-white relations, had almost no significance for field missionaries, although it was probably of some consequence for faraway authorities. See the latest treatment of the issue in Terry Jay Ellingson, *The Myth of the Noble Savage* (Berkeley and Los Angeles: University of California Press, 2001).

the object of much knowledge or interest in Europe, except to a select few. A Church of England minister in Leghorn, Andrew Burnaby (1734?–1813), reminded his friend, future U.S. president George Washington, that the aboriginal nations were "in this part of the World" rather "little talked of," as Corsicans were "in yours" (that is, in the British continental colonies), although both the aboriginal peoples and Corsicans could be "a Subject of very interesting Conversation."[32] Some, of course, were better informed than others. A number of North American bishops, such as Edmund Burke (1753–1820), who ended his career as bishop of Sion and vicar apostolic in Nova Scotia, and Hubert, had had direct experience of western aboriginal societies.[33] In the 1830s and 1840s, during the great missionary revival and the erection of many western dioceses, more and more bishops, let alone missionaries, became involved in the aboriginal missions. For their part, the officials of the Sacred Congregation "de Propaganda Fide" were rather keen on studying and filing the reports they regularly received from North America, and so were the officials of the Propagation de la Foi in Lyons.[34] But whatever one did not know from personal experience tended to conform to a stereotypical image of the North American Indian that grew apace with one's remoteness from the regions where contact really took place. The Sulpician superior in Paris, Jacques-André d'Émery (active 1789–98), threatened by the French Revolution, was willing to send all his confrères to North America, which he was convinced was still "populated by savages, Protestants, and some Catholics." Now was the time, he enthusiastically suggested, "to start to convert the savages, recall the Protestants, and confirm the Catholics in their faith."[35] So much for two hundred years of colonization and missionizing. About a generation later, the prefect of the Sacred Congregation de Propaganda Fide, the Barnabite Francesco Fontana (1750–1822), was enthralled by the new

---

32. Andrew Burnaby to George Washington, Leghorn, April 29, 1765, Library of Congress, Washington Papers, 1741–99, Series 4, General Correspondence, 1697–1799, fols. 94v–96r.

33. For Edmund Burke's years in the West, see Michael Power, "Father Edmund Burke: Along the Detroit River Frontier, 1794–1797," Canadian Catholic Historical Association, *Historical Studies* 51 (1984): 29–46.

34. The real title of this missionary agency was *Association de la Propagation de la Foi*, later *Oeuvre de la Propagation de la Foi*. Established in Lyons on May 3, 1822, the association issued the *Annales de la Propagation de la Foi*, a quarterly published since 1822. The *Annales* printed recent letters originating in mission territories. See Jean-Claude Baumont, "La renaissance de l'idée missionnaire en France au début du XIXe siècle," in *Les réveils missionnaires en France du Moyen-Âge à nos jours (XIIe-XXe siècles): Actes du colloque de Lyon (29–31 mai 1980) organisé par la Société d'Histoire Ecclésiastique de la France et le concours de la Société d'Histoire du Protestantisme français*, ed. Guy Duboscq and André Latreille (Paris: Beauchesne, 1984), 210–21.

35. Jacques-André d'Émery to Dugnani, Paris, September 5, 1790, APF, FV, vol. 26, fols. 200rv–201rv.

prospects for conversion among the "most recently discovered" innumerable northwestern Canadian aboriginal nations. He insisted that Joseph-Octave Plessis (1763–1825), the bishop of Québec, be more precise in his letters. The latter was asked to advise "on the best way to convey the light of the Gospel to these barbaric peoples."[36] Plessis, however, was much less enthusiastic. That region was still roamed by "nomadic and most ferocious peoples," he explained, and was so far away that it would better be entrusted to missionaries from Russia or California.[37] In a similar vein the Vincentian Felice De Andreis (1778–1820) described his station in St. Louis, which he had just reached, as "at the extremity of the Earth, on the banks of the Mississippi, with nothing between us and the Pacific Ocean, which separates us from China, but a few days of walking in a country that is only inhabited by beasts, or by savages who differ but little from these beasts."[38]

In spite of their recourse to negative stereotypes (barbarism, nomadism, ferociousness), faraway jurisdictional authorities were in fact rather open-minded and willing to help. To my knowledge, there is hardly any instance in the Roman correspondence in which a marriage dispensation was denied or a doctrinal matter not interpreted in favor of the aboriginal peoples. If anything, the Holy See tended to be fascinated by the aboriginal persons they met in Rome, and sometimes they fell right into the traps prepared by their alleged missionaries or by those who pretended to speak on their behalf. Sent by the bishop of New Orleans, the Sulpician Louis-Guillaume-Valentin Dubourg (1766–1833), the scoundrel priest Angelo Inglesi (c. 1795–1825) traveled all around Europe in 1821 collecting money and enticing young priests to come and participate in the conversion of Louisiana's aboriginal nations. Giovanni Giuseppe Vincenzo Argenti (active 1808–22), an official at the Dataria Apostolic, reported to his trusted correspondent in Dublin, Archbishop John Thomas Troy (1739–1823), that Inglesi spoke "of vast lands and of the needs of those savage peoples, ready to embrace Catholicism."[39] In the late 1820s the case of Jean-Baptiste-François Fauvel (1796–after 1830), a Québec minor cleric who ended up as a bogus missionary in Green Bay, Michigan, and that of J. Delaunay (active 1826–29), a

---

36. [Francesco Fontana] to Plessis, [Rome], March 13, 1819, APF, Lettere, vol. 300, fols. 131rv–133rv.
37. Plessis to Propaganda, Rome, November 17, 1819, APF, CP, vol. 146, fols. 676rv–679rv.
38. Felice De Andreis to Carlo Domenico Sicardi, St. Louis, [February 24, 1817?], APF, C, AC, vol. 8, fols. 32rv–37rv.
39. Giovanni Giuseppe Vincenzo Argenti to John Thomas Troy, Rome, May 19, 1821, Archives of the Archdiocese of Dublin, Roman Correspondence, Troy, AB2/28/1, no. 135, fol. 170rv.

Frenchman who styled himself "leader of the Osages" of upper Louisiana, are well documented.[40] In 1826 Fauvel accompanied to Paris and Rome a Mohawk chief of Akwesasne, Joseph Teorogaron Anouaren, a self-proclaimed descendant of the Mohawk saint Kateri Tekakwitha (1656–80). After being received with great honors by all of the Catholic dignitaries in Paris, he proceeded to Rome in full Iroquois regalia. There Pope Leo XII (Annibale Sermattei della Genga, 1760–1829) blessed him and gave him a relic and two medals. The party disappeared as soon as someone began to question their veracity. In fact, three years later, their hoax was exposed by the western missionaries, who accused Teorogaron of being a drunkard and Fauvel a simoniac and lascivious cleric.[41] Delaunay led a small group of Catholic Osages (a chief, his wife, and a warrior) willing to help their nation to become "civilized" through France to Rome. Although Delaunay had managed to survive by "exhibiting the savages" and through the assistance of the French embassy, the indebted party was now stranded in Rome, unable to return home.[42] Yet the Holy See officials had learned their lesson. A warrant for Delaunay's arrest was issued and the exploitation of the Osages ordered to cease forthwith.[43] Not all aboriginal persons who went to Rome were "bad Indians," however. In the hope of preparing some aboriginal youngsters for the priesthood, the American Catholic Church and the Holy See went to great lengths to pay for their education at the Urban College, where young students from all over the world had been welcomed for almost two centuries. In 1832 two students from L'Arbre Croche, in Michigan, entered the Urban College. They were William Maccatebinessi or Maccodabinasse (d. 1833), also known as Blackbird or Oiseau Noir, and Augustin Kiminitchagan (active 1834–40), also known as Augustin Hamelin. Unfortunately, the former died in Rome, and the latter soon returned

---

40. Quotation in J. Delaunay to [Pius VIII], Rome, June 30, 1829, APF, Acta, vol. 192, fols. 304rv–305rv. For a review of the presence of persons of aboriginal origin in Rome and their changing image, see Giovanni Pizzorusso, "Indiani del Nordamerica a Roma (1826–1841)," *Archivio della Società Romana di Storia Patria* 116 (1993): 395–411; and Pizzorusso, "Gli indiani del Nordamerica in due riviste della prima metà dell'Ottocento: L'*Antologia* e il *Diario di Roma* (1821–1834)," in *Gli indiani d'America e l'Italia: Atti del Convegno di Studi, Torino 14–15 ottobre 1996*, ed. Fedora Giordano (Alessandria: Edizioni dell'Orso, 1997), 115–27.
41. Edward Dominick Fenwick to Propaganda, Cincinnati April 8, 1829, APF, C, AC, vol. 10, fols. 94rv–95rv; Fenwick to Mauro Cappellari, Cincinnati, May 12, 1829, fols. 138rv–139rv; [Cappellari] to [Propaganda], [Rome], [August 1829], APF, Acta, vol. 192, fols. 298rv–301rv.
42. Quotation in Delaunay to [Pius VIII], Rome, June 30, 1829, APF, Acta, vol. 192, fols. 304rv–305rv. See also Louis-Pierre-Vincent-Gaston-Gabriel Bellocq to Giovanni Soglia Cerroni, [Rome], July 1, 1829, APF, Acta, vol. 192, fols. 303[a]rv–303[b]rv.
43. [Cappellari] to [Propaganda], [Rome], [August 1829], APF, Acta, vol. 192, fols. 298rv–301rv.

home owing to health problems, although he never renounced his Catholic upbringing.[44] When Kiminitchagan became a chief in his own Ottawa Nation, the Holy See congratulated him and advised him to seek "the civilization, peace, and happiness" of his people by using "great moderation."[45]

With respect to the issue of the conversion of the aboriginal peoples, then, the period from 1760 to 1830 was characterized by a contradictory attitude within the Catholic Church. The farther the distance from the real aborigines, the stronger the impulse to assist them in their salvation and to trust in their goodwill. The closer one got, however, the less sympathy was felt, cultural or otherwise, and the weaker the conviction that these primitive peoples could be civilized and converted. There is little that is new in this contradiction, as it may be observed, with slight variations, throughout the missionary history of North America in the early modern age. From 1760 to 1830, however, two variations occurred within this familiar pattern, provided by the motivations offered by the British Crown and by the threat represented by the Protestant churches, respectively.

After the Treaty of Paris (1763), the British Crown realized rather quickly that in spite of its wish to create an English-speaking and Anglican North American empire, a substantial number of its subjects continued to be French-speaking Catholics. These subjects included newly arrived Irish and Scottish immigrants, as well as most of the aboriginal nations. In order to keep the loyalty of the latter, the British Crown resorted to the same tactics that the French Crown had used for a century—it pressured the Catholic hierarchy to send missionaries to live in the aboriginal villages by granting them an allowance, as long as they performed their duties well. These allowances were disbursed directly by the provincial governor. Since they were not deducted from the periodical allowances, donations, and privileges that the Crown offered to British North American bishops, the bishops' only objection to the posting of their missionaries in the aboriginal villages might be that their clergy were not

---

44. For the most recent literature, see Pizzorusso, "Indiani del Nordamerica a Roma," 403–8; Roger Antonio Fortin, *Faith and Action: A History of the Archdiocese of Cincinnati, 1821–1996* (Columbus: Ohio State University Press, 2002), 29–30, 408n13; and Gregory Evans Dowd, *War Under Heaven. Pontiac, the Indian Nations, and the British Empire* (Baltimore: Johns Hopkins University Press, 2002), 21.

45. [Mai] to Augustin Wummelin [Augustin Hamelin], [Rome], August 20, 1836, APF, Lettere, vol. 317, fols. 704rv–705r. Two years later more room was made available for a prospective aboriginal student from Nova Scotia, although the Urban College was said to be full, "given the special importance of the matter," provided that they would not suffer on account of the Roman climate. See [Fransoni] to Colin Francis MacKinnon, [Rome], March 17, 1838, APF, Lettere, vol. 318, fols. 260rv–263r.

sufficient in number to provide for the needs of the population of European origin, which invariably came first.

The need for Catholic missionaries to be used with the aboriginal peoples was felt in the Maritime Provinces of British North America immediately after the Seven Years' War. As soon as Briand, the newly appointed bishop of Québec, returned home, he received delegations of aborigines, British officers, and local merchants, all of them imploring him to send missionaries to the aboriginal villages. This was the only way to resume trade, they maintained.[46] The province of Québec and its Acadian appendage were, however, rather exceptional, as almost nowhere else in the British Empire did the Catholic Church enjoy such religious freedom.[47] To be sure, although official Catholic emancipation came later to the Atlantic Provinces, unofficial tolerance was indeed the rule very soon after the Treaty of Paris.[48] Still, prior to the War of American Independence, in the province of Massachusetts it would have been difficult to respond positively to the request that came from sixty Penobscot families who wanted a Catholic missionary. According to the provincial law, any priest caught on land, except on account of a shipwreck, was subject to perpetual imprisonment and even death. The only solution, Governor Thomas Hutchinson (1711–80) suggested to the secretary of state, was to remove the Penobscot to Nova Scotia.[49] The secretary of state was well aware that in Nova Scotia there was a Québec priest, Charles-François Bailly de Messein (1740–94), who was being paid to minister to the local aboriginal nations, so much so that, when informed that the missionary had absented himself from his station for two years, he immediately ordered that his allowance be stopped and that no successor be appointed, unless the aboriginal nations strenuously insisted.[50] Examples of the disbursement of such allowances are very numerous throughout the 1830s, and the practice

---

46. Jacrau to Pamphili Colonna, Québec, August 20, 1766, AAQ, 1 CB, IV, no. 188.
47. For the most recent literature on similar legal situations, see Philip Graeme Lawson, *A Taste for Empire and Glory: Studies in British Overseas Expansion, 1660–1800* (Aldershot: Variorum, and Brookfield, Vt.: Ashgate Publishing Company, 1997), article no. 3, (originally published 1989), 134; article no. 6 (originally published 1991), 308; Eric Jarvis, "His Majesty's Papist Subjects: Roman Catholic Political Rights in British West Florida," *Gulf South Historical Review* 16 (fall 2000): 6–19; Peter M. Doll, *Revolution, Religion, and National Identity. Imperial Anglicanism in British North America, 1745–1795* (Madison, N.J.: Fairleigh Dickinson University Press, and London: Associated University Presses, 2000), 120–21.
48. Murphy and Perin, *Concise History of Christianity*, 135–36.
49. Thomas Hutchinson to William Legge, Earl of Dartmouth, Boston, [17] April 1773, National Archives, London, Colonial Office 5, box 762, fols. 153rv–158rv.
50. Francis Legge to W. Legge, Halifax, August 25, 1774, ibid., Colonial Office 217, box 50, fols. 147rv–159rv; W. Legge to F. Legge, [London], October 5, 1774, fols. 160rv–161rv.

was regarded as customary.[51] In fact, the exceptional case was the one in which these allowances were withheld or reduced. Allowances seem to have been less customary in the West, probably because of the absence of a well-established provincial government. Never, however, did these allowances take the form of a salary. In this way the Crown reserved to itself a way to reward the loyalty of the beneficiaries and ensure their gratitude.[52] In the United States, in principle, the government did not officially intervene in religious matters. Some treaties with the aboriginal nations, however, did just that. For example, article 16 of the Treaty of Fort Meigs, otherwise called the Treaty with the Wyandots, etc. (September 29, 1817), implicitly recognized the Catholicism of the Ottawa, Chippewa, and Potawatomi nations by allowing them to grant to the rector of Sainte-Anne-du-Détroit full possession of some of their lands at Macon, near the Raisin River (Rivière-aux-Raisins), Michigan, for the future education of their children.[53] Salaries were also paid in the same years to missionaries in the Osage country in Missouri.[54]

In 1816 Plessis valued the Crown's annual expenditure for the aboriginal missionaries at £500,[55] a sum that must be weighed against the £50 that were normally granted to each of them.[56] For some missionaries, these allowances were barely sufficient to justify their employment. Plessis joyfully announced that he had finally found a missionary for the Abenaki/Malecite of Sainte-Anne-de-Frédéricton, but immediately after the bishop's death that same missionary, Charles-Joseph Asselin (1798–1856), let it be known that he had been obliged to accept that post owing to Plessis's wish that the Crown's allowance not be wasted. In fact, Asselin explained, he did not even know the language of the aboriginal nations to which he was to minister.[57] When the allowance

51. Plessis to John Coape Sherbrooke, Québec, October 14, 1816, AAQ, 210 A, IX, no. 13.
52. At the same time the regular disbursement of a salary to the Catholic Church was being debated in London with regard to Ireland. See Thomas Bartlett, *The Fall and Rise of the Irish Nation: The Catholic Question, 1690–1830* (Savage, Md.: Barnes & Noble Books, 1992), 250–51.
53. Charles Kappler, ed., *Indian Affairs: Laws and Treaties*, 6 vols. (Washington, D.C.: U.S. Government Printing Office, 1904–41), vol. 2, *Treaties, 1778–1883* (1904), 150.
54. Thorne, *Many Hands of My Relations*, 140.
55. Plessis to Lorenzo Litta, Québec, November 23, 1816, APF, C, AS, vol. 2, fols. 269rv–270rv.
56. This was certainly the figure for the Maritime Provinces. See George Robert Ainslie to Plessis, Sydney, March 23, 1818, AAQ, 312 CN, VII, no. 11; Michael McSweeney to Bernard-Claude Panet, Fredericton, March 24, 1828, AAQ, 311 CN, I, no. 31; no. 42, McSweeney to Panet, Fredericton, September 30, 1828; no. 44, Ferdinand Belleau to Panet, Sainte-Anne-de-Frédéricton, January 6, 1829; no. 52, Belleau to Panet, Sainte-Anne-de-Frédéricton, June 19, 1830.
57. Plessis to Patrick McMahon, Québec, October 27, 1825, AAQ, 210 A, XII, no. 359; Charles-Joseph Asselin to Panet, Sainte-Anne-de-Frédéricton, February 19, 1826, AAQ, 311 CN, I, 14.

was suspended, Asselin's successor, Michael McSweeney (1796–1836), threatened to leave the mission altogether.[58] It appears that in the Maritime Provinces the monetary and political inducement provided by the British Crown persuaded the Catholic hierarchy and some of its missionaries to take care of the aboriginal missions more than they would have done had they been left to their own devices.

The second variation at work in the period 1760–1830 was the threat represented by the Protestant churches. Of course, the inroads of Protestantism, both in Europe and elsewhere, had always been one of the main psychological impulses behind the missionary drive from the Council of Trent (1545–63) onward. In North America, however, after a short ecumenical period in which the betterment of the Christian human being had been deemed to be more important than confessional success,[59] in the late 1810s Protestant aboriginal missions began to be a real threat, or at least Catholics felt them to be so, from the Maritime Provinces all the way to the distant West.[60] In most cases the danger that came from dissenting denominations made the common interest of the British Crown and the Catholic Church even stronger. Answering Plessis's plea for assistance with regard to the Mi'kmaq Nation, the lieutenant-governor of Cape Breton Island, George Robert Ainslie (1776–1839), emphasized their common interest in the matter: "I shall be, at all times ready to give every encouragement in my power to Missionaries who will instruct Indians or others in the duties of Christians, inculcating more especially, loyalty to the King and attachment to the Mother Country, but shall be at least equally so to discourage the introduction of those pests of Society, and foes to Great Britain and Royalty, the Methodists. There is no danger of this kind from those of the creed of your Reverence, and my protection, limited in its extent, shall always be afforded them."[61] In the missionaries' letters, names and figures took the place of what

---

58. McSweeney to Panet, Fredericton, January 3, 1827, AAQ, 311 CN, I, no. 28; no. 40, McSweeney to Panet, Fredericton, December 26, 1828.

59. Murphy and Perin, *Concise History of Christianity*, 123–25; James Harold Lambert, *Monseigneur, the Catholic Bishop: Joseph-Octave Plessis, Church, State and Society in Canada; Historiography and Analysis* (Ph.D. diss., Université Laval, 1981), 706–93; Joseph Anthony Agonito, *The Building of an American Catholic Church: The Episcopacy of John Carroll* (New York: Garland Publishing, 1988), 146–204.

60. For the most recent literature, see J. H. Archer, "The Anglican Church and the Indian in the Northwest," Canadian Church Historical Society *Journal* 28 (1986): 19–30; Mark A. Noll, *A History of Christianity in the United States and Canada* (Grand Rapids, Mich.: William B. Eerdmans Publishing Co., 1992), 187–89; Carol L. Higham, *Noble, Wretched, and Redeemable: Protestant Missionaries to the Indians in Canada and the United States, 1820–1900* (Albuquerque: University of New Mexico Press, and Calgary: University of Calgary Press, 2001), 1–87.

61. Ainslie to Plessis, Sydney, March 23, 1818, AAQ, 312 CN, VII, no. 11.

had until then been general fears. A former Catholic mission on Lake Erie had become Protestant, Burke informed Rome in 1816.[62] An Anglican minister, John West (1778–1845), was in Saint-Boniface, Provencher warned in 1824.[63] Fifty baptized Huron children were lured away from near Detroit, in Upper Canada, to a Methodist school in the center of Ohio, reported the Sulpician Gabriel Richard (1767–1832) in 1826, a move that Étienne-Thédore Badin confirmed two years later.[64] In the same year Badin invited Charles Bretennière, superior general of the Soeurs de la Retraite Chrétienne in Marseilles, to assist in establishing new schools for the people of French-Canadian and aboriginal origin in Detroit, Mackinaw, Vincennes, and Illinois country, where Protestants had recently invested 500,000 francs.[65] Badin, a missionary who had spent most of his life in the American West, was even more detailed in a report that he prepared for the pope, Leo XII, in the same year. In the diocese of Cincinnati, Protestant missionaries had built thirty-two schools since 1824, with a current enrolment of 916 students.[66] At Mackinaw, New York Presbyterians were hard at work and especially successful in the field of education.[67] Nor were Protestant churches threatening in the far West only. They were also rather active in the Kingston region of Upper Canada,[68] and in New Brunswick, where the new missionary at Sainte-Anne-de-Frédéricton, Ferdinand Belleau (1805–after 1845), accused the local "New Light ministers, who for many years vainly tr[ied] to obtain some fixed allowances from the government." "Knowing that a Roman Catholic priest were advantaged in this regard," Belleau explained, "they most zealously try to convince the public opinion of the odiousness of this missionary." This had happened first with Asselin and now with him, who stood accused of being the cause of diminished Sunday attendance among the aboriginal faithful, while the number of aboriginal drunkards and thieves had increased during his mandate.[69] Although it is difficult to prove, I would argue that the real danger

62. Burke to Litta, Rome, February 12, 1816, APF, C, AS, vol. 2, fols. 261rv–262rv.
63. Provencher to Propaganda, near Saint-Boniface, July 3, 1824, Brevis relatio, APF, SOCG, vol. 937, fols. 703rv–704rv.
64. Richard to Jean-Paul Rigagnon, [Detroit], January 26, 1826, APF, C, AC, vol. 8, fols. 381rv–398rv; Badin to [Cappellari], Rome, January 2, 1828, APF, C, AC, vol. 9, fols. 534rv–537rv.
65. Badin to Charles [Bretennière], Marseilles, October 16, 1826, APF, C, AC, vol. 8, fols. 686rv–687rv.
66. Badin to Leo XII, [Rome], [November 1826], APF, C, AC, vol. 8, fols. 13rv–22rv.
67. Pierre Déjean to Rigagnon, during his mission with the Miamis, November 26, 1827, APF, C, AC, vol. 9, fols. 585rv–588rv.
68. Alexander McDonell to Cappellari, Kingston, September 13, 1823 [1827?], APF, C, AC, vol. 8, fols. 115rv–116rv.
69. Belleau to Panet, Sainte-Anne-de-Frédéricton, June 19, 1830, AAQ, 311 CN, I, no. 52.

represented by the Protestant churches provided yet a second impulse, together with the British Crown's inducement, for the Catholic Church to take care of the aboriginal missions, which ran a real danger of being left to their own almost nonexistent resources.

The years from 1760 to 1830 seem to confirm the tendency that I have observed for the previous period, namely, that while missions to the aboriginal peoples of North America continued to be one of the proclaimed objectives of European expansion, these missions had long since lost the central relevance they had prior to 1660. The years after the Seven Years' War also confirmed another tendency that was already observed with regard to the early missionary era, that of a major difference between missionaries in the field and faraway jurisdictional authorities or would-be missionaries. In fact, this difference became even wider after 1760. Missionaries in the field acted mostly according to their own conscience and personal whims, which almost invariably showed little personal sympathy for the aboriginal peoples and certainly no attraction to their societies and cultures. Faraway jurisdictional authorities, on the other hand, although prey to the customary stereotypical representations of the aboriginal cultures, proved to be more open-minded, optimistic, and often fascinated by them. This pattern is very much in line with the pre-1760 period, and might be said to be typical of all missionaries and church officials who dealt with "primitive" societies. What was typical of the 1760–1830 era and provided variations on familiar themes was, first, the unexpected alliance between the Catholic Church and the British Crown.[70] This was part of a more general political alliance that was to last well into the twentieth century. This alliance affected the aboriginal missions positively as well. The second variation was the threat represented by the Protestant churches, which had now become a real competitor in the field. This threat provided another major reason for the Catholic Church to continue its involvement with the aboriginal peoples.

---

70. On this alliance, see Codignola, "Roman Catholic Conservatism in a New North Atlantic World, 1760–1829," *William and Mary Quarterly,* 3d ser., 64 (October 2007): 717–56.

Policing Wabanaki Missions in the Seventeenth Century

CHRISTOPHER J. BILODEAU

During the King Philip's War (in Maine, 1675–78), many Wabanaki Indians of what is now northern New England fled from the violence and moved to the southern shore of the Saint Lawrence River near Québec. There they encountered Jesuit missionaries at the mission village of Sillery. Wabanakis continued to move there even after the conclusion of the war, and the mission grew throughout the 1670s and early 1680s. In 1683, when Sillery and its environs had become too small to accommodate the incoming flood of refugees, the governor-general of New France, Joseph-Antoine le Febvre de la Barre, his intendant, Jacques de Meulles, and the Jesuit superior-general of the missions, Thierry Beschefer, decided to move the mission to a site on the banks of the Chaudière River, renaming it St. François de Sales, after the French saint famous for his *Introduction to a Devout Life*.[1]

There were a number of reasons why the Wabanakis had become so interested in the French and Catholicism by the 1670s. First, the brutal years of warfare with the English during the King Philip's War destabilized Wabanakia, and many Wabanakis yearned for security. This relatively new threat from the English only exacerbated Wabanaki anxiety about warfare, as they had already suffered through the decades-old off-and-on hostilities with the Mohawks of the Hudson River valley.[2] With those hostile Indian nations to the west and a belligerent

---

I would like to thank Dan Usner, Mary Beth Norton, Jon Parmenter, Alyssa Mt. Pleasant, Allan Greer, and the members of the Cornell European History Colloquium of the fall of 2005 for their helpful comments and guidance with this essay.

1. Reuben Gold Thwaites, ed., *The Jesuit Relations and Allied Documents: Travels and Explorations of the Jesuit Missionaries in New France: 1610–1791*, 73 vols. (Cleveland: Burrows Brothers, 1896–1901), 62:265–67 (hereafter cited parenthetically in the text by volume and page number).

2. Colin G. Calloway, *The Western Wabanakis of Vermont, 1600–1800: War, Migration, and the Survival of an Indian People* (Norman: University of Oklahoma Press, 1990), 69–74; and Harald E. L.

European colony to the south, the Wabanakis looked north, to the French of Canada, for aid.[3] Second, Wabanaki shamans had steadily lost power and legitimacy among their people, as they failed to perform effective acts of ritual medicine in the face of almost a century of chaotic change (31:191–93, 201–3; 60:235–37).[4] Third, when the missionaries cared for the Indian sick, fed the hungry, and acted in other humanitarian ways during a time of stress, the Wabanakis interpreted those acts through the lens of reciprocity. The Indians believed that proper moral conduct rested overwhelmingly on reciprocal relations between people and *manitous,* or spirits, and so took the utmost care in negotiating their world. The Wabanakis understood these acts of kindness and healing within their own social and cultural framework, and believed the missionaries acted in proper ways.[5] Fourth, and finally, the missionaries' message of redemption and power through Jesus Christ, a vision of the world that explained all events within a seemingly coherent and meaningful narrative, helped to allay fears that many Wabanakis harbored during those tumultuous times.

But the Wabanakis did not simply convert to Catholicism. Across Wabanakia, most Indians seemed to have the same general reaction to Catholicism: an enthusiasm for its ritual and appreciation of its cosmology—though interpreted in their own idiom and understood through their own categories—but an indifference to missionary prescriptions of "proper Catholic behavior."[6] The majority of Wabanakis in those missions along the St. Lawrence River valley hoped to tap into what they believed to be the power of Christ, Mary, and the saints, but they did not believe they had to change their lives and customs in important ways in order to do so. Throughout their writings, the missionaries

---

Prins, *The Mi'kmaq: Resistance, Accommodation, and Cultural Survival* (Fort Worth, Texas: Harcourt Brace College Publishers, 1996), 112–14.

3. Calloway, *Western Wabanakis,* 79–80; P.-Andre Sévigny, *Les Abenaquis: Habitat et Migrations (17e et 18e siècles)* (Montréal: Les Editions Bellarmin, 1976), 124–26.

4. The Jesuit Pierre Biard, who proselytized among the Mi'kmaqs of what is now the Canadian Maritimes in the 1610s, wrote that those Indians questioned the power of shamans to cure diseases brought through European contact as early as 1612. Biard went on to note that the shamans complained that "their Devils have lost much of their power, if compared with what it is said to have been in the time of their Ancestors," and they blamed that loss on the French. See Thwaites, *Jesuit Relations,* 2:77.

5. This had been occurring for years. See ibid., 31:185–87, 201–5; 63:73, 81–85; and Kenneth M. Morrison, *The Embattled Northeast: The Elusive Ideal of Alliance in Abenaki-Euramerican Relations* (Berkeley and Los Angeles: University of California Press, 1984), 82–85.

6. For the best work on Wabanaki understanding of Catholicism—indeed, the best work on all Algonquian understanding of religious interaction with Catholic missionaries—see Kenneth M. Morrison, *The Solidarity of Kin: Ethnohistory, Religious Studies, and the Algonkian-French Religious Encounter* (Albany: State University of New York Press, 2002).

repeatedly condemned certain Wabanaki beliefs and actions, while the Wabanakis understood these same beliefs and actions as normal and justifiable ways of living their lives and comprehending their world. Why radically change their lives, they reasoned, simply because of Catholicism?

This reasoning, of course, befuddled the missionaries. They wanted most of all for the Wabanakis to acknowledge that how they lived on earth determined their placement in the eternal beyond. With the introduction of Catholic ritual into Wabanaki society, the missionaries also hoped to persuade the Indians to behave in ways they deemed just and pious along Catholic lines. This was clearly the most important goal of the missionaries in the late seventeenth and early eighteenth centuries in Wabanakia.[7]

Of course, what was "just and pious along Catholic lines" has been open for debate for two millennia, and the missionaries had their own ideas on the subject. Though many missionaries, as James Axtell notes, condensed the lessons of Catholicism into two overarching rules—"to believe in [God], and to be firmly resolved to keep his commandments"—they took for granted just how those rules should be followed and did not recognize how much their judgments were influenced by the French, religious-ordered, Counter-Reformation culture in which they lived.[8] Certainly, much Indian behavior that the missionaries deemed inappropriate violated the Ten Commandments. But other practices, such as eating to engorgement, taking revenge on enemies, torturing captives, sexual promiscuity, excessive drinking, and many others fell outside the purview of the Commandments. Their prohibition was due, in Axtell's phrase, to "French ethnocentrism."[9]

Persuading the Wabanakis to act in prescribed ways was an extremely difficult task for the missionaries.[10] Therefore, in their attempt to persuade the

---

7. Christopher Vecsey calls this aspect of the mission project making "the natives normative members of the faith." See Vecsey, *The Paths of Kateri's Kin* (Notre Dame: University of Notre Dame Press, 1997), 14.

8. Thwaites, *Jesuit Relations*, 13:169, quoted in James Axtell, *The Invasion Within: The Contest of Cultures in Colonial North America* (New York: Oxford University Press, 1985), 106.

9. Ibid., 107.

10. As it was with American Indians across North and South America. See Vecsey, *Paths of Kateri's Kin*, 29. It should be noted, however, that this does not mean that the Wabanakis disdained Catholicism, or even that they were not Catholics. If the criteria for being a Catholic meant a firm understanding of theology, or living a pure and sinless life as delineated by Catholic doctrine at the time, then a very low percentage of people—even in Europe—could call themselves Catholic. This was especially true among the poor. See Louis Châtellier, *The Religion of the Poor: Rural Missions in Europe and the Formation of Modern Catholicism, c. 1500–c .1800* (Cambridge: Cambridge University Press, 1997), 147–61.

Wabanakis to think in the ways in which they wanted them to think and do the things they wanted them to do, the missionaries had to police them.

To this end the missionaries of Sillery and St. François de Sales adopted a number of strategies. First, the missionaries delegated their authority to specifically chosen Wabanakis in order to spread, as widely and deeply as possible, a network of surveillance. Such delegation was as much a logistical necessity as it was a calculated strategy. With too few missionaries among too many Indians, the missionaries were forced to expand their ranks in ways that their missionary orders, which lacked personnel to send to Wabanaki missions, could not. Delegating authority to specially chosen Indians, ones who lived among their brethren and understood the difficulty many Indians would have in living a Catholic life, gave the priests a potentially important avenue of regulation. Second, the missionaries, especially the Jesuit Jacques Bigot, also attempted to use the prestige and power of the government in Québec to routinize certain kinds of behavior among the Indians. They hoped to harness the power of Québec, and the authority of the governor of New France, to bolster their claims, settle disputes, and legitimate their use of violence in quelling any resistance to missionary authority. Overall the missionaries succeeded in gaining some Wabanaki allegiance through these strategies. But ultimately they failed to gain the amount of control they wanted.

Missionaries started complaining about Wabanaki behavior almost immediately after the Indians began to fill the mission at Sillery in 1675. They believed that the Wabanakis led morally corrupt lives that endangered their souls. The Jesuit Jacques Vaultier wrote in 1677 from Sillery that these Wabanaki refugees were "altogether averse to what we preach to them" and that "their Licentious life," which was "strongly opposed to the christian law," would prevent them from embracing Catholicism. The missionaries especially complained about excessive drinking, which they regarded as the Wabanakis' "greatest failing" (66:175–77; 60:233–35, 239).

In order to combat such behavior, the missionaries attempted, at times systematically, at times in an ad hoc manner, to regulate Indian activities. One of the first tasks of creating a mission and regulating its inhabitants had to do with the control of space. Most obviously, the missionaries attempted to control where the Wabanakis were and when they were there. The missionaries recognized that they had little power to influence any Indian nation when the Indians were away from the village. Therefore they offered the Wabanakis incentives to remain sedentary. This was a strategy that missionaries pursued not only in North America but throughout the world. Father Jean Morain, among a group of Mi'kmaq called the Pemptegwets, wrote in 1677 that their lifestyle created problems for the mission. "Their Nomad and Wandering life is a great obstacle to their Instruction," he wrote. But he had great hopes that "the Fields that have been offered them for the cultivation of Indian corn, and the Chapel that is to be built for them, will induce them to become stationary to some extent,—or, at least, to come Here more constantly throughout the spring" (60:269).[11]

But the missionaries succeeded only partially in keeping the Wabanakis within areas that they could manage, and even then only with later generations of the Indians (67:29). And the task of controlling them only became more difficult the larger the mission grew. When Wabanaki refugees began gathering at Sillery in the 1670s, and then at St. François de Sales in the 1680s, the missionaries became inundated with work. The rising population made the burden of running the mission overwhelming. The problem became even worse when the Jesuit Vincent Bigot was transferred by the superior-general of the order to Québec, leaving the entire, rapidly expanding mission of Sillery, and then St. François de Sales, to his brother and fellow Jesuit Jacques Bigot (62:109, 115–17). The missionaries simply lacked the personnel to run the mission as effectively as they wanted to.

So, in order to maintain the gains he believed he had made, Jacques Bigot resorted to a strategy that he hoped would expand his influence among the Indians: the delegation of authority within the missions. First Bigot targeted respected members of the Wabanaki community and tried to convert them. Missionaries, especially the Jesuits, also had used this tactic throughout the world.[12] What made it potentially successful was the relationship between political power and kinship within Wabanaki social life. It was a strategy that had already been used in Sillery. Jacques Vaultier noted in a 1677 letter that he administered the sacrament of baptism to a number of the elders, including "one of their captains, named Pirouakki." Vaultier extolled Pirouakki's "excellent qualities— the goodness of his heart, the gentleness of his nature, his judicious management, and his natural eloquence," which "gave him great authority over the members

---

11. Biard also believed that the Indians had to become sedentary. See Thwaites, *Jesuit Relations*, 3:143–45.

12. For this strategy in New France, see Axtell, *Invasion Within*, 77.

of his tribe." Vaultier went on to praise Pirouakki's "incredible ardor to become a Christian, and to incite the others to procure the same happiness for themselves." Vaultier wrote that Pirouakki expressed immediate enthusiasm when approached about attending mass. Upon his first visit to the church, Pirouakki "brought with him those over whom he had more special authority, because they were his nearest relatives." He told his relatives to follow his lead "in the harangues he delivered to them almost every day," and he especially warned them against drinking alcohol (60:241–43).

As stipulated by the unwritten law of reciprocity, the conversion of one Wabanaki sachem like Pirouakki could potentially persuade those related to or politically aligned with that sachem to convert as well.[13] Missionaries realized that Indian political relations based on kinship and reciprocity could facilitate their attempts at converting large numbers of Indians. This tactic thus had both direct and indirect effects on the web of power and authority within Wabanaki villages. At first glance it seems relatively simple: the missionary attempted to convert the Indians as efficiently as possible by targeting those with the most influence. When seen in this way, the missionary did not delegate power at all, but consciously attempted to gain a religious foothold within the community. Converting tribal leaders and elders to a religion in which the missionary was indispensable to its practice would lead to the growth of his power and prestige. He hoped that the community would bestow power upon him.

But when one analyzes this tactic more closely, one finds that it had a second and more complicated dimension. Converting Wabanaki sachems within a community worked to link Indian leaders to a series of colonial institutions, such as the Society of Jesus or the Catholic Church or the government of New France at Québec. Such institutions maintained and dispensed their own authority, but an authority based in part on the power and prestige given to them by the very groups they hoped to colonize. The Wabanakis, for example, legitimated the Catholic Church by believing that its missionaries were powerful, that they had "charisma." Thus a circular calculus of authority occurred when missionaries converted sachems to Catholicism. The Wabanakis bestowed respect and deference on the missionaries who standardized and routinized it into a charismatic authority that was transferred to the church itself. This authority was then channeled, again through the priest, back onto those Wabanaki elders

---

13. The most famous and possibly most important sachem of the region who had converted was Membertou, a Mi'kmaq who was dubbed a Catholic in 1610 (converted might be too strong a word, considering that Abbé Fléché, the secular priest who baptized him, could not speak a word of Algonquian). See Vecsey, *Paths of Kateri's Kin*, 139–40, and Thwaites, *Jesuit Relations*, 1:75.

who converted to Catholicism. Their prestige among the community was augmented by their relations with the priests. And, as the missionaries were priests within the Catholic Church, they had clear links with those in power in the city of Québec. Any group of Wabanakis linked to them would therefore benefit both materially and symbolically from that link.[14]

For example, Wabanaki sachems who had converted to Catholicism would be the favored sachems for the trade of goods and gifts—called "presents"—that would necessarily accompany any Indian nation's relationship with the government of New France. The Catholic sachems would then control the dispersal of such goods to the members of their communities. Through this dispersal of goods they would enhance their reputations as men who were generous, humane, and sensitive to the protocols of reciprocity, which translated into the accumulation of political power and prestige within the community. In this way the priest played a vital role in delegating, dispersing, channeling, and structuring power that flowed from the Wabanaki communities to organizations like the government of New France and then returned to specifically chosen Wabanaki men and women.[15]

Missionaries delegated authority, as well, in a second and more common way by granting it directly to particular Indians. They attempted to create a hierarchy in which certain well-chosen Indians—called *dogiques,* or catechists—had a power over the rest of the laity but answered directly to the missionaries. The missionaries based this hierarchy on the benefits and interests that they explicitly granted to these Indians, and this new hierarchy competed with other hierarchies already in place in Wabanaki communities. Common throughout Wabanakia and beyond, this method can best be seen in the numerous writings of Jacques Bigot.

Bigot resorted to this strategy of delegation because he simply could not do all of the work that his mission imposed upon him. After his brother Vincent was

---

14. This paragraph and the previous one were informed by Max Weber's "The Sociology of Religion," found in his *Economy and Society: An Outline of Interpretive Sociology,* 2 vols. (Berkeley and Los Angeles: University of California Press, 1978), 1:439–51; Pierre Bourdieu, "Legitimation and Structured Interests in Weber's Sociology of Religion," in *Max Weber, Rationality and Modernity,* ed. Scott Lash and Sam Whimster (London: Allen & Unwin, 1987), 119–36; and Pierre Bourdieu, "Genesis and Structure of the Religious Field," in *Religious Institutions,* ed. Craig Calhoun (Greenwich, Conn.: JAI Press, 1991), 1–44.

15. Here the priest fulfilled his role as one who systematized and rationalized the religion to which he devoted his life. For a discussion on the complicated relationship between cultural capital and delegation that has informed some of the ideas behind this paragraph, see Pierre Bourdieu's essay "Delegation and Political Fetishism" in his *Language and Symbolic Power* (Cambridge: Harvard University Press, 1991), 203–19.

transferred to an Iroquois mission and was not replaced, Bigot called the Sillery Wabanakis together for a council. "Two days after [Vincent] left," Bigot wrote in 1682, "I gathered all the savages together in order to appoint a person to take charge of the prayers that [Vincent] was wont to direct. This man's chief occupation would be to proceed promptly wherever I might send him; to stop or to prevent misconduct; and to inform all who might come to this mission of the customs observed in it." He recognized immediately the potential for conflict that this policy would create and acknowledged that the person he would choose for the task "would have some trouble at the outset." He settled on a man—carefully gaining "the consent of the two captains" before making his choice—named Etienne Neketucant, who, Bigot claimed, "during the 2 years that he has spent here, seems Never to have committed the slightest fault." Almost immediately after he was appointed, Etienne and a man named "Francois Xavier haurawereunt" went across the river to face a number of Indian canoeists who had stopped at Sillery, telling them they could not drink and foiling some Frenchman's plans, Bigot believed, to get them drunk (62:109–11).

Bigot coupled this tactic of delegating authority to *dogiques* who policed Wabanaki behavior with a curfew, which by definition attempted to control both time and place of Indian activities, and he charged his *dogiques* with enforcing it. Again in 1682 he wrote that after the night's prayers he had forbidden anyone to leave the mission site to drink alcohol at local French settlements. When he learned of any Indian leaving the village after prayers, he would send the *dogique* and "any companion that he chooses" to go out "on my behalf to warn those who are outside to come in." Bigot often accompanied the *dogique,* no matter what time of night it was. "I have warned the dogique to make these rounds frequently," he wrote, insisting that this delegate "has always obeyed me, and has also induced some others to accompany Him on this duty" (62:125). Whether Bigot wrote the truth here remains unknown, but he believed he had to limit Wabanakis' movement and sociability and keep the Wabanakis within missionary guidelines of proper behavior, and he used *dogiques* to do so.

Bigot also developed a tactic that he used to insert himself into certain dimensions of Wabanaki life to which he lacked access. When he wanted to criticize certain Wabanakis for their actions, Bigot let his *dogiques* "make the first attack." He directed them to confront a wayward Indian and chastise him for his transgressions. He then told them to tell the Indian "to come to find me, after they have spoken to him." After his *dogiques* had explained the missionary's displeasure to the Indian, Bigot himself would then confront him, asking, "'Has such a one spoken to thee on my behalf? What dost thou think?' And then I talk to him in good earnest about The fault that he has committed" (63:77).

In part, this strategy was linguistic and cultural: Bigot believed that native speakers could "explain themselves much better than I" (63:77). Never one to let a potential advantage slip away, he tapped into that skill for his own purposes. Bigot wanted to couple his notions of good behavior with the Indians' superior ability to communicate in their own language and within their own idiom. He hoped it would make his job that much easier. In this way he granted a measure of power to these *dogiques* to speak on his behalf, thereby giving them the symbolic capital that he represented and had the ability to dole out as he pleased. Simultaneously he hoped to gain a greater reach within the lives of the Wabanaki mission villagers by using natives who might achieve a level of intimacy that a Jesuit missionary could not.

But Bigot did more than create an indigenous Christian police force. By 1682 he was enlisting native teachers as well. One Indian man would gather up each unbaptized Wabanaki in the village for a meeting with Bigot in the church at noon. That Indian would also teach the catechism and hymnody every day to all the boys in the cabin. For the women, Bigot enlisted a Wabanaki named Jeanne, who taught the catechism and hymns to the girls (62:113–15).

Another woman, Margueritte, also helped him at the mission at Sillery by teaching the catechism to her relatives—twenty-five of them in all—who had traveled to Sillery from other areas of Wabanakia. Bigot reported happily that social pressure aided his cause. One of Margueritte's relatives expressed extreme regret that she could not get baptized with three adult children, as she had once become "slightly intoxicated" and therefore Bigot had refused her the sacrament. Bigot marveled at not only what he believed was Margueritte's piety but also at her skills in helping him teach "proper" behavior. For one month she taught a group of Wabanakis "so assiduously that all these fervent Catechumens learned in that short space of time Everything that the older Christians knew" (62:25–27). As more Wabanaki Indians poured into Sillery and St. François de Sales during 1683 and 1684, many "visited the Cabin of Margueritte, where several persons have already undertaken to Instruct them." Without the help of Margueritte and others like her, Bigot insisted, he would be unable to handle the situation as it was (63:67). He hoped that both men and women Indian catechists would play important roles in the inculcation of Jesuit ideals of morality and proper living, so that these lessons would not just be learned at mass or through the priest himself.

As these examples illustrate, the delegation of authority empowered two people at once. When a missionary delegated authority to a Wabanaki, that Indian gained prestige and distinction within an Indian community—at least within that part of the Indian community that respected the missionaries. It would therefore be in the best interest of a *dogique* to make sure that the source of authority and distinction—the missionary—maintained his position within the community, for his removal would spell one's own marginalization. Missionaries like Bigot hoped for this investment when they granted authority to the Indians. By giving Indians the authority to police in their name, the missionaries hoped to make themselves indispensable to the total village.[16]

But this task was far from easy. Bigot wrote in 1684 that, during the spread of an epidemic fever, he was constantly on the move, trying to administer the sacraments, teach the sick, and prepare the dying for baptism. He faced a logistical problem: the Indians were spread out "in Cabins in the Country; some were at Coste de St. Ignace, others at St. Michel, others at the fort very near me." These sites were roughly half a league apart, and Bigot was forced to travel extensively (63:83–85). In this situation, the missionaries were forced to delegate authority out of desperation. They needed a way to make their presence felt, to ensure that the Wabanakis acted as proper Catholics. But they simply could not be everywhere at once, teaching, monitoring, judging, policing, scolding, and punishing. And so they had to delegate. Missionaries hoped that delegating authority would expand their influence and power, create a larger space that their presence, their specific practices and rites and rituals, would fill. They understood well that if they had to be physically present to enforce "proper Catholic behavior," they would only lose their influence.

The missionaries among the Wabanakis used another strategy to gain as much control as possible over mission life: they attempted to exploit the complicated relationship missions had with the French government of Québec. Missionaries among the Wabanakis acted, obviously, as religious and spiritual leaders within these villages, but they also acted as de facto representatives of the French government. They used both of these roles—roles that were by no means separate

---

16. Here, the Wabanakis who received authority from the missionaries were fulfilling their roles in what Bourdieu describes as "a process of *systematization and moralization of religious practices and representations.*" They, in part, were the new ranks within the Catholic Church, attempting to take Catholic practices (as defined by the missionary) and simultaneously standardize them within and tailor them to the locality of Wabanakia. See Bourdieu, "Genesis and Structure of the Religious Field," 7–8, and his "Legitimation and Structured Interests," 133.

within the everyday lives of early modern mission priests—to aggrandize and perpetuate their power in any way they could.[17] Again, it was Jacques Bigot who excelled in using this tactic, especially in his attempts to eradicate the problem of alcohol abuse in his missions.

The missionaries saw the Indian use of alcohol as a massive problem throughout New France; but how to curtail it? For government officials in Québec, abolishing alcohol in the colony was out of the question. They never made alcohol illegal in New France. In 1660 the bishop of Québec, François Xavier de Laval de Montigny, declared that he would excommunicate from the Catholic Church anyone caught selling alcohol to the Indians. This declaration had almost no measurable effect other than to enrage government officials who supported the trade. The government enjoyed the sizable income in fur that the trade brought to New France and did not want that income threatened in any way. They successfully demanded that this edict (and a second one in 1662) be repealed.[18]

As for the missionaries, they insisted on the traffic's illegitimacy, preaching sermon after sermon to the Indians on the links between drinking, moral depravity, and eternal damnation. Many Indians agreed but continued to drink. The French Crown decided in 1679 to permit the trade but prohibited the transport of alcohol into Indian villages. That prohibition did little, however, to stem the sale to and consumption of alcohol by the Indians, and the policy only infuriated the church. In the words of Peter C. Mancall, "the king and his advisors made a specific economic point: New France needed the fur trade to survive, and brandy lubricated the fur trade." This situation incensed many clerics in Québec and elsewhere but left them with few weapons to attack the problem. It created a dissonance between what could be described as "mission law" and "colonial law": behavior deemed unacceptable in a mission would not necessarily be understood as illegal within the colony as a whole.[19]

In the 1680s Jacques Bigot attempted to implement a solution, one that attached the legal authority of the colony of New France to the Jesuit mission law against drinking, regardless of the legal stance of the government. Bigot's

17. Here I agree with the argument of Alvin H. Morrison that the French missionaries of Wabanakia were highly political men whose work could not be separated from the political aims of the governor-general and the French Crown. See his "Dawnland Decisions: Seventeenth-Century Wabanaki Leaders and Their Responses to the Differential Contact Stimuli in the Overlap Area of New France and New England" (Ph.D. diss., State University of New York at Buffalo, 1974), 88. Kenneth M. Morrison argues against this notion of political priests in his *Embattled Northeast*, 133–35.
18. Peter C. Mancall, *Deadly Medicine: Indians and Alcohol in Early America* (Ithaca: Cornell University Press, 1995), 140–44.
19. Ibid., 144–48; Axtell, *Invasion Within*, 64–67.

writings from 1685 reveal both the extent of drunkenness as a problem in his missions and his extraordinary attempts to try to regulate it. He wrote that he placed complete sobriety at the center of his mission's goals, "with continual exhortations, continual warnings, continual public prayers for the total abolition of that wretched vice." He claimed that the Indians themselves opposed alcohol consumption, especially the Wabanaki refugees who were coming to the St. Lawrence Valley from Maine. "We are going away from the English solely because they tormented us too much, and would give us nothing but liquor for all our peltries," Bigot claimed these Indians told him. But he also wrote that the Indians said that "we see here many frenchmen who wish to do the same" (63:117, 123).

Still, he thought he saw a Wabanaki weakness he could exploit. According to Bigot, the governor-general of New France at the time, Le Febvre de la Barre, expressed concern over Indian alcohol consumption, for "he looks upon our Savages as his children. All our savages love and respect him, and regard him as a saint" (63:119). Whether that was in fact the case is not altogether clear. What is clear is that Bigot believed that the governor-general had an authority among the Indians that the missionary thought he could use.

With that authority in mind, Bigot began a series of tactics—which he termed "Holy juggleries" (63:106–7)—in which he lied to mission Indians about his relations with the governor-general and attempted to create unprecedented authority over Indian behavior. This tactic resulted in the creation of a system that grafted the authority of the governor-general onto whatever mission laws Bigot wanted to enact.

In a letter dated 1685, Bigot wrote that a member of the Algonquin nation who had been staying at St. François de Sales for a number of days[20] was found one Sunday "in a state of intoxication" with his brother, also a guest at the mission. Out of control, the Algonquin attacked everyone in his cabin with "burning firebrands." He nearly burned down the cabin itself. "As his Cabin was near mine," Bigot reported to Father la Chaise, in Paris, "I immediately heard the cries of those whom the drunkard was tormenting. I go to the Cabin; I call for assistance; I cause the drunken man to be bound, and carried to a cellar where there is nothing to drink or to seize."[21]

The next day Bigot requested from Québec a military force of "archers" to cart the offending Algonquin off to prison. But he insisted that this power

---

20. The mission of Sillery was moved to St. François de Sales in 1683. However, Bigot wrote on this letter that it was written at Sillery, though dated November 8, 1685. Bigot might have called the new mission Sillery, or he simply miswrote the name of the mission. See Thwaites, *Jesuit Relations*, 63:137.

21. Quotations in this paragraph and the next are from ibid., 63:101–3.

came from Governor-General La Barre himself, who had "already informed me of his intention to prevent the evils of intemperance, as far as lay in his power, and to secure the observance of the orders that he found we had already given here to check such disorderly conduct." Bigot then asked the governor-general to speak to the assembled mission Indians on the imprisonment and eventual expulsion of this Algonquin and the evils of drinking. "You see all the Pious juggleries which I employed to inspire terror in the others," Bigot boasted, "especially in those who are here only for a time, and whose sole object in coming seems to be to disturb the piety and fervor of all the good christians who properly compose this mission."

Bigot often used the authority of the governor-general in his quest to regulate Wabanaki drinking. In one incident he attempted to send two female relatives to jail for getting drunk. Both had fled the mission, but the next day one returned, repentant. Bigot went to their cabin and told her, "as a friend" and in front of her relatives, that they should return to Québec before sunrise the next day and put themselves in prison. Bigot told them "that this would appease the Great Captain [the governor-general of Québec], and that I might perhaps obtain the remission of some days' imprisonment." Both women obeyed. Bigot followed them later to Québec, and when he returned he told the relatives of the two women, "I had, with great difficulty, obtained the favor that those two Savage women should remain only three days in prison; and that all were forbidden to go to deliver them before the three days had expired." Bigot claimed that everyone believed he had secured for these women a light sentence (63:109–11).

In another example, Bigot told the relatives of a Soquoqui woman who had been caught drunk that she should surrender herself to the prison in Québec as well. She initially resisted and fled the mission, only to return after two days, very ill. Her relatives, fearing for her safety, asked him for his advice. He waited for one day to answer, to leave them "in suspense," and then told them that he had talked to the "Great Captain," who supposedly told Bigot that because the woman was sick he would only fine her one *escu*, which she should donate to the hospital in Québec. He also prohibited her from entering the city for two months. The woman and her relatives thanked the missionary for being able to gain from the governor-general "so light a sentence." Bigot also succeeded in having the Frenchman who got this Soquoqui drunk pay a fine, in order to show the Indians that "the wicked French are punished equally with the wicked savages." He ended on the overly optimistic note that "if we choose to display a little firmness in repressing the evils of intemperance, we can obtain what we wish from our Savages" (63:111–13).

These "pious juggleries" did not always work as Bigot hoped. On certain occasions he overreached his power and was simply ignored by Indians and Frenchmen alike. In another attempt to stop the Wabanakis from drinking he sent "orders" to Québec policing authorities, telling them to incarcerate any Indians they found drunk. "No heed was paid" to his demand, Bigot complained, and "most of the Savages who became drunk escaped from Quebek without being taken." In order to rectify the situation Bigot lied to his mission Wabanakis by stating that "the Great Captain" knew of those drunken Indians and had ordered Bigot to inform him about any Indians who did this in the future. "In such a case," Bigot said, La Barre "would at once send archers for him, in order that the drunkard might, by the hardships of the prison, make reparation to God for his sin." The governor-general, Bigot claimed, had only the best interests of the Wabanakis at heart, for he "wished to show Holy compassion for all the christians of this mission, and, by that order, prevent them from casting themselves into the dungeons of hell." This subterfuge highlights the lengths to which Bigot had to go to counter his growing powerlessness in the face of alcohol consumption in the Wabanaki community (63:103).

But the situation only spurred the missionary on. Bigot not only remained undeterred, he redoubled his efforts to gain some kind of control over conduct within the mission. He thus came up with his most audacious attempt at aggrandizing power, which the Wabanakis dubbed the "Holy pillage." Again he used the authority of the governor-general to build his case against Indian intoxication. For the "better observance of his orders," Bigot wrote, he told his Wabanaki laity that the governor-general "desired that I should, with a Holy audacity, take away from every Savage who I found intoxicated some petty effects belonging to his Cabin, in order that the effects so taken might Serve to pay the Archers who would come to put that drunken Savage in prison." Bigot claimed that the Wabanakis began calling this tactic "the Holy pillage" or "a pillage that is effected for the purpose of obeying God and of establishing prayer." Bigot told them that he disliked being "compelled to do a thing which might perhaps seem harsh to some," and he was at pains to make sure that his laity knew "very well how much I loved them, and what trouble I took on their behalf." But he had to uphold La Barre's supposed order even if he had to "do violence to myself on that point." No one was exempt from the order—neither sachem, nor *dogique*, nor the most recent neophyte. He followed this speech with a prayer session devoted to those who had been caught in drunkenness, "in order to obtain for them a sincere sorrow for that sin, and a firm resolution to commit it no more" (63:103–5).

He put his strategy into practice soon thereafter. Only three days after his speech an Indian was found drunk, and Bigot "plundered him for the holy purpose." The Catholic sister of the drunken man criticized her brother, saying, "Why art thou astonished that our Father should take this in thy Cabin? Knowest thou not that he told us that he would piously plunder those who became intoxicated?" Though this statement strains credulity, "such are the expressions she used," Bigot insisted. After the offending Indian sobered up, he fled the fort, and Bigot summoned archers from Québec to find him. He "thoroughly instructed [the archers] in the part that they had to play in order to impress the imaginations of the Savages," he wrote. The Indian came back of his own volition, begging forgiveness from Bigot, the governor-general, and God. Bigot told him that he would talk to the "Great Captain" about obtaining a pardon for him, even though his penalty was to be twelve days in prison—a standard penalty when archers were involved. Bigot wrote that he easily gained a pardon for this Indian but that he did it in such a way as "to inspire all our other Savages with still greater dread of drunkenness." He went on to write, "It would take too long were I to relate all the Holy juggleries of which I made use," but he did touch on the central strategy of the tactics: "I seemed to take our savages' part, while I was doing whatever I could against them" (63:105–7).

Believing in the potential of the "Holy pillage," he attempted to expand its reach by not only using it on Indians who got drunk but threatening to use it on those he considered likely *to get* drunk. During a feast he gave for a group of Wabanaki refugees from Acadia (what is now Nova Scotia and New Brunswick), Bigot strolled through the village and stopped at the cabins of certain Indians who had trouble with alcohol. He would confront them by saying, "My child, thou wilt never be able to keep away from drink; I must rob thee holily in advance, to pay those who will come to take thee to prison when thou art drunk." Laughing, he would grab some item, only to give it back immediately. The Indian would laugh at Bigot's artifice, but, Bigot wrote, the missionary's tactic would also "compel him to assure me that he would never get drunk again." Bigot also teased those who returned from a successful hunt laden with furs, as "I would jokingly rejoice that I would have ample things to take when they got drunk." But he would then change his demeanor and ask them seriously if it was better to buy blankets for their wives and children than to buy alcohol, get thrown into prison, and lose their furs to the missionary. He would then invoke the governor-general: "Does not the great Captain manifest a holy compassion for thee by forbidding thee to get drunk, so that thou mayst employ the proceeds of thy hunting solely in procuring provisions for thyself and thy family? He considers solely thy welfare in this. Does he derive any benefit from it?" Bigot wrote that on this point the Indians all agreed that the governor-general "does well in forbidding us to get drunk." Of course, Bigot did not outline the "benefit" that the governor-general would in fact have gained from a stable missionary village filled with strong healthy warriors who fought under the banner of New France and produced furs and consumed goods for the colony's market economy. But he did outline in remarkable detail the tactics he used in his attempt to regulate Wabanaki behavior (63:115–17).

As a final tactic of regulation, Bigot coupled the authority of the governor-general with his denigration of anything having to do with drinking to create a broad strategy to influence the political structure of the village. Bigot wrote to Father La Chaise in 1685 that he had told his St. François de Sales Wabanakis of a fictitious conversation he had had with the governor-general. When the Wabanakis were about to choose new sachems for their village, Bigot told the Indians that La Barre did not want the Wabanakis to support potential sachems who had previously abused alcohol. Bigot said that La Barre—"whom I afterward secretly inform of all his jugglery"—had told him "to keep me informed even more minutely regarding the conduct in this respect of the savages who are to be proposed as captains." After Bigot told the Indians what the governor-general had supposedly said, he spoke to one of them who had been tapped as a potential sachem. Bigot told him that unfortunately he could not give the governor-general a stellar recommendation for his candidacy because he had been caught drunk roughly one year before.[22]

Bigot feared that this Indian's standing within the village (which was great), when coupled with his previous drinking, might possibly lead him to shun "the interests of prayer"—in other words, Bigot's interests. The missionary then talked to the governor-general (this time for real, it seems), and "on my return hither I stated, with an appearance of some sorrow, that the great Captain wished to put off for a year the election of one of the captains who had been proposed, until it were proved that he continued to lead a good life." As for the other Indians up for appointment, Bigot stated that the governor-general gave his blessing "that all three should govern the mission together in perfect harmony."

22. The governor-general did not have the power to choose sachems within Wabanaki villages. However, Bigot here implies that a mechanism was in place by which the Wabanakis had to present their new sachems to the governor-general for his approval. This protocol was most probably a formality. If the governor-general did have veto power over the election of Wabanaki sachems, then it seems unlikely that Bigot and La Barre would look for other strategies to procure the same end. Thwaites, *Jesuit Relations*, 63:119–21.

These three men, whom Bigot named "the Captains of the prayer, in the Ceremony of their election," had supported the Jesuit cause and the conversion of the Wabanakis to Catholicism for some time and had worked against "the evils of intemperance among their people" (63:121–23). Here Bigot attempted to create, in a sense, a small Indian Catholic hierarchy, one based on forms of knowledge and interest that would privilege the missionary's ideals over indigenous ones, and he used the authority attached to the governor-general to do it.

But the efficacy of Bigot's strategies, and the strategies of his fellow missionaries, remained partial. That he felt the need to use the office of the governor-general in such diverse ways and in so many instances only underscores his lack of control over much of mission life. Drinking continued to be a problem in all of Wabanakia.[23] And, of course, drinking was not the only issue that the missionaries felt they needed to address. The missionaries were clearly willing to do much in order to achieve the general ends of gaining more souls for the faith.

The missionaries believed that all sorts of problems plagued Wabanaki mission life. Missionaries across Wabanakia complained of Indians who drank until they were intoxicated[24] and believed that the Wabanakis had a penchant for vengeance (29:83), were susceptible to envy (62:117), and were prone to slander (62:117–19).

But in their project to eradicate this behavior, they were only partially successful. The ambiguity of Wabanaki Catholicism during the late seventeenth and early eighteenth centuries led to a religious structure that seemed blatantly contradictory both to the missionaries and to many European and American interpreters who came after them. The Indians simultaneously professed an attachment to Catholicism yet remained indifferent to moral precepts that the missionaries insisted should necessarily come with its practice—a contradiction that struck the missionaries as absurd.

But by embracing Catholicism at all, even with their reservations about the missionaries' moral proscriptions, the Wabanakis brought forces into their societies that created hierarchies that benefited the French. The missionaries, as sole executors of Catholic ritual, were placed in positions of power that kept

---

23. For a later example at St. François de Sales, in 1710, see the letter of Father Joseph Aubery to Father Joseph Jouvency in ibid., 66:177–79. For another example, this time among the Norridgewocks, see the Jesuit Sébastien Râle's complaint about the trade with the English, who were providing these Indians with alcohol, in James Phinney Baxter, *The Pioneers of New France in New England, with Contemporary Letters and Documents* (Albany, N.Y.: Joel Munsell's Sons, 1894), 101–2.

24. It should be noted that they complained about anyone—Indian or European—who drank until they were intoxicated. Among many examples, see Thwaites, *Jesuit Relations,* 29:77–79; 63:101.

them in Wabanaki villages, even when their presence caused internal political stress. As well, the entrenchment of French missionaries within the sacred lives of the Wabanakis reinforced the growing diplomatic and economic ties between the two groups, binding them together in ways that at times became onerous yet were necessary during warfare. Finally, the lack of enthusiasm for some aspects of Catholic morality on the part of the Wabanakis—an Indian group central to French pretensions to North American domination—guaranteed governmental and missionary attention and vigilance in attempting to stamp out any un-Catholic behavior. Tensions over religious issues blended with political and economic tensions to create rifts within and between mission villages. Overall, religious relationships in Wabanakia were based on conflict and tension, which dovetailed with other aspects of Wabanaki-French life in northern New England and southern Québec during a time of war.[25]

25. See Christopher J. Bilodeau, "The Economy of War: Violence, Religion, and the Wabanaki Indians in the Maine Borderlands" (Ph.D. diss., Cornell University, 2006).

The Moravian Missionaries of Bethlehem and Salem

ROWENA McCLINTON

Mid-eighteenth- and early nineteenth-century Moravians missionaries David Zeisberger of Ohio, Pennsylvania, and Canada, and husband-and-wife team John and Anna Rosina Gambold of Springplace Mission (near Chatsworth, Georgia), strove valiantly to establish meaningful and permanent missions among Indians in North America. Theirs are stories of life-and-death struggles against nature's harshness and man's brutality. Canoeing through strange waters whose banks harbored mottled rattlesnakes, the Moravians faced a Euro-American populace suspicious of peoples of non-English tongues. Their persistence in speaking German gave rise to other qualms as well, for they remained adamant in their refusal to take oaths or bear arms. Yet these embattled Moravian missionaries persevered by sheer force of will with patience and loyalty.[1]

Their resilience to adversity had deep, almost impenetrable roots. Moravians, or the Unity of the Brethren, had clung together as a viable pre-Reformation people, though a "hidden seed" for centuries in central Europe, determined to withstand oppression at all costs. Emerging in 1722 as remnant descendants of Czech reformer and martyr Jan Hus and going by the name Hussites, they joined hands with German Pietists who surfaced after the Thirty Years' War (1618–48) to form the Renewed Moravian Church in 1727 on Count Nicholas Ludwig von Zinzendorf's[2] estate in Herrnhut, Saxony.[3] To avoid persecution

---

1. John Gottlieb Ernestus Heckewelder, *Thirty Thousand Miles with John Heckewelder*, ed. Paul A. W. Wallace (Pittsburgh: University of Pittsburgh Press, 1958), 30, 31.

2. For the most definitive biography of Zinzendorf, see John R. Weinlick, *Count Zinzendorf: The Story of His Life and Leadership in the Renewed Moravian Church* (Bethlehem, Pa.: [Moravian Church] Department of Publications and Communications, 1989). For a discussion of Quaker and Moravian stances on personal military service, see Adelaide L. Fries, "Parallel Lines in Piedmont North Carolina Quaker and Moravian History," paper presented at the annual meeting of the North Carolina Friends Society, August 3, 1949, 11–12.

3. Peter de Beauvior Brock, *The Political and Social Doctrine of the Unity of Czech Brethren in the Fifteenth and Early Sixteenth Centuries* (The Hague: Moulton and Co., 1957), 46–81, 98, and 191;

and possible extinction, many Brethren became missionaries. Their impulse to evangelize prompted them to focus on the "forgotten peoples of the earth," and by the late 1730s the Brethren had extensive mission enterprises in Greenland, Africa, and the Caribbean, as well as on the eastern seaboard and, later, the interior of America as far west as present-day northwestern Georgia.[4]

Self-preservation brought the Moravians to the New World, and their outreach to the Indians induced them to remain. From the two mission-intent congregations, Bethlehem and Salem, these two remarkable sets of missionaries, Zeisberger and the Gambolds, became diligent workers among Indians and recorded their contacts almost daily. The ethnographic materials generated by the Zeisberger *Diaries* assume an additionally valuable character for scholars prepared to compare them with those spawned by the Gambold Springplace Diary.[5] What makes this contrast unique is that the latter's principal author, Anna Rosina Kliest Gambold, was female. Furthermore, the settings of both works differ in period and location. Zeisberger's heroic missionary service spanned sixty years, but within those six decades he encountered many hostilities, multiple tribes and tribal alliances, and constant displacements; his very

---

and Peter de Beauvoir Brock, *Pacifism in Europe to 1914* (Princeton: Princeton University Press, 1972), 36–41. During the German War of Liberation, many Moravians became imbued with nationalism, and congregations in Saxony and Prussia officially abandoned their position on noncombat. In 1815 Prussia, now controlling all Saxon congregations, withdrew the grant of exemption, and the Brethren registered no objection to the state. In 1818 the Pennsylvanian Moravian stand on armed participation ended when that synod "officially withdrew the ban on members performing military service." Whether to bear arms or take a conscientious objector's position was left up to the individual. Somewhat later, on July 4, 1831, the more conservative North Carolina Brethren adopted a position that allowed their young men to bear arms. See Peter Brock, *Pacifism in the United States: From the Colonial Era to the First World War* (Princeton: Princeton University Press, 1968), 327–29; and Rudolph Rican, *The History of the Unity of the Brethren: A Protestant Hussite Church in Bohemia and Moravia,* trans. C. Daniel Crews (Bethlehem, Pa.: [Moravian Church] Department of Publications and Communications, 1992), 9.

4. The Moravian settlement of British North America gave rise to systematic Moravian government that divided the Atlantic eastern seaboard into two headquarters for the Moravian Church. Eventually, the northern province's official capital of government became Bethlehem, Pennsylvania (founded in 1741), named for the House of David and birthplace of Christ. In 1766, Salem, now Winston-Salem, North Carolina, was pronounced the southern province's seat of authority, some thirteen years after the founder of the Renewed Moravian Church purchased 98,985 acres of land from John Carteret, Earl Granville, Lord Proprietor of the northern section of North Carolina. Zinzendorf selected the tract's name, *Wachovia,* as a reminder of the fine meadows of *der Wachau,* now Austria, the site of one of the Zinzendorfian ancestral estates. Zinzendorf's *Wachau* is located in the vicinity of the Melk Monastery, west of Vienna. Joseph Mortimer Levering, *A History of Bethlehem, 1741–1892, with Some Account of Its Founders and Their Early Activity in America* (Bethlehem: Times Publishing Company, 1903), 270–71.

5. See Rowena McClinton, ed., *The Moravian Springplace Mission to the Cherokees,* 2 vols. (Lincoln: University of Nebraska Press, 2007) (hereafter *Moravian Springplace Mission*).

survival depended on his moving from one missionary post to another.[6] Between 1772 and 1782 Zeisberger mainly served three mission posts in Ohio and Pennsylvania country: Friedenstadt, Schönbrunn, and Gnadenhütten.[7] John and Anna Rosina Gambold, by contrast, lived from 1805 to 1821 at Springplace Mission and established a school for Cherokee youth; Cherokee leaders dictated its success because of their interest and fortitude.

Both Zeisberger and the Gambolds believed they could introduce the better elements of European culture to Indians. Count Zinzendorf's instructions to missionaries reflected the European values that it pays to work hard and remain independent. The count urged missionaries to earn the esteem of the "heathen" with humility but to wear blinders and remain immune to every danger, snare, and conceit.[8] In obeying these edicts, Moravian missionaries positioned themselves outside political arenas and on the periphery of what Native American scholar Richard White calls "middle ground."[9] Although Moravians tended not to get involved with politics,[10] their stances on nonviolence, which went hand in hand with their Pietist but sympathetic behavior toward Indians, drew the ire of policymakers and settlers. Settlers continued to settle the backwoods, and their combatant nature often led to bloodshed. Unlike backwoodsmen who acted upon the belief that Indians had no more of a soul than a buffalo, and that the killing of either was the same thing,[11] Moravians refused to accept militancy as a way to negotiate differences.

It was their reputation for nonviolence, I believe, that gave Zeisberger and the Gambolds access to Indian thought and customs and that in turn allowed these missionaries to contribute significantly to Indian ethnography. What is

---

6. See Reverend William H. Rice, D.D., *David Zeisberger and His Brown Brethren* (Bethlehem, Pa.: Moravian Publication Concern, 1908); and Edmund De Schweinitz, *The Life and Times of David Zeisberger, the Western Pioneer and Apostle of the Indians* (Philadelphia: J. B. Lippincott and Co., 1870; reprint, New York: Arno Press, 1971).

7. See Carola Wessel, "Connecting Congregations: The Net of Communication Among the Moravians as Exemplified by the Interaction Between Pennsylvania, the Upper Ohio, and Germany (1772–1774)," in *The Distinctiveness of Moravian Culture: Essays and Documents in Moravian History in Honor of Vernon H. Nelson on His Seventieth Birthday*, ed. Craig D. Atwood and Peter Vogt (Nazareth, Pa.: Moravian Historical Society), 153–72.

8. Joseph Edmund Hutton, *A History of the Moravian Church*, 2d ed. (London: Moravian Publication Office, 1909), 174–76; and A. J. Lewis, *Zinzendorf, The Ecumenical Pioneer* (Philadelphia: Westminster Press, SCM Press, 1962), 92.

9. Richard White, *The Middle Ground: Indians, Empires, and Republics in the Great Lakes Region, 1650–1815* (New York: Cambridge University Press, 1991).

10. Ibid., 389–91.

11. John Heckewelder, *Narrative of the Mission of the United Brethren Among the Delaware and Mohegan Indians, from its Commencement, in the Year 1740, to the Close in the Year, 1808* (Philadelphia: McCarthy and Davis, 1820; reprint, Arno Press and New York Times, 1971), iii, 42–43.

striking in their diaries is the emphasis given to the Indian point of view. Careful observers of Indian cultures, they focused, however, on the conversion of the "heathen"[12] to Christianity, but not necessarily to the Moravian Church. Moravians believed that the Holy Spirit selected persons to become Christians.[13]

Yet, portraying Indian sensibilities as critical to Indian survival, these Moravians left indelible evidence of the kinds of obstacles Indians faced in times of both war and peace. One barrier was the destructiveness of alcohol. Earlier Indian interpreter and assistant to the proprietor of Pennsylvania Conrad Weiser told Moravian missionary John Martin Mack of Bethlehem of his 1737 visit to the Indian town of Otseninky (near modern Binghamton, New York) on the north branch of the Susquehanna River. It was a time of great famine, and game was scarce. Weiser observed that the region's Indians were desperate, and that the people said, "Rum will kill us and leave the land clear for the Europeans without strife and purchase."[14] The missionaries, who did not themselves abstain from alcohol, did not judge Indians inferior or defective because of alcohol abuse; rather, they displayed sympathy and concern for the problems they faced. Alcohol, Zeisberger noted, flowed quite freely, and he revealed his concern about the ways in which settlers ridiculed Indians and cruelly tried to undermine Indian society.

The following episode from Zeisberger's diary illustrates this point.

> In the evening, actually it was already night, he [Shawnee Chief Gischenatsi] came to our lodgings with another *Shawnee* and a *Mingo Indian*. He talked with *Isaac*, who understands *Shawnee* pretty well

---

12. Spangenberg wrote the treatise on Moravian perceptions of the "heathen," which included those who had not entered into a covenant relationship with God and Christ. He conceptualized the bond as resembling the way "God called the people of Israel to be his people and to bless and protect them as his people." Thus God consented to enter into a covenant with "a certain race of men," a people who recognized God's calling as a reciprocal agreement binding one to the other. According to Spangenberg, God wanted to manifest his glory in them in a "peculiar, distinguishing manner." He postulated that other peoples, though no fault of their own, lacked knowledge of God's contract and historic perception to share "in this peculiar covenant of grace," so they were generally considered aliens and commonly called "heathen." Spangenberg admonished Moravians in this way: "Do not be terrified by the inhuman wickedness prevailing among the heathen and do not be deceived by appearances, as though the heathen were already good sort of people." August Gottlieb Spangenberg, *An Account of the Manner in which the Protestant Church of the Unitas Fratrum, Or United Brethren, Preach the Gospel and Carry on their Missions among the Heathen* (Barby, December 12, 1780), 1, 2, 45–46.

13. Edward Langton, *History of the Moravian Church: The Story of the First International Protestant Church* (London: Great Britain East Midland Allied Press, 1956), 55–60.

14. Quoted in Heckewelder, *Thirty Thousand Miles,* 29, 30.

and can also speak it a little, and asked him about *Gekelemukpechünk* and what things are like there and about the affairs of the *Wyandot* there. *Isaac* told him all the news he had heard about this. Then he told him what things were like in the *Lower Towns* from where he came, and that there was much drunkenness. This was causing great harm. He warned his young people urgently, but they no longer wanted to obey him and he could hardly keep them from robbing the *Traders* any more. They were beating each other to death; a great many had died recently and he did not know what would come of this. He pointed to me and said, Presumably he is coming here to tell us good things. You all may go wherever you want. Perhaps you will manage to do more than I have. Perhaps they will listen to you and obey. The White people have done this as long as I have known them. They always tell us they possess great understanding and wisdom from above. They just deceive us in this, however, in any way they want to, because they consider us fools. They say the Indians do not know anything or understand anything and are poor people. Indeed this is partly true. Now because the White people realize the Indians' weaknesses and inability, they always have a certain power over us. Therefore it is very easy for them to deceive the Indians and trick them into thinking that they only mean well for the Indians, although they are deceiving them. They come and bring *Rum* into our *Towns,* offer it to the Indians and say, here, drink, which they do until they become foolish and act like crazy people. Meanwhile the White people stand there, point their fingers at them, laugh at them, and say to each other, There, you see what great fools the *Shawnee* are.[15]

Just as Zeisberger displayed compassion for Indians when they drank in the presence of whites, so did the Gambolds. Because of Springplace's longevity,[16]

---

15. David Zeisberger, *The Moravian Mission Diaries of David Zeisberger, 1772–1781,* ed. Hermann Wellenreuther and Carola Wessel, trans. Julie Tomberlin Weber (University Park: Pennsylvania State University Press, 2005), 165–66. For the definitive text pertaining to alcohol and Indians, see Peter C. Mancall's *Deadly Medicine: Indians and Alcohol in Early America* (Ithaca: Cornell University Press, 1995).

16. Beginning in 1829, the discovery of gold at Dahlonega, Georgia, intensified rapacious white settlement in the Cherokee Nation. In 1830, encouraged by President Andrew Jackson's policy of Indian displacement, Congress passed the Indian Removal Bill. Georgia's laws required that all whites within "Georgia boundaries" swear an oath of allegiance to the state; the Brethren refused to obey Georgia's laws. On January 1, 1833, Georgia citizens, using bayonets, forced Moravian missionaries Henry G. Clauder and his wife, Eder, from the Springplace buildings. George R. Gilmer,

1801 to 1833, and the relatively peaceful times both the Cherokees and Gambolds experienced, Springplace missionaries had the advantage of keeping many of the same students in their mission school over a period of time. Consequently, their relatives felt comfortable at Springplace,[17] as Cherokees insisted that their offspring live at the mission itself.[18] They expected Moravian missionaries to accommodate and accept Cherokee traditions. As a result, the mission was the place where each culture encountered the other, and where each challenged the other to appreciate cultural differences while clinging to their respective spiritual values.[19]

Along the lane that led from the Federal Road[20] to the mission environs, the Gambolds witnessed Cherokees going to ball play, a mini-warrior sport, and they associated ball play and all-night dances with the immoderate consumption of alcohol. To the missionaries' dismay, Springplace figured in some of the more overtly religious practices associated with the ball play. The Cherokees used the nearby limestone springs from the Conasauga River for purification

---

Sketches of Some of the First Settlers of Upper Georgia, of the Cherokees, and the Author (New York: D. Appleton and Co., 1855), 392; J. Taylor Hamilton and Kenneth G. Hamilton, *History of the Moravian Church: The Renewed Unitas Fratum, 1722–1957* (Bethlehem, Pa., and Winston-Salem, N.C.: Interprovincial Board of Christian Education, Moravian Church in America, 1967; reprint, 1979), 294; and Thurman Wilkins, *Cherokee Tragedy: The Story of the Ridge Family and the Decimation of a People* (New York: Macmillan, 1970), 214.

17. In 1800 the Salem Moravians negotiated for thirty-five acres of land on which to build the mission. Initially the Cherokees rented them twenty-five. Land was not individually owned—only the improvements on the Cherokee land. In 1814 the Cherokee Council granted the Moravians the requested acreage. Thereafter they referred to this as new land and to their original purchase as old land. Kenneth G. Hamilton, trans. and ed., "Minutes of the Mission Conference Held in Springplace," *Atlanta Historical Bulletin* 15 (winter 1970): 50, 51.

18. David Zeisberger and the Reverend John Gottlieb Ernestus Heckewelder, another Moravian missionary, converted far more native people than the nineteenth-century missionaries to the Cherokees did; earlier missionaries insisted that Christian Indians live at the mission outpost. See also Wellenreuther and Wessel's introduction to Zeisberger's *Moravian Mission Diaries* for a detailed and comprehensive overview of eighteenth-century Moravian mission theology and goals. For definitive studies of Zeisberger, see Earl P. Olmstead, *Blackcoats Among the Delaware: David Zeisberger on the Ohio Frontier* (Kent: Kent State University Press, 1991); and De Schweinitz, *Life and Times of Zeisberger*. For a comprehensive study of Heckewelder, see Heckewelder, *Thirty Thousand Miles*.

19. For major contributions to our understanding of cultures in contact, see James Axtell, *The Invasion Within: The Contest of Cultures in Colonial North America* (New York: Oxford University Press, 1985); Colin G. Calloway, *New Worlds for All: Indians, Europeans, and the Remaking of Early America* (Baltimore: Johns Hopkins University Press, 1997); and White, *Middle Ground*.

20. Finished in 1805, the Federal Road connected Augusta, Georgia, with Nashville, Tennessee. See John Goff, *Place-Names of Georgia: Essays of John H. Goff*, ed. Francis Lee Utley and Marion R. Hemperley (Athens: University of Georgia Press, 1975); and Kenneth G. Krakow, *Georgia Place Names* (Macon, Ga.: Winship Press, 1975).

rites before and after ball play. Furthermore, ball players sought spiritual and physical strength from juice extracted from the roots of wild crabapple trees that grew on the site.[21]

Missionaries had other objections. Players stripped nearly naked, and indeed so did some of the spectators. As was the custom during the competition, Cherokees made bets on which side would win and gambled away their garments.[22] Unclothed Cherokees who walked home from ball play along the lane that led to the Federal Road horrified the missionaries, who opposed not only the Cherokees' nakedness but also young and old of both sexes walking side by side.[23] In addition, some parents came into the mission intoxicated before and after the game, and the Gambolds believed they set a bad example for the students.

Within the confines of the mission, a ball player known as The Tyger, a Cherokee leader whose father was Onandago, threatened to attack his family physically.[24] Both alcohol use and corporal punishment were European introductions, and some Cherokees had gradually adopted these alien customs into their culture. As foreign ways crept into their social constructs, a few Cherokees questioned European influence. In 1811 the Moravian missionaries heard that the highly respected Chief Koychezetel, also known as Warrior's Nephew,[25] warned his fellow Cherokees: "The Mother[26] of our Nation was not pleased because you punish each other severely. Yes, you whip until blood flows."[27] A foreign concept, corporal punishment had displaced the traditional punishments of ostracism and slight scratching.[28]

Moravians reported that children begged their fathers in particular not to overindulge in "brandy-wine." So pervasive was the problem of alcohol abuse that the missionaries recorded many incidents of Cherokees arriving at the mission inebriated and demanding food and shelter. Anna Rosina Gambold recorded the following incident involving The Tyger:

21. James Mooney, "The Cherokee Ball Play," *Journal of Cherokee Studies* 7 (spring 1982): 14, 20.
22. Ibid., 23.
23. *Moravian Springplace Mission*, 2:74.
24. The Tyger, Big Tyger, or Tyger was the leader of a faction in the 1820s that wanted to overthrow the existing Cherokee government and banish Christian missions. See William G. McLoughlin, *Cherokees and Missionaries, 1789–1839* (New Haven: Yale University Press, 1984), 225.
25. Ibid., 84–85.
26. Selu, or Corn, the fictive ancestral first female of the Cherokees.
27. *Moravian Springplace Mission*, 1:411.
28. Charles Hudson, *The Southeastern Indians* (Knoxville: University of Tennessee Press, 1976), 322–24. For further study of the Cherokee cosmic world, see Charles Hudson, *Elements of Southeastern Indian Religion* (Leiden: E. J. Brill, 1984), 1–15.

In the mission, when The Tyger met Dawzizi again, his father addressed him in the following manner: "You concern yourself very much about mother, but you abandon me to stand alone like a dog."[29] With eyes full of tears, Dawzizi's answer was, "Father, I must protect my mother from you, when you are drunk. I love you as much, but your behavior hurts me. There is nothing I want as much as for you but to abstain totally from drinking brandy-wine." At this his father seemed touched and was silent.[30]

In addition, throughout the early nineteenth century familial tensions had heightened because United States policymakers had urged Cherokees to adopt an inheritance law. Intermarriage with Scots traders had agitated those relationships, and the Cherokees began to alter their political structure in order to make their legal system understandable to white America. In 1808 these increasing demands led the Cherokee National Council to pass an inheritance law that allowed goods to be passed along the father's side instead of the mother's.[31] As the Cherokee were traditionally a matrilineal society, this law provoked disagreements between the genders.[32] Cherokee men began to assume a relationship to their offspring and assert authority in areas where women had previously been the negotiators and powerbrokers.

In spite of The Tyger's pleadings, he finally succumbed to what was traditionally understood: The mother ruled in the family. In the face of such impassioned family relationships, the Moravians displayed compassion and agreed, in this case, that Dawzizi could come and live with them.[33] "Oh," his mother said, "he has my complete approval. Here he is in good hands. At home he would become a drunkard just like his father."[34] The attempt at male dominance subsided as female power prevailed in this situation.

---

29. A German Script symbol, resembling a German Script "X" and standing for the Latin *pergendum,* placed at the end of "dog," denotes et cetera.

30. *Moravian Springplace Mission,* 2:75.

31. *Laws of the Cherokee Nation: Adopted by the Council at Various Periods* (Tahlequah, Cherokee Nation: Cherokee Advocate Office, 1853; reprint, 1973), 3.

32. This is an example of tensions between the genders, as Cherokee fathers began to claim kinship in the matrilineal system. For a definitive study of Cherokee gender change, see Theda Perdue, *Cherokee Women: Gender and Culture Change, 1700–1835* (Lincoln: University of Nebraska Press, 1998).

33. Although Dawzizi had been a student at the mission school since 1810, his parents came and took him home whenever they chose. Now his mother signaled to the missionaries that he would be in their care from then on.

34. *Moravian Springplace Mission,* 2:75.

Though misuse of alcohol caused familial distress and outrage, the missionaries also noted that The Tyger and his wife lived together on the best terms; it was only her husband's strong passion for "brandy-wine" that caused his good-natured wife grief. Anna Rosina Gambold portrayed the couple as "very diligent people."[35]

Cherokee men and women alike were concerned in this instance about a son who would face an entirely different world from theirs. Furthermore, the Cherokee Nation believed that the Moravians offered their children the language and other skills to coexist with encroaching frontiersmen and protect the Cherokee ancestral domain.

While the Gambolds in particular offered the practical knowledge they thought Indians would need to survive in a hostile environment, both they and Zeisberger portrayed the Indians as needing, most of all, spiritual uplifting by becoming Christian. In their view, the Holy Spirit was the only medium through which this goal could be realized. John Gambold lamented that the Holy Spirit's influence could not draw more Cherokees to the sufferings of Jesus.[36]

While Indians faced massacres like the 1782 one at Gnadenhütten and would soon face their forced removal from the American South (1838–39), the chief concern of the Moravians was the welfare of their immortal souls; human suffering in the here and now was secondary. In this sense, the historical Moravian Christian belief system held little room for human frailty. Moravians believed in the humanity of mankind but not in every man's innate ability to determine his own life course. Thus the missionaries thought of Indians as human objects worthy of assistance but not as persons to be completely respected for their humanity.

In some ways, both Zeisberger and the Gambolds understood their limitations. Zeisberger noted that Indians lacked faith in him, and the Gambolds noted the abject spiritual poverty of the Cherokees' plight. Their "hearts still ached and now fervent sighs for the salvation of these poor heathens rose to the *Redeemer of the World*."[37]

Moravian spiritual dissonance thus detached missionaries from the perplexing issues facing Indians but simultaneously allowed them to seek their own spiritual sustenance.[38] Indians lived in a practical, temporal world, while

35. Ibid.
36. Ibid., 2:439.
37. Ibid., 2:74.
38. For some similar thoughts about the effectiveness of Moravian missionary works, see Jon F. Sensbach, *Rebecca's Revival: Creating Black Christianity in the Atlantic World* (Cambridge: Harvard University Press, 2005), 237–45.

Moravians found solitude and peace in a sphere of spiritual harmony that held out hope only for those the Holy Spirit had touched. Thus Moravian missionary activity among Indians was well meant but perhaps misguided. Yet the copious documents Moravians bequeathed us have left both challenges and lasting contributions to scholars of Indian cultures. Scholars must cull from the materials ways to portray Indian struggle and survival beyond what Moravians thought humanly possible and recognize the host of vast ethnographic insights made by Moravian missionaries that scholars would not have known otherwise.

"Incline Your Second Ear This Way":

Song as a Cultural Mediator in Moravian Mission Towns

WALTER W. WOODWARD

On December 11, 1781, three days after the Delaware war chiefs Captain Pipe and Buckagahitas had delivered thirty white American scalps to the commander of the British fort at Detroit, the fort's commander met with Buckagahitas and his warriors in council.

As the protocols record, Buckagahitas, holding the war belt under which the Delawares had been fighting, metaphorically complained to the British Major that the axe his people had used against the enemy had become dull, and only the British could sharpen it again. They could do so, Buckagahitas said, by supplying him and his 240 warriors "with rifles and other implements of war." Not just any weapons would do, for the enemies the Delawares faced were well armed. "We want good Kettles, Tomahawks, and other necessaries for warriors . . . the Tomahawks we received formerly were of no use as they would break to pieces not only on the heads of the enemy, but on the smallest branch in the woods." Buckagahitas demanded that Major DePuyster order them "good, strong tomahawks."[1]

As revealed in the treaty minutes, this was a fairly dramatic piece of theater: the war ally capitalizing on a moment of victory to demand better material support. Something that may easily be overlooked, however, is that this piece of intercultural theater was actually a musical. Before Buckagahitas uttered a word, he stood before the assembled English and Indian councilors and sang his war song, a genre of Indian music distinct in tune and timbre, in which the singer recounted not only his own exploits in the late war but the heroic exploits of his ancestors, too. Buckagahitas was not the only vocalist that day.

---

1. Appendix, Document no. 5, "Protocol of the Conference at Detroit, 1781," in David Zeisberger, *The Moravian Mission Diaries of David Zeisberger, 1772–1781*, ed. Hermann Wellenreuther and Carola Wessel, trans. Julie Tomberlin Weber (University Park: Pennsylvania State University Press, 2005), 568–72 (hereafter cited parenthetically in the text by page number).

Between his oratorical description of the dull tomahawks and his demand for better weapons, his warriors also sang their war songs. In the protocols, the descriptions of these performances take ten words. In the talks themselves, the songs probably represented by far the longest segment of the council meeting.

Music, especially song, was a pervasive and essentially important aspect of eighteenth-century Native American culture. It fulfilled an array of functions and was called upon as a core element of interpersonal, spiritual, and intercultural communications. Similarly, music, especially song, was a pervasive and critically important aspect of Moravian mission culture. As in Delaware society, David Zeisberger and other Moravian missionaries called upon music to carry much of the burden of interpersonal, spiritual, and intercultural communication. Song was a bridge that helped enable the Indian Brothers and Sisters to transition from exclusively native life-ways and religious beliefs to accommodate life and religious practice within the different and more regulated society of the Moravian missions. Indian and Moravian beliefs about the power of music combined with Moravian mission ideology to make song a primary medium for intercultural communication and conversion.

The new scholarly effort to understand the significance of sound in the world we have lost argues that all historians can benefit from paying closer attention to the presence of music and song in our sources. Peter Hoffer has asked us to think about the "sensory imperialism" of the colonial era.[2] Richard Rath has suggested that sounds constituted identity, especially among Native Americans.[3] I join with historian Michael McNally in believing that music making was both a subtle and a supple agent of cultural mixing.[4] David Zeisberger's Moravian mission diaries, through what they reveal about song, provide a useful case study of the resilience of cultures in transition when faced with the forces of cultural change.

Importance of Song in Eastern Woodlands Cultures

Native American cultures were song societies. Social relations, personal identity, and intercultural communications were created and confirmed vocally. Song was a powerful medium that fulfilled many functions. European chroniclers,

---

2. Peter Charles Hoffer, *Sensory Worlds in Early America* (Baltimore: Johns Hopkins University Press, 2003).
3. Richard Cullen Rath, *How Early America Sounded* (Ithaca: Cornell University Press, 2003).
4. Michael McNally, *Ojibwe Singers: Hymns, Grief, and a Native Culture in Motion* (New York: Oxford University Press, 2000).

from their earliest contacts, noticed the importance of song to Indian life-ways. From John Smith, William Strachey, and John Eliot in the seventeenth century, to nineteenth-century recorders Henry R. Schoolcraft and John Long, observers commented on the manner in which music pervaded Native American cultures.[5] "The Savages are great singers," noted the Jesuit father Paul Le Jeune in 1634. "They sing, as do most of the nations of the earth, for recreation and for devotion, ... they nearly all take pleasure both in singing and in hearing others sing; and although I told them that I did not understand anything about it, they often invited me to sing some song or prayer."[6]

Virtually every aspect of Native American life was shaped by and expressed in song. Hunting, planting, harvesting, sickness, healing, gaming, dreaming, life-cycle changes, lullabies, diplomacy, war making—even death had its own characteristic song form.[7] Songs helped mediate and shape social relations both within and among Indian groups.[8] Songs were part of communal healing activities, intercultural treaty and war making, and most other spiritual and ceremonial rituals. Song was the most important element in worship, in the ceremonies of age- and status-defined peer group societies, and in gambling games.

Indian song was commonly performed in combination with dance. Europeans writing about these ceremonies, overawed by the antic gestures, often focused attention on the disconcerting dances, but a purposeful song accompanied every dance. The Baptist minister David Jones, who visited the Delaware community of Gekelemukpechünk in the Ohio country in 1772, noted the inseparability of the two: "They are most indefatigable dancers, continuing almost every night in the winter to near 12 o'clock. Their musick is only a skin stretched over a keg. On this the musician beats with one stick. As an assistant, another stands up shaking in his hand a gourd that has parcels of grains of corn in it. But as they dance, all sing, so that the echo of their united voices may be heard at a great distance."[9]

---

5. Robert Stevenson, "English Sources for Indian Music Until 1882," *Ethnomusicology* 17 (September 1973): 399–442.

6. Quoted in Reuben Gold Thwaites, ed., *The Jesuit Relations and Allied Documents: Travels and Explorations of the Jesuit Missionaries in New France, 1610–1791*, 73 vols. (Cleveland: Burrows Brothers, 1896–1901), 6:181–82.

7. See, for example, Frances Densmore, *Chippewa Music*, 2 vols. (Washington, D.C.: U.S. Government Printing Office, 1910); John Roberts Columbo, ed. *Songs of the Indians*, 2 vols. (Ottawa: Oberon, 1983).

8. McNally, *Ojibwe Singers*, 27. Establishing proper social relations is a pervasive theme of surviving native song repertoires.

9. David Jones, *A Journal of Two Visits Made to Some Nations of Indians on the West Side of the River Ohio, in the Years 1772 and 1773* (Burlington, N.J.: Isaac Collins, 1774; reprint, New York: Arno Press, 1971), 57.

Native people sang, and paid close attention to songs, because songs were functional—they *did* things.[10] And they did things powerfully, because they originated in the spaces that linked the spiritual world to the material one. The idea of composing songs was an alien concept to native singers. The inspiration that led one to a new song was a special gift from the spiritual world, intended specifically for the recipient's and/or his or her people's education, direction, protection, or empowerment. In this sense, McNally has suggested, it may be helpful to understand all Indians' sung music in terms of prayer.[11]

Dream songs, given to recipients during dream states or as parts of visions, were spiritual messages instrumental in shaping individual identity. So was the death song, an agonizing final performance often expected of captive Indian warriors. As the eighteenth-century chronicler Jonathan Carver described it, death songs were the ultimate expression of individual courage, endurance, and manhood.

> The prisoners destined to death are soon led to the place of execution . . . bound to a stake, with faggots heaped around them, and obliged, for the last time, to sing their death song. The warriors . . . now perform in a more prolix manner this sad solemnity. They recount with an audible voice all the brave actions they have performed, and pride themselves in the number of enemies they have killed. In this rehearsal they spare not even their tormentors, but strive by every provoking tale they can invent, to irritate and insult them. Sometimes this has the desired effect, and the sufferers are dispatched sooner than they otherwise would have been.[12]

Music symbolized and personalized supernatural power. *Powaws* and other individuals thought to have supernatural powers had a special relationship with music. Eastern woodland Indians employed both antiphony—call-and-response singing—and strophic forms—verse and chorus singing. The lyrics of songs, however, seem to have been less important than the songs' functions. Music and performance were judged less by what they said than by what they

---

10. McNally, *Ojibwe Singers*, 30.
11. Ibid., 32.
12. Jonathan Carver, *Three Years Travels, Through the Interior Parts of North-America, for More Than Five Thousand Miles . . . Together with a Concise History of the Genius, Manners, and Customs of the Indians . . . and an Appendix, Describing the Uncultivated Parts of America That Are the Most Proper for Forming Settlements, by Captain Jonathan Carver, of the Provincial Troops in America* (Philadelphia: Printed and sold by Joseph Crukshank in Market-Street, and Robert Bell in Third-Street, 1784), 141.

accomplished. To the degree that a song fulfilled the religious, social, personal, political, or military functions expected of it, it became a welcome addition to the song kit. Not surprisingly, Native American song repertories often included thousands of items.[13]

The Importance of Song in American Moravian Communities

Moravian communities, too, shaped much of their social and spiritual activity around music. Singing was a standard and significant part of every day's routine. Mornings began with discussion of the *Loosungen,* or watchwords, often reinforced with a hymn composed of a scriptural verse or verses set to music.[14] Evenings usually concluded with the singing hour, a time of song and spiritual reflection. Throughout the year the calendar was filled with a series of special holy commemorations and love feasts in which songs were the focal point of ritual activity. In addition to their daily spiritual activities, Moravians celebrated ten holy festival days commemorating events in the life of Christ, and fifteen special days of commemoration celebrating key moments in the development of the Unity. Over and above these often highly musical occasions, the Brothers and Sisters celebrated another fifteen or more annual festival days in which age, gender, and marital status–based peer group choirs (all children, small boys, big boys, single brethren, single sisters, married couples, widows and widowers, widows alone) performed (565–67).

Song was so central to Moravian spiritual practice that observers from other religious groups thought it was the foundation of their faith. In the 1790s the minister John Bennett noted with Episcopal superiority, "Their worship consists principally in singing, and hence, perhaps, their societies are called choirs.... There is certainly a great mixture of good in this people. What a pity, that they cannot join with us in offering a rational service."[15] Moravian tradition had long held that song was a fundamentally spiritual activity that allowed God to work in a nonrational or suprarational manner, providing evidence of God's

13. Bruno Nettl, Victoria Lindsay Levine, and Elaine Keillor, "Amerindian Music," *Grove Music Online,* ed. L. Macy, www.grovemusic.com/ (accessed July 16, 2004).
14. See, for example, Bernhard Adam Grube, *Dellawaerisches Gesang-Büchlein* (Bethlehem, Pa.: Johann Brandmüller, 1763); David Zeisberger, *A Collection of Hymns for the Use of the Christian Indians of the Missions of the United Brethren, in North America* (Philadelphia, 1803).
15. John Bennett, *Letters to a Young Lady, on a Variety of Useful and Interesting Subjects: Calculated to Improve the Heart, to Form the Manners, and Enlighten the Understanding,* 2 vols. (Hartford: Printed by Hudson and Goodwin, 1791), 1:71–72.

presence that superseded rational analysis. Johann Alsted, the seventeenth-century professor at Herborn who tutored the famed Moravian educator Jan Comenius, held that God was the author of all music, and that he intended it to be used to advance piety and unity. Vocal music was the noblest of all musical forms, and when joined with instrumental music it became "an incredible means of moving the affections and senses." Alsted believed that the chief force of music came from the emotional power it derived from accommodating text to the affections.[16] The ability of music to add affective power to scriptural text was its great attraction for Moravian clerics, and as the Brethren, under the influence of Count Nicholas von Zinzendorf, adopted a focus on the nonrational experience of Christ's heart, wounds, and Passion, song became increasingly central as a medium of Moravian spiritual practice.[17]

In discussing Moravian theology and mission method, Hermann Wellenreuther, relying on the works of Count Zinzendorf, has emphasized the visual aspects of mission work. "Visualization of the sufferings on the cross" was what made Moravian theology distinct. "To paint for the eyes," Wellenreuther notes, was the essence of the mission method. He relates the visions promoted by Zinzendorf to the spiritual vision quests of Native Americans (56). A focus on the visual may well have been the essence of spirituality for Moravians such as Count Zinzendorf, surrounded by the compelling paintings of Moravian artists such as Valentine Haidt. But out on the Ohio frontier, sounds, rather than sights, conveyed the essence of spiritual meaning. David Zeisberger seems to have used visual referents such as a crèche scene in at least some of his services, but he recognized that conversion to the "truth" of the wounded Christ often came about as the result of aural experience (517). Time and again he distinguished between those Indians who could hear Christ's message and those still deaf to the truth. In the year-end summary for 1779, for example, Zesiberger noted the power of the *Loosungen* as the source of daily food for the Brothers and Sisters. The messages and sung verses had served to instruct, admonish, and comfort the Indian converts, and, he noted, paraphrasing a biblical injunction, "we are happy to see that the Brothers and Sisters have ears to hear" (518).

---

16. Johann Heinrich Alsted and John Birchensha, *Templum Musicum, Or, the Musical Synopsis of the Learned and Famous Johannes-Henricus-Alstedius* (London: Will Godbid for Peter Oring, 1664).

17. Craig D. Atwood, *Community of the Cross : Moravian Piety in Colonial Bethlehem* (University Park: Pennsylvania State University Press, 2004), 43–112; Henry Whitfield, *Strength Out of Weaknesse, Or a Glorious Manifestation of the Further Progresse of the Gospel Among the Indians in New-England* (London: M. Simmons for John Blayne and Samuel Howes, 1652), 29; Jean Fittz Hankins, "Bringing the Good News: Protestant Missionaries to the Indians of New England and New York" (Ph.D. diss., University of Connecticut, 1993), 109.

Moravians such as Zeisberger were not the only missionaries who recognized the value of music in seeking Indian conversions. The Puritan missionary John Eliot had taught the "praying Indians" of Natick to sing translated psalms in "Indian tongue, and Indian meter, but to an English tune." Massachusetts governor John Endecott, who visited Eliot in 1651, found that the Indians sang the psalms "cheerfully and prettie tuneablie."[18] In the eighteenth century, New Light ministers such as Eleazar Wheelock incorporated the innovative musical style of singing hymns using vocal harmony rather than traditional unison singing into the music he taught students at Moor's Indian Charity school in Lebanon Crank (now Columbia), Connecticut.

Wheelock's school became a center of musical proselytizing to the Indians. One of his students, a Mohegan named David Fowler, was commissioned by Wheelock as a schoolmaster to the Iroquois town of Oneida in New York. Within three weeks of his arrival, Fowler reported to Wheelock that his students could already "carry three parts of several tunes neatly." Fowler's brother, Jacob, experienced similar success while a schoolmaster at Conajohare.[19] Samson Occom, another Mohegan student at Wheelock's mission, not only compiled, edited, and published a book of hymns in 1774, but several of his own sacred compositions became standards of nineteenth-century Protestant liturgy.[20] Samuel Kirkland, the first non-Indian student to attend Wheelock's school, became one of the most effective Protestant missionaries among the Iroquois. His efforts were clearly enhanced by the singing school he maintained six nights a week among the Seneca. Kirkland translated psalms into the Seneca language, and believed his Indian singers were the finest in the region.[21] Wheelock himself had no doubt about the importance of music in gaining Indian converts. Writing to the Connecticut minister Nathaniel Whitaker, he noted, "Many of them Say, they never knew such pleasure before—That it is worthwhile to be Christians, if they had nothing more by it, than the Pleasure of singing Praises to God."[22]

New Light missionaries like Wheelock and his emissaries effectively incorporated music into their conversion efforts, but the Moravians appear to have

---

18. John Endecott to John Eliot, reprinted in Whitfield, *Strength Out of Weaknesse*, 29; Hankins, "Bringing the Good News," 109.

19. Hankins, "Bringing the Good News," 300; James Dow McCallum, ed., *The Letters of Eleazar Wheelock's Indians* (Hanover: Dartmouth College Publications, 1932), 97, 117.

20. Joanna Brooks, "Six Hymns by Samson Occom," *Early American Literature* 38, no. 1 (2003): 73.

21. Hankins, "Bringing the Good News," 301.

22. Eleazar Wheelock to Nathaniel Whitaker, April 11, 1767, Wheelock Papers #767261.4, Dartmouth College, Hanover, New Hampshire, quoted in ibid., 302.

used it most pervasively and persuasively. Jean Hankins has noted that "it was the Moravians' liturgical use of music which truly set them apart not just from the Congregationalists but from all other religious groups in America, including the Roman Catholics," and that, for the Indians, "the most appealing part of the Christian liturgy may have been the music." John Sergeant, the first missionary from the New England company to the Indians at Stockbridge, Massachusetts, marveled at the Moravians' "Wonderful Success."[23]

How effective were Moravians' music-centered conversion efforts in the Ohio country? Most historians have argued that the Moravian missions generally were indeed more successful than their other Euro-American counterparts.[24] Although David Zeisberger's recordkeeping categorizations are inconsistent, the number of baptisms performed in the Ohio mission towns seems to compare favorably to the number of baptisms obtained in the Pennsylvania Indian towns as reported by Jane Merritt.[25] Furthermore, given the instability in the region generated by the threats and actuality of war in the years between 1774 and 1780, the number of Indians who accepted the risks of staying with the mission whites seems quite remarkable. David McClure, a Congregationalist minister who spent two days at the Moravian missions in Ohio, concluded that the Moravians had found "the best mode of Christianizing the Indians."[26] Merritt has noted, and Zeisberger's *Diaries* confirm, that Indians came to the towns for an array of reasons, of which desire for conversion was only one. Hunger, sickness, and the search for security undoubtedly attracted many to the towns. It is also clear, however, that for a substantial but indeterminate number of people, the Moravian religion, as preached and "chanted into being" by Zeisberger, Heckewelder, and

23. Ibid., 306, 299.
24. R. Pierce Beaver, "American Missionary Motivation Before the Revolution," *Church History* 31 (June 1962): 225–26; James P. Ronda and James Axtell, *Indian Missions: A Critical Bibliography* (Bloomington: Indiana University Press, 1978), 30–32; Henry Warner Bowden, *American Indians and Christian Missions: Studies in Cultural Conflict* (Chicago: University of Chicago Press, 1981), 157–58; David S. Lovejoy, *Religious Enthusiasm in the New World: Heresy to Revolution* (Cambridge: Harvard University Press, 1985), 168.
25. Merritt has determined that there were a maximum of 505 Indian converts in Pennsylvania in the twenty-two year period between 1742 and 1764. The Ohio missions counted 269 baptized members in their year of highest population, 1778, their seventh year of settlement. The totals are problematic, however, since some of the migrants to Ohio had been baptized previously. Jane Merritt, *At the Crossroads: Indians and Empires on a Mid-Atlantic Frontier, 1700–1763* (Chapel Hill: University of North Carolina Press, 2003), 105, table 1.
26. Ibid., 302. John Sergeant, "Mr. Sergeant's Letter Finished," *The Christian History, Containing Accounts of the Revival and Propagation of Religion in Great Britain and America (1743–1745)*, July 16, 1743, no. 20, 1; Franklin B. Dexter, ed., *Diary of David McClure, Doctor of Divinity, 1748–1820* (New York: Knickerbocker Press, 1899), 51.

the converted Indian Brothers and Sisters, was a primary reason for residing in the Ohio towns.[27]

One of the elements that made the mission towns desirable living places for Indians was the syncretic approach to cultural conversion adopted by the missionaries. While would-be residents had to agree to adhere to a number of Christian principles and reject former practices that challenged the Christian faith or social order, the Ohio mission towns also incorporated important aspects of traditional Delaware culture (563–64). The division of labor, for instance, continued to reflect the gendered expectations of Delaware society. Women cultivated the fields and men did the hunting, though the missionaries were concerned not to allow them to remain away too long. Face painting and other ways of presenting an aggressive or "savage" countenance were prohibited (as was engaging in warfare), but some Delaware Brothers continued to wear their hair in the style associated with warriors.[28] Unintentionally, but usefully nonetheless, the Moravian choir system incorporated native social categories. The separate choirs for men and women, and the gender-specific choirs for older children, mirrored native social divisions and acknowledged the transitional nature of Indians entering adolescence.

Zeisberger's sensitivity to the operation of Delaware politics suggests that he was deeply aware of the nuances of Delaware cultural interpretation. The patient pressure he applied, through repeated protocol-sensitive requests, in an effort to acquire from Delaware leaders special status for the mission community as an independent subordinate member of the Delaware Nation, reflects a practical commitment to embracing cultural syncretism in the mission process. Cultural syncretism also helped ameliorate two of the greatest problems Indians faced when making the decision to join the mission community. Playing games of chance was a common pastime in Delaware communities. It involved the exchange not only of goods but of good fortune. One of the attractions of gambling games was that they incorporated assumptions about spiritual favor. Major gambling events were accompanied by rituals invoking spiritual aid. Zeisberger described one such occasion:

> The Indian game of dice is the most popular of amusements. They may devote days in succession to it, always gambling on the throwing.

---

27. Richard Rath writes of "worlds chanted into being" in *How Early America Sounded.*
28. John Gottlieb Ernestus Heckewelder, *Thirty Thousand Miles with John Heckewelder,* ed. Paul A. W. Wallace (Pittsburgh.: University of Pittsburgh Press, 1958), 194.

Among the Mingoes I have observed that two towns brought together goods, blankets, strowds, shirts, linen and played for them. In this case the game lasted eight days. The dice are placed in a dish, lifted up and thrown forcibly on the ground. The people of the two towns met daily during the period named and every inhabitant of each town threw the dice once. This done they parted for the day and each party separately offered a sacrifice in the evening. In connection with the sacrifice they had their special ceremonies, consisting in a man going several times around a fire, throwing tobacco into it and singing a song. Afterwards the whole company danced. This continued for eight days. When the winners bore away the spoil in triumph.[29]

Such games of chance were among those aspects of native culture residents of Indian towns gave up when they agreed to "renounce and abhor all Jugles, cheats, lies, and deceits of Satan" (564). But they did not have to give up belief in the power of chance altogether, merely assign to it a much higher purpose. Unlike other Christian denominations, which rejected all forms of gambling on religious and moral grounds, the Moravian Brothers elevated chance to the highest level of spiritual discernment. Through drawing lots, Moravians determined the will of the Church's Elder (Jesus Christ) and used chance to guide their most difficult and sensitive decisions.[30] Gambling as a native pastime was proscribed more because it was sacrilegious than because it was inherently evil.

An even greater obstacle to conversion—because of its pervasive practice and multiplicity of uses in Delaware culture—was dancing. Here, however, as in many other areas of cultural conflict, song proved to be a potent and elastic medium of intercultural accommodation. Using song to counter the spiritual, social, and ritualistic aspects of native dancing made sense, for, after all, every Delaware dance was integrally related to an accompanying song, and song was central to Moravian religious practice.

From earliest settlement Zeisberger worked to make Moravian spiritual songs accessible to the Delawares and to integrate them into their daily round of activities. He already had access to the *Dellawaerisches Gesang-Büchlein,* a group of Moravian hymns translated into Delaware in 1763.[31] These hymns—usually

---

29. Archer Butler Hulbert and William Nathaniel Schwarze, eds., *David Zeisberger's History of the Northern American Indians* (Columbus, Ohio: F. J. Heer, 1910), 118–19.

30. See, for example, Zeisberger, *Moravian Mission Diaries,* Appendix, Document no. 1, "Protocol of the Conference at Langundo-Utenünk on 12 August, 1772," 555–59.

31. Grube, *Dellawaerisches Gesang-Büchlein.*

scriptural verses translated and set to popular Moravian tunes—presumably formed the basis for the songs rehearsed during the evening's singing hour and for choir festivals and love feasts. Sensitive to the numerous variants of Delaware dialect, Zeisberger, shortly after the establishment of Schönbrunn, initiated a project to "revise some of the hymns which have been translated into the Indian language." In doing so, one of the people with whom he probably collaborated was Brother Anton, a Delaware who had assisted Bernhard Adam Grube in producing the original Delaware hymnbook.[32]

The daily singing hour, though often shorter than an hour, took place in the evening, the time of day when dancing usually began in the Delaware villages. While Moravian rules explicitly rejected dance, the vocal performances may have included kinesthetic components that further commended them as a suitable alternative to the Delawares' former practices. We know little about the actual manner in which the singing hour and other services were conducted, but books on psalmody and choral singing from the period frequently suggest a communal kinesthetic component to the vocalizing. In the 1779 publication *Select Harmony*, the itinerant choir master Andrew Law noted that "some gestures, when used with solemnity, are proper in singing as well as in speaking, such as looking up, when singing the words God, Christ or Heaven."[33] Thomas Walter, author of a frequently reprinted guide to singing, noted that one could learn tempo by raising and lowering one's hand rhythmically.[34] This may have provided the basis for the very energetic gesticulation that accompanied the genre known as shape note singing, hymnals for which first appeared in Philadelphia around 1798.[35] Zeisberger also was familiar with the postural contortions practiced by the highly regarded vocalists in the Pennsylvania utopian community of Ephrata. There, according to the Anglican observer Joseph Duche, the singers sat singing in "a solemn and dejected manner," with heads tilted fully backward and lips barely parted, producing "music such as thrilled to the very

32. Brother Anton died in Schönbrunn on September 5, 1773. Zeisberger, *Moravian Mission Diaries*, 96, 157.

33. Andrew Law, *Select Harmony, Containing in a Plain and Concise Manner, the Rules of Singing, Together with, a Collection of Psalm Tunes, Hymns and Anthems* (Cheshire, Conn.: Printed by William Law, 1779), 2.

34. Thomas Walter, *The Grounds and Rules of Musick Explained, Or, an Introduction to the Art of Singing by Note* (Boston: Printed by J. Franklin for S. Gerrish, 1721), 20.

35. Frank J. Metcalf, "'The Easy Instructor': A Bibliographical Study," *Musical Quarterly* 23, no. 1 (1937): 89–97; the complete copies of this text date from the edition published at "Hopewell Near Trenton: Thomas Smith & Co., 1803," though an incomplete (but textually different) version, perhaps from 1799, has survived. See also Sibley Music Library Watanabe Special Collections, www.esm.rochester.edu/sibley/specialc/shapenotes/shape1.htm.

soul."[36] We don't know whether Zeisberger incorporated physical movements into communal singing, but he did make them part of prayers. When Thomas the Onondaga and his son Nicholas were accepted into the congregation amid many tears, the "congregation fell down," prostrating themselves, before Zeisberger prayed (253). On other occasions, Zeisberger noted, "in the dust we prayed to our Lord and Chief Elder" (480). Rituals such as prostrate prayer and foot washing suggest that the Brothers were not averse to incorporating physicality into spiritual rituals.

Whether or not physical expressions were intentionally incorporated into the singing hour to augment their appeal as an alternative to traditional song and dance rituals, singing hymns and verses became a popular evening activity among the Indians, which pleased Zeisberger a great deal. "Every evening they [the Indian Brothers and Sisters] hold their own singing services in their houses," Zeisberger recorded, "and instead of hearing nothing except for noise and heathen entertainment as in the savages Towns, here you hear the Lord being praised and the crucified Savior being preached" (520).[37] In the fall of 1777, after the Indian Brothers had returned from a fourteen-day hunt—a great occasion for celebratory song and dance in traditional Indian communities—Zeisberger noted, "The Brothers and Sisters encouraged each other, and it was sweet and uplifting to listen to the occasional singing and preaching in their houses" (418).

Moravian spiritual songs did much more than serve as an alternative to traditional Indian song and dance rituals. They also helped the Moravian Brothers surmount or offset essential linguistic and theological problems they encountered in attempting Indian conversion. All would-be Protestant missionaries needed strategies to overcome two obstacles: (1) Indians' inability to read scripture; and (2) the difficulty of presenting fundamental Christian theological concepts in ways that made sense to native listeners. Conrad Weiser, the German trader, religious seeker, and longtime Pennsylvania agent to the Iroquois, once described the problem to the Lutheran leader Henry Muhlenberg. "When one tries to explain to them something of the revealed word of God, in the first place, their language lacks the essential phrases and expressions with which to convey the spiritual and heavenly truths and make

---

36. Quoted in E. Gordon Alderfer, *The Ephrata Commune: An Early American Counterculture* (Pittsburgh: University of Pittsburgh Press, 1985), 114–15.
37. See also Zeisberger, *Moravian Mission Diaries,* 176, 296, 512, 518, 566.

them understandable; at best one is able to express with their phrases a natural theology and the historical truths of the Word of God."[38]

Weiser, who was so respected among the Iroquois that they gave him the name Tarachiawagon, "he who is holding up the heavens," suggested to Muhlenberg that music would play an essential role in overcoming these obstacles. He believed that successful missionary work required three things: (1) one or two missionaries would have to live among the Indians to learn their language, custom, dress, and manner of life; (2) they would have to translate religious truths into the Indians' language to make them as clear as possible; and (3) they would need to learn Indian melodies and tones, presumably to provide a medium for transmission of the religious concepts into an accepted spiritual medium.[39]

Weiser's suggested strategy was very much like the one implemented by Zeisberger in the Ohio mission towns. Early in 1772 Zeisberger and the Brothers made an effort to incorporate and rationalize their use of the Christian concepts they had translated into the Delaware tongue. "We want to use more words in the Indian language such as 'amen, hallelujah, lamb, agape,'" the Brothers noted, "and we want to define rules for writing these words in order to avoid using too many K's and write them in a more uniform style." These regularized, easier-to-sing translations would be incorporated into the verses that constituted the text of most Moravian Indian hymns. The Brothers and their Indian helpers (Brother Anton?) agreed that "no verse is to be introduced without being first reviewed and revised by those Brethren responsible for this" (558–59).

Incorporating standardized Christian concepts into musical verse vetted by Indian converts accomplished a lot. The frequent repetition of biblical verses set to music in practices, singing hours, love feasts, and regular services allowed some Indians to develop a firm knowledge of the most important Moravian scriptural tenets, even without acquiring literacy. Thus, when the native Brother Johann Martin was questioned by the American General Macintosh regarding his spiritual knowledge, Martin told him, "I cannot actually read the Bible, but still I know it is written and we have been taught this by our teachers. The *General* can read the Bible and will know if what I say is the truth." The general was

---

38. Henry Melchior Muhlenberg, *The Journals of Henry Melchior Muhlenberg*, trans. Theodore G. Tappert and John W. Doberstein, 3 vols. (Philadelphia: Muhlenberg Press, 1942–58), 1:167.

39. I would like to thank Laura Luder, whose 2003 senior independent study paper at Dickinson College, entitled "Muhlenberg and Weiser: Faith and Indian Relations on the Frontier," led me to this quotation, which in turn caused me to start thinking about the importance of song in intercultural communications. The quotation is from the *Journals of Muhlenberg*, 1:168.

"completely amazed" when Martin answered the theological queries to his "complete satisfaction" (483, 482).

Chunking out verses and putting them individually to music also allowed Indians less proficient in language skills to select, learn, and make use of scriptural passages that seemed particularly meaningful or providential to them. Learning through repetition was essential. During periods of intensified conversion, the ability to teach scripture through song became especially important. In the spring of 1775 Zeisberger noted, "We cannot lead the Indians enough in the verse, He that loveth father or mother more than me is not worthy of me.... When you think you are finally finished, then you must begin again, especially since there are always more people coming to us" (273–74).

For all Indians to some degree, and especially for those who had difficulty understanding scriptural concepts in either the original or in translation, music offered yet another alternative: a chance to achieve knowledge of spiritual "truth" as a transcendent emotional experience. In the early spring of 1775 Zeisberger recorded the story of some Indian strangers visiting the congregation at Schönbrunn who were "very emotional and were touched" by the service they attended. "One of them who heard about the Savior for the first time said that although he really could not understand what was preached, much less remember it, he believed it was all the truth" (262). Love feasts, such as the annual Christmas festival, which were primarily musical events, could become extremely emotional. The 1776 Christmas love feast was one such occasion.

> What can you say about such a Christmas Eve celebration? I have never seen one like it. From beginning to end it was nothing but a service of very loud crying, and many thousands of tears were shed. At the beginning Brother *David* wanted to control this but there was nothing he could do. The tears had to flow freely, because they broke out like a flood. All who were there, young and old, with children in their arms, were transported and a stream of tears was shed for Baby Jesus in his manger. (349–50)

Song played a critical role in inculcating Christian concepts in the young, and the young played a special role in conveying the power of music to their parents. It is easy to forget, unless one keeps in mind the diaries' annual population assessments, that the mission towns were teeming with children. Young children always represented a very significant proportion of the population of the Moravian towns, usually between 40 and 50 percent, despite relatively high rates of infant mortality. Belief in the power of music as a medium of learning for the young was widespread in the eighteenth century. Zeisberger contemporary and educational theorist Benjamin Rush noted, "Singing aids the memory in acquiring a knowledge of words and the ideas connected with them. A song is always learned sooner than the same number of words set to music."[40] In September 1774 Zeisberger "began singing instruction with the children to teach them some new verses" (227). This new institution expanded upon the singing hour held each evening. The singing instruction may have been a natural response to the increasing number and advancing ages of the children in the settlement, or it may have been intended to prepare the children for a special role in the upcoming Advent celebrations. The year before, at the children's service during the Christmas love feast, Zeisberger had noted that "there was a blessed feeling. . . . The children sang very sweetly of the Savior's birth and incarnation, so that the older people shed many tears during this" (176). Weeks later, the impact of the children's performance was still being felt. "It awakened our hearts to praise that He revealed Himself especially graciously among our children in the recent holidays and allowed Himself to be felt among them" (179). The impact of the 1774 singing lessons was also significant, not just on the children and their parents but on the unconverted Indians who attended the Christmas Eve children's service. Of this service, Zeisberger reported, "There were also many adults and strangers present who could not keep from crying when they heard the children singing alone so sweetly. Some of them came and told us of their spiritual concerns and their desire for the bath of Holy Baptism" (250–51). Zeisberger was well aware of the close affective ties between Indian parents and their children, and he may have seen the singing lessons as serving a dual function: providing important scriptural knowledge to the young and, through their song performances, applying powerful emotional persuasion on the older Delawares. It is tempting to wonder whether the tears of the adults on hearing children singing Christian hymns were shed as much for a way of life being lost as they were for the kingdom of heaven being gained.

The emotional impact of Moravian music on the Indian children may have become a problem. In Lichtenau, under the unstable and threatening conditions encountered in 1776, the entire congregation, and especially the children, seemed to have experienced a kind of spiritual crisis. On January 8, during the baptism of a boy named Johannes, Zeisberger noted that "most of our children

---

40. Benjamin Rush, *Medical Inquiries and Observations, upon the Diseases of the Mind* (Philadelphia: Thomas Dobson, 1818), 288.

and adults shed many tears." This in itself was not unusual. But four days later Zeisberger found it necessary to bring all the children together for a special service. "For some time now," he reported, "they have been emotional and sensitive. Their parents are often concerned and do not know how to comfort their children adequately when they cry bitter tears for baptism" (354). The children had apparently learned to be terrified of dying without baptism before the Brothers considered them qualified to receive that sacrament.[41] Zeisberger does not tell us how the crisis was resolved, but the crisis itself is a complex testament to the powerful potential of the Moravians' musically centered spiritual education.

It would, of course, be incorrect to assume that the intercultural bridge made by Moravian music was unidirectional. Even as the Delawares embraced the songs of the Brothers, they adapted them to many of the uses to which native music had traditionally been put. Sung verse, for instance, was used by Moravian Indians to care for and comfort the sick, just as Delaware *powaws* had used communal music to treat illness. Zeisberger reported numerous instances of sung verse giving comfort to diseased patients. The final sickness of Brother Timothaeus, who died in the fall of 1780, is indicative of how Christian songs may have become syncretic rituals incorporating aspects of native healing rituals. Brother Timothaeus, the *Diaries* note, was "especially glad to listen when the Brothers and Sisters sang verses for him, which Brother *David* did many times as well. He always folded his hands during this, as he did when he received the blessing even though he had already lost his ability to speak" (544).

Christian music sung by Indians also became a tool of diplomatic expression, as when Indian Brothers went to visit Shawnee towns in early 1773. The Shawnees requested, and the Brothers agreed, "to hold services for them and also to sing verses" (127). In another instance, when a chief from Shenango petitioned to come reside in the Moravian town, the community sang "our prayer of Thanksgiving" for the service the Savior provided (160–62). After a particularly favorable meeting with the Delaware war chief White Eye, Zeisberger used a verse hymn to characterize the outcome of the meeting, noting, "The King loves us rather well" (166n286).

41. This nonscriptural sung verse, taken from a Moravian children's hymnbook, may help explain why children found religious instruction fear-inducing.

> When I at night recline my head,
> Or in the Morning rise from Bed
> Lamb! I direct my eyes to Thee
> And thy pale Blood drained Body See

An excruciating fusion of Christian song with traditional native practice occurred on March 8, 1782, when ninety Indian Brothers and Sisters used prayer and sung Christian verse to substitute for the traditional Delaware death song. The ninety had returned to Gnadenhütten II from a location near Detroit, to which they had been driven as captives by combatant warriors allied with British. The winter of 1781–82 had been extremely harsh, and by the end of February the captive Christian Indians faced starvation. For that reason their captors allowed a portion of the community to return to Gnadenhütten to retrieve food stores they had cached there. Once near their old homes, they encountered a Pennsylvania militia group, who pretended to befriend them, got the Indians to show them where their stores were hidden, and took their weapons into custody for safekeeping. They then became belligerent and accused the Christian Indians of being hostile warriors and having killed whites. Although the Indians vehemently protested their innocence and demonstrated their Christian knowledge, the militia leaders held a council and sentenced them to immediate death.

According to Brother John Heckewelder, the Indians tried to make a deal with their captors:

> Finding that nothing would satisfy them, but putting them to Death, they [the Christian Indians] told them, That they were willing to die, tho innocent, that God knew their Innocence, that they, when they had first converted unto Jesus Christ and baptized, had made a covenant to live for him, and according to his Will, Word, and Pleasure as long as they lived in this world—that they were sensible they had not always fulfilled their promise for which they were sorry, and would beg a Days time for the purpose of praying and preparing for Death, and being answered that a few hours should be granted to them for this Purpose, they fell on their knees praying and singing hymns.[42]

The Indian men were shut up in one house, the women in another. And for a time, Christian hymns did the duty of the death song—offering defiance to the enemy and hurling their own culture's message of faith and deliverance against them. The whites grew impatient with the Indians' ceremony, and the ninety Christian converts were clubbed to death and scalped by the militiamen.

On the surface, this appears to be an appropriation of Christian forms to traditional native purposes in which Christianity ultimately triumphs. The Moravian

---

42. Heckewelder, *Thirty Thousand Miles*, 194–95.

Brothers and Sisters, faced with imminent death, used hymns as death songs, remaining true to the faith they had adopted. No doubt, for some, if not many, of the Indians slaughtered there, that was true. But for others, the immanence of death and the ultimate test of faith propelled them back to their native roots. Many died not with Christian songs on their lips, but Indian death songs.

We know this through the account of militiaman Henry Brackenridge, who, after the fact, offered up a rationale for why the Christian Indians had been considered dangerous. Brackenridge said he believed "the greater part of the men put to death were warriors," and cited as his evidence "their singing the war song when ordered out to be tomahawked."[43] The war song was not a war song, nor was it a sung verse of scripture. Rather, it was a decision, made in the final moment of life, to die as an Indian, singing a native death song. For some, then, the cultural bridge to Christianity created by song became, at the end, a bridge too far.

43. Hugh Henry Brackenridge, "Account of John Slover," in *Narratives of a Late Expedition Against the Indians; with an Account of the Barbarous Execution of Col. Crawford; and the Wonderful Escape of Dr. Knight and John Slover from Captivity, in 1782* (Philadelphia: Printed by Francis Bailey, 1783), 31.

III.

Indigenous Perspectives

Munsee Social Networking and Political Encounters with the Moravian Church

Siegrun Kaiser

The Moravians are well known for their mission work among the Algonquian of the eastern woodlands. Their memoirs and reports were the sourcebook for James Fennimore Cooper's *Leatherstocking Tales* and as such shaped Americans' image of eastern Native American tribes.[1] Drawing from Heckewelder's history, Cooper's novels depict the Delaware and Mahican as the prototype for a noble but vanishing people who had lost the power struggle with colonists and Iroquois and therefore made perfect candidates for conversion. Ethnologists and historians have discussed their response to Moravian mission approaches in some detail.[2]

A third group of Eastern Algonquian, the Munsee, also encountered the Pietists from Herrnhut. As close neighbors of the Mahican and Delaware tribes, they were frequently mentioned in Moravian publications and played an interesting role in David Zeisberger's recently translated Ohio diaries.[3] In contrast to the

---

I wish to thank the conference participants and Clio Caleb Church, Delaware-Muncie; Marvin DeFoe, Red Cliff Band of Lake Superior Chippewa Indians; Vinzenz J. Leppert, historical researcher, Forest County Potawatomi; Mark Peters, Munsee-Delaware Nation; and Darryl K. Stonefish, Moravian of the Thames Band of the Delaware Nation.

1. Edwin Link Stockton, *The Influence of the Moravians upon the Leatherstocking Tales,* Transactions of the Moravian Historical Society 20 (Nazareth, Pa.: Moravian Historical Society, 1964).

2. Stefan Hertrampf, *"Unsere Indianer-Geschwister waren lichte und vergnügt": Die Herrnhuter als Missionare bei den Indianern Pennsylvanias, 1745–1765,* Mainzer Studien zur Amerikanistik 35 (Frankfurt am Main: P. Lang Verlag, 1997); Siegrun Kaiser, *Die Delaware und die Herrnhuter Brüdergemeine: Konflikte einer Missionierung, 1741–1806* (master's thesis, Johann Wolfgang Goethe-Universität, Frankfurt, 1992); Siegrun Kaiser, "Four Cases of Delaware Indian Land Loss and the Moravian Church," in *Religion and Identity in the Americas,* ed. Brigitte Hülsewiede and Ingo Schröder, Bonner Amerikanistische Studien 28 (Möckmühe: Verlag Anton Saurwein, 1997), 135–52; Carola Wessel, *Missionsvorstellung und Missionswirklichkeit der Herrnhuter Brüdergemeine in Nordamerika im 18. Jahrhundert* (master's thesis, Universität Göttingen, 1989).

3. The Munsee are mentioned in David Zeisberger, *The Diary of David Zeisberger, a Moravian Missionary Among the Indians of Ohio, 1781–1791,* ed. and trans. Eugene F. Bliss, 2 vols. (Cincinnati: Robert Clarke and Co. for the Historical Society of Ohio, 1885; reprint, St. Clair Shores, Mich.:

mission outcome with the Delaware, the relationship of the majority of the Munsee with the Moravian Church was never harmonious. In the diary section describing the outbreak of the Revolutionary War, Zeisberger viewed them merely as opponents of his mission goals.

To get a better picture of Munsee cultural resistance, we must also turn to yet-unpublished German diary excerpts from Moravian missions at Wyalusing, Schechschequannünk, Goschgoschünk, Lagundo Utenünk, Sandusky, Petquottink and Goshen, New Fairfield, Westfield, Renew, and New Westfield.[4] At these locations we discover a pattern: when Moravian missionaries moved into an established Munsee village setting, they did not find many followers or were not allowed to remain for very long. They were more successful with founding exile settlements in western Pennsylvania, Ohio, Canada, and Kansas with families relocated from their homelands. In general, the Munsee refused to incorporate Christian theology, while, during periods of forced removal, their families had to depend on missionaries' support in economic and legal matters.

Munsee Phratries and Their Political Function

The Munsee homeland was an area stretching between Manhattan Island, the lower Hudson River, and the upper Delaware River. In the early seventeenth century their linguistically and culturally related bands were known under various names, such as the Canarsee, Esopus, Hackensack, Haverstraw, Warrawawankongs, Wiechquaeskeck and Minisink.[5] During this time many of the southern Munsee cooperated in defending their settlements against Dutch hegemony and formed temporary alliances such as the so-called Manhattan

---

Scholarly Press, 1972); Merle H. Deardorff, "Zeisberger's Allegheny River Indian Towns, 1767–70," *Pennsylvania Archaeologist* 16, no. 1 (1946): 2–19; Lawrence H. Gipson, ed., *The Moravian Indian Mission on White River: Diaries and Letters, May 5, 1799, to November 12, 1806*, Indiana Historical Collections 23 (Indianapolis: Indiana Historical Bureau, 1938); Archer Butler Hulbert and William Nathaniel Schwarze, eds., "The Diaries of Zeisberger Relating to the First Mission in the Ohio Basin, 1767–69," *Ohio Archaeological and Historical Quarterly* 21, no. 2 (1912): 1–125; Linda Sabathy-Judd, ed., *Moravians in Upper Canada: The Diary of the Indian Mission of Fairfield on the Thames, 1792–1813* (Toronto: Champlain Society, 1999).

4. "Moravian Mission Records Among the North American Indians," Moravian Church Archives, Bethlehem, Pa. (hereafter MAB), (New Haven: Microfilm Publication 1970). I discussed the history of Munsee-Moravian encounters in "Die Munsee: Migrationsgeschichte und Ethnische Identität" (Ph.D. diss., Goethe-Universität, Frankfurt, 2003). See urn:nbn:de:hebis:30-48743; http://publikationen.ub.uni-frankfurt.de/volltexte/2007/4874.

5. Ives Goddard, "Delaware," in *Handbook of North American Indians*, ed. William C. Sturtevant, vol. 15, *Northeast*, ed. Bruce G. Trigger (Washington, D.C.: Smithsonian Institution, 1978), 237–38.

Confederacy. Later on, these local bands created temporary unions during the Kieft War (1643–45), Peach War (1655), and the Esopus Wars (1658–64). When New Holland was turned over to the British, the Munsee and neighboring tribes united in the River Indian Confederacy. Their cooperation enabled them temporarily to maintain political sovereignty and defend themselves against Iroquois and European trade and land control.[6] Only a small percentage of the original population survived devastating wars, epidemics, and the often horrible scenarios along the frontier. After 1650 the Munsee retreated into a secluded region above the Delaware Water Gap on the back of the Kittatinny Mountains. They named their principal village Minisink, "the place where stones are gathered together." For a time Minisink became the spiritual center and the seat of the last council fire in their original homelands.[7]

The term *Munsee* only came into use during their exile in order to incorporate the survivors of "people, who had come from [or left from] Minisink."[8] At the same time, most Munsee kept referring to themselves as "the Wolves" or "the Turkeys." While the Central Algonquian of the Great Lakes region classed the Munsee and other refugees from the East Coast as Wabenaki, "the Easterners," the Moravians freely added new group terms such as "Christian Indians" or "Moravian Indians," when commenting on their converts. Historians mostly termed the Munsee a subgroup of the Delaware, even after Zeisberger had distinguished the Munsee as a separate "nation" from the Delaware.[9]

These varying terms have confused historians who have written about the tribal level of ethnic groups. The transitional use of names is a well-known problem in ethnohistory. Darlene Johnston (Anishnabe) argues that "the introduction and

---

6. Ted J. Brasser, "The Coastal New York Indians in the Early Contact Period," in *Neighbors and Intruders: An Ethnohistorical Exploration of the Indians of Hudson's River*, ed. Laurence M. Hauptman and Jack Campisi (Ottawa: National Museum of Canada, 1978), 151–56; Allen W. Trelease, *Indian Affairs in Colonial New York: The Seventeenth Century* (Ithaca: Cornell University Press, 1960).

7. "Gnadenhütten Diary, 7. Juli 1748," MAB, reel 4, box 116, folder 4; "Gnadenhütten Diary, 29. März, 1753," MAB, reel 5, box 117, folder 4; Carl J. Fliegel, *Index to the Records of the Moravian Missions Among the Indians of North America* (New Haven: Research Publications, 1970), 888; James Mooney, "Munsee," *Handbook of American Indians North of Mexico*, Bureau of American Ethnology Bulletin 30, vol. 1 (Washington, D.C.: U.S. Government Printing Office, 1907), 957.

8. William A. Hunter, "Documented Subdivisions of the Delaware Indians," *Bulletin of the Archaeological Society of New Jersey* 35 (1978): 31.

9. David Zeisberger, *Herrnhuter Indianermission in der Amerikanischen Revolution: Die Tagebücher von David Zeisberger, 1772 bis 1781*, ed. Hermann Wellenreuther and Carola Wessel (Berlin: Akademie Verlag, 1995), 367, 447n1206; "Information about the Munsee (Muncie, or Christian) Indians Gained by Mrs. J. W. King in an Interview with Mrs. Josephine A. Plake, One of the Members of the Tribe," n.d. (ca. 1935), Franklin County Historical Society, Ottawa, Kansas, Chippewa and Munsee file; Mark Peters, interview by author, September 15, 1996, Munceytown, Ontario, Canada.

recording of different names bestowed by outsiders creates the potential for confusing a change of names with a change of people."[10] She recommends greater exposure to the aboriginal viewpoint as a means of developing greater sensitivity and more accurately interpreting documentary gaps in the reconstruction of Algonquian history. Her conceptual guide through the historical sources is the totemic identity of clan members. Totemic identity relates to the creation of mankind, with the totemic animal being the cultural hero. The totemic ancestor is a fact of descent history and cannot be questioned by outsiders or related to their own origin stories.[11] Totemic identity is provided after birth by assigning the child to its clan, which is a matter of inheritance and not of choice. In her work on the Anishnaabeg of the Great Lakes, Johnston demonstrates that totemic identity goes back to the creation of mankind and has remained largely unchanged in the centuries since contact began.[12] Murdock and Tooker also define a clan as a group of people who identify themselves by a common eponym, usually an animal figure. The clan eponym symbolizes the common descent and history, territory, and character of a people.[13] Among the Munsee, a newborn was assigned to its mother's clan and was expected to live up to the characteristics of its clan eponym. A clan bundle was used during ceremonies to define history as well as a set of standards for social, cultural, political, and moral life. This clan relationship can therefore reflect actual blood relation as well as shared interests and experiences. A phratry, a union of clans and lineages, denotes clan totems that can be related in character, share a similar habitat such as air, water, or land, and therefore go back to a common origin. Reflecting older and younger clans in the hierarchy of animals, the eponyms describe the migrations and social networks of a people.[14] John Heckewelder observed that the Munsee Wolves (members of the Wolf phratry) traced their origins to the underworld, whence they got their role as hunters and providers of deer meat: "As to the Wolf . . . they consider him as their benefactor, as it was by his means that the Indians got out of the interior of the earth. It was he,

10. Darlene Johnston, "Connecting People to Place: Great Lakes Aboriginal History in Cultural Context," paper prepared for the Ipperwash Commission of Inquiry, 2004, www.ipperwashinquiry.ca/transcripts/pdf/P1_Tab_2.pdf.

11. This is also emphasized by Marvin DeFoe, Red Cliff Band of Lake Superior Chippewa, who states that Big Beaver is not just a symbolic figure of creation but the actual creator of the Great Lakes and its inhabitants. Marvin DeFoe, interview by author, September 21, 2004, Washington, D.C.

12. Johnston, "Connecting People to Place," 3–4.

13. George Peter Murdock, *Social Structure* (New York: Macmillan, 1949); Elisabeth Tooker, "Clans and Moieties in North America," *Current Anthropology* 12, no. 3 (1971): 357–76.

14. Theresa M. Schenck, *The Voice of the Crane Echoes Afar: The Sociopolitical Organization of the Lake Superior Ojibwa, 1640–1855* (New York: Garland Publishing, 1997), 61.

they believe, who by the appointment of the Great Spirit, killed the deer whom the Monsey found who first discovered the way to the surface of the earth, and which allured them to come out of their damp and dark residence. For that reason, the wolf is to be honored, and his name preserved for ever among them."[15] While Moravian missionaries had a hard time finding proselytes among the Munsee, they nevertheless provided insight into Munsee clan history. Their writings corroborate other colonial observations that the predominant clans of the Munsee bands belonged mainly to round-footed fur mammals called *Tu'ksi't*. Nora Thompson Dean (Delaware) explains that, among round footers, the Wolf clan related to fox, bear, dog, and other clans of pawed animals.[16] Moravian comments on the signers of written documents such as letters, receipts, and land surrenders help to determine the clan affiliation of some of the mission settlement inhabitants. For example, the mixed Munsee-Mahican Shekomeko was a village with a strong faction of Wolves, as their representative, Shawasch, signed his documents with his eponym of a wolf.[17] At the village of Wyalusing, the Turkeys must have had great influence, as Papunhank, who made strategic decisions for the village during the 1760s, was of the Turkey totem.[18] Members of both the Turkey and the Wolf phratries were to be found at the Munsee villages of Coshecton, a refugee camp of Minisink, Esopus, and Wappinger Indians on the upper Delaware River in 1746, and in Wyalusing, Pennsylvania. They were the leading phratries in Munceytown, the Munsee of Ohsweken in Ontario, the Munsee living in New York, and the group that later removed to Kansas. There is no indication that the Turtle phratry played a strong role in Munsee society.[19]

15. John Heckewelder, *History, Manners, and Customs of the Indian Nations Who Once Inhabited Pennsylvania and the Neighboring States* (Philadelphia: Historical Society of Pennsylvania, 1876), 253. Revised from the original in 1819 by William C. Reichel.
16. Nora Thompson Dean, "A Reply to 'A Further Note on Delaware Clan Names,'" *Man in the Northeast* 9 (1975): 63.
17. "Receipts with Indian Signatures, Catalog 1742–1772," MAB, reel 33, box 313, folder 7.
18. "Deed for the Sale of Friedenshütten, June 22, 1772," in Earl P. Olmstead, *Blackcoats Among the Delaware: David Zeisberger on the Ohio Frontier* (Kent: Kent State University Press, 1991), 9.
19. In 1835 the Munsee clans at Munceytown were of Wolf, Beaver, Otter, and Mole. "Chippewa and Munsee Tribe to John Colbourne, March 10, 1835," National Archives, Ottawa, Ontario, Canada, RG 10, vol. 57, frames 59.222–59.225; Robert S. Grumet, "That Their Issues Be Not Spurious: An Inquiry into Munsee Matriliny," *Bulletin of the Archaeological Society of New Jersey* 45 (1990): 22; Mark R. Harrington, "Some Customs of the Delaware Indians," *Museum Journal* (University of Pennsylvania) 1, no. 3 (1910): 52; "Ethnological and Linguistic Field Notes from the Munsee in Kansas and the Delaware in Oklahoma" (1912), Truman Michelson Papers, MS 2776, National Anthropological Archives, Smithsonian Institution, Washington D.C.; Frank G. Speck and Jesse Moses, *The Celestial Bear Comes Down to Earth: The Bear Sacrifice Ceremony of the Munsee-Mahican in Canada as Related by Nekatcit*, Scientific Publications 7 (Reading: Public Museum and Art Gallery, 1945).

Today, the Stockbridge-Munsee of Wisconsin still follow the pattern of traditional clan responsibilities. They hold Bear clan members responsible for protection and Wolves for hunting game for the community.[20] The Martin clan of the Lac Du Flambeau Band of Lake Superior Chippewa provides warriors to protect the village and is known as a master of defense strategies.[21] During a gathering of the Delaware Nation Council at Moraviantown, the Wolves were described as follows:

> The Wolf clan are a people that can be easily detected.... The Wolf clan people are pretty straight forward and, in fact it can be said a lot of the time, lack diplomacy. The wolf clan are ready to argue anybody no matter what the issue. The outcome of the issue argued doesn't matter as long as they argued. The Wolf clan will easily explode and really cause a big ruckus but they just as easily get over it and immediately after the big unpredictable storm, they forget and forgive as though nothing happened and the sky is just cloud clear and blue. The Wolf clan are pretty ambitious especially if they really believe in something and usually they do mostly what they believe in. The Wolf clan are a people of action, never the dull moment.[22]

A second group of Munsee belonged to the Turkey phratry or *palé*. They were related to two-footed animals, such as birds, and were described as careful negotiators. Their political spectrum ranged from the more traditional ways of the Wolves and the ultraloyal and pro-American style of the Turtles.[23]

Among the northern neighbors of the Munsee, the Mahican, the Wolf phratry was also dominant. We have several indications that representatives of this phratry cooperated closely with various alliances to defend the original homelands.

---

20. Bill Terrio works to fulfill the responsibilities of the Wolf clan as he organizes food for the elderly program on the reservation. Bill Terrio, interview by author, May 2 and October 17, 1996, Stockbridge-Munsee Reservation, Bowler, Wisconsin.

21. "O-Do-I-Daym-I-Wan: The Clan System," flyer, n.d., George W. Brown Jr. Museum and Cultural Center, Lac Du Flambeau, Wisconsin.

22. "4th Annual Lenape Gathering," Moraviantown, Ontario, August 27–29, 1996," flyer, Moraviantown, Ontario.

23. Some of the few Turkey phratry members who achieved political success were the Munsee Papunhank and the Delaware White Eyes, who both tried to establish a reservation for their people. There are other indications that the Turkeys moved away into Indian country after agreements with the British colonies failed. An example for this tactic is the retreat of Welapachtschiechen, leader of the Turkeys, who moved directly to Ohio after signing the Walking Purchase Treaty (February 12, 1777), in Zeisberger, *Herrnhuter Indianermission*, 357–58; Ives Goddard, "A Further Note on Delaware Clan Names," *Man in the Northeast* 7 (1974): 106–9.

The River Indian Confederacy of the early seventeenth century was probably an intertribal alliance of the *Tu'ksi't,* or Wolves. A few decades later these clan-related Munsee and Mahican began to explore new hunting grounds and allies in the Great Lakes area. When traveling west, the Eastern Algonquian pioneers could easily expand their social network by relating to the round-footed clans of the Central Algonquian. We do not understand all of their clan relations, but the French called bands of Esopus, Minisink, Sokoki, Mahican, and other Eastern Algonquians traveling west *Loup* (wolves).[24]

Did a phratry defined by similar clan characteristics have distinguishable political strategies? The Wolf core of the Munsee clearly differed from the Turtle phratry, who often cooperated with British and American officials. The Munsee Wolves openly opposed European colonialism. Minisink was the center of such an alliance of the Wolf phratry. In 1723, Munsee, Nantikoke, and Mahican of related clans cooperated against the British, an alliance that was still referred to in 1766.[25]

Throughout the eighteenth century, the Munsee of the Wolf phratry remained within an intertribal northern network. Between 1720 and the outbreak of the Revolutionary War, some bands found permanent shelter among the Haudenosaunee and were adopted into the Wolf clans of the Cayuga and Seneca in upstate New York. Others went further, to Ohio, where they joined related members of the Central Algonquian of the Great Lakes region. The Wolves of the Wyandot invited these Munsee to resettle among them.[26]

Neither at Minisink nor at most of the early exile villages, such as Assinink, was the intrusion of missionaries appreciated. The Munsee of these locations expressed a reserved attitude toward direct interference with any delegate or representative of the British colonies, who they claimed were responsible for the forced surrender of their land.[27] Throughout the eighteenth and nineteenth

---

24. Ted J. Brasser, *Riding on the Frontier's Crest: Mahican Indian Culture and Culture Change,* National Museum of Man Mercury Series, Ethnology Division, Paper no. 13 (Ottawa: National Museums of Canada, 1974), 23–24; Sylvester K. Stevens and Donald H. Kent, *Wilderness Chronicles of Northwestern Pennsylvania* (Harrisburg: Pennsylvania Historical Commission, 1941), 29.

25. "Conference Minutes and Pro Memoria of Gnadenhütten, Pennsylvania, 5 April 1753," MAB, reel 6, box 119, folder 1, item 1; "Friedenshütten Diary, 17. September 1768," MAB, reel 7, box 131, folder 5.

26. Ted J. Brasser, "Mahican," in *Handbook of North American Indians,* ed. William C. Sturtevant, vol. 15, *Northeast,* ed. Bruce G. Trigger (Washington, D.C.: Smithsonian Institution, 1978), 20; Kaiser, "Munsee," 85–136; Speck and Moses, *Celestial Bear Comes Down to Earth,* 11, 23; "Friedenshütten Diary, 27. Juni, 9. August 1765," MAB, reel 7, box 131, folders 2–3.

27. Norman Pettit, ed., *Jonathan Edwards: The Life of David Brainerd* (New Haven: Yale University Press, 1985), 576.

centuries, the Delaware and Seneca noted the Munsee spirituality and strong emphasis on preserving traditional values. "The Munsee ... are held in high esteem for their former bravery and, strange to say though natural enough in the regard held by Indians for such matters, for their indifference to economic and material affairs and devotion to those of a spiritual nature."[28] In relating these statements to the responsibilities of the Munsee clans as protectors (Wolves) and negotiators (Turkeys), we can conclude that phratries reflected a policy that also determined how to deal with Europeans. On February 10, 1777, Zeisberger wrote in his diary of Lichtenau, Ohio, that five converts had traveled to Coshecton to report to their clan relatives, here called "Freundschaften," or friendships, why they had joined the Moravians. A decision to interact with Europeans had to be evaluated by the standards of clan responsibilities.[29]

Three decades later, Algonquian Wolves would even judge other Wolves for signing lands away too easily. In the final clash between the British and Americans in the War of 1812, most Munsee sided with the Shawnee Tecamthi, who had united several North American tribes against the United States. Tecamthi's name, *Tû'kûmthi* (Jumping-at-Him), or *Nila Ni Tekamthi* (One Who Lies Waiting to Cross the Path of Living Creatures), describes the characteristics of a mountain lion. The Shawnee Tecamthi and his brother Tenskwatawa both belonged to the Wolf phratry, which was known as the most belligerent of the Algonquian groupings, as their members often contributed to warrior societies. Tenskwatawa prosecuted the leader of another member of the Wolf division, the Delaware Tetepachsit, who had signed away the White River lands in present-day Indiana. He executed Tetepachsit and two Moravian converts for being traitors of Wolf politics.[30]

First Meeting Ground with the Moravians: Removal, Disease, Starvation, and Family Ties

The first encounter between Munsee and Moravians took place along a tributary of the Hudson River. The multitribal village Shekomeko had been founded in

28. Frank Gouldsmith Speck, "A Study of the Delaware Indian Big House Ceremony, in Native Text Dictated by Witapanóxwe," Publications of the Pennsylvania Historical Commission, vol. 2 (Harrisburg: Pennsylvania Historical Commission, 1931), 18.
29. See the entry for February 10, 1777, in Zeisberger, *Herrnhuter Indianermission*, 357.
30. Bil Gilbert, *God Gave Us This County: Tecamthi and the First American Civil War* (New York: Anchor Books, 1989), 8–11; Alanson Skinner, "The Mascoutens or Prairie Potawatomi Indians, Part I: Social Life and Ceremonies," *Bulletin of the Public Museum of Milwaukee* 6, no. 1 (1924): 27.

the early eighteenth century when survivors of the colonial encounter began to resettle in locations less exposed to the intruding Dutch, German, and British traders and settlers. In 1740 the situation had become so dire that the Wyachtonok-Mahican and Munsee of Shekomeko invited the Moravian missionary Christian Heinrich Rauch to live and work among them. It took two years for the Moravians to convert a Munsee, when the veteran warrior Hendrick was renamed Michael and baptized into the Moravian faith.[31]

A few years before Rauch's arrival at Shekomeko, the Munsee and Delaware had lost their land west of the Delaware River through the forged arrangement known as the Walking Purchase Treaty of 1737. The lands east of the Delaware River toward the Hudson River roughly enclosed a triangle of still unceded land where some Munsee families tried to remain as long as possible. While Rauch was working at Shekomeko in the Hudson Valley, Moravian Church leaders were active in buying parcels of lands released by the Walking Purchase Treaty. The church planned to establish a strategic headquarters for their economic and spiritual enterprises in North America. When they purchased land in the Lehigh Valley to build their new town of Bethlehem, they were probably aware of the ongoing process in Pennsylvania of dispossessing the local Algonquian.[32]

Between 1727 and 1765, most of the native settlements of the area were gradually deserted. Munsee activity shifted from Minisink on the Delaware River to Assinink and several villages along the Chemung River in present-day upstate New York. This cluster of villages became the new strategic and religious center for those Wolf Munsee who were dwelling under the wings of the Haudenosaunee. As the Six Nations likewise opposed British intrusion into their territory, they supported the Munsee in their refusal to allow any missionary activity in their settlements. Between 1742 and 1763, Moravian Church founder Nikolaus Ludwig von Zinzendorf and his missionary colleagues made numerous unsuccessful attempts to establish a *Civitas Indiana-Germana,* a sovereign state of Moravian and Iroquois communities.[33]

---

31. Heckewelder, *History*, 206–7.
32. For a disscussion on the Walking Purchase Treaty, see Francis Jennings, "The Scandalous Indian Policy of William Penn's Sons: Deeds and Documents of the Walking Purchase," *Pennsylvania History* 37 (1970): 19–39. Zinzendorf knew about the treaty negotiations but misinterpreted the fate of the local Munsee and Delaware families during the forced migration phase that followed. Efforts to entrust their children to his care were viewed as a vivid interest in Christianity, whereas they could be interpreted as a pledge to remain in the area or a means of physical survival. See "Zinzendorf's Account of his Experience Among the Indians," in William C. Reichel, ed., *Memorials of the Moravian Church* (Philadelphia: J. C. Lippincott & Co., 1870), 127.
33. Nikolaus Ludwig von Zinzendorf, "Division of the Field and Plan of Operations," in Reichel, *Memorials of the Moravian Church*, 136–40; Kaiser, *Delaware und die Herrnhuter Brüdergemeine*, 67–74.

Meanwhile, Bethlehem prospered and became a trade center for local manufacturing. The few Munsee and Mahican who had remained in this area were attracted by the new town's independent economy and outstanding craftsmanship. The direct-marketing strategy of the Moravians enabled exiled Algonquians to take their furs, baskets, brooms, and other products to the "Rose Store" and trade them for necessities. The Mahican Joshua Jr. spent almost his entire life in the Moravian missions and was known for his expertise in building spinets. He and other converts recited songs, a way in which Algonquians and Germans could communicate well.[34]

But adaptations to Christian life were often a result of starvation or miraculous healings within the Moravian sphere. Following traditional matrilocality, single women were reported to ask for acceptance into the mission for themselves and their daughters and grandchildren.[35] After 1747 the Moravians report welcoming Mennissing (Munsee from Minisink) and Sopus (Esopus) into the mission settlement at Gnadenhütten on the Lehigh River. These individuals came to visit their relatives and usually shifted between the relocated Munsee villages in Haudenosaunee territory to the north and their new exile villages in western Pennsylvania.[36]

Despite the Moravians' many efforts to keep the Munsee in the missions, and after repeated approaches to the various exile villages, only seven Munsee baptisms were recorded between 1742 and 1754. This number contrasts with the 138 Delaware baptisms for the same period.[37] It reflects a decision on the band or even the phratry level not to interfere with the church. For the Munsee and Mahican of the Wolf phratry, the Moravian settlements served

---

34. Lawrence W. Hartzell, "Joshua Jr.: Moravian Indian Musician," *Transactions of the Moravian Historical Society* 26 (1990): 1–19. Joshua's father, Joshua Sr., belonged to the Wolf clan. Joshua Junior's clan eponym on a treaty of 1772 shows a "small wolf," probably a fox. This means that Joshua Jr. belonged to a division of "pawed" clans in relation to the older Wolf clan. Olmstead, *Blackcoats Among the Delaware*, 9.

35. An example of the preference of widows, older women, and their children to settle in the missions is the Erdmuth family of Friedenshütten. Fliegel, *Index to the Records of the Moravian Missions*, no. 565; "Friedenshütten Diary, 5. Januar 1766," MAB, reel 7, box 131, folders 2–3.

36. "Gnadenhütten Diary, 7. Juli 1748," MAB, reel 4, box 116; folder 4; "Gnadenhütten Diary, 29. März, 1753," MAB, reel 5, box 117, folder 4; "Gnadenhütten Diary, 9. Mai 1751," MAB, reel 5, box 117, folder 2: "viele Ind. zu Besuch, etl. von der Susqueh. ungefehr 30. Meilen obig Wajomik von der Menissinger Nation es war auch ein Mahicander dabei"; "Gnadenhütten Diary, 7. Juni 1751," MAB, reel 5, box 117, folder 2; "Gnadenhütten Diary, 28. März 1753," MAB, reel 5, box 117, folder 4: "Einige Delaware Ind. u. 3 von der Menissinger Nation, unseres Benjamin Anverwandten, 20 Meilen obig Wajomick an der Susquehanna kamen zum besuch her."

37. Kaiser, *Delaware und die Herrnhuter Brüdergemeine*, 176, Liste der getauften Delaware und Mennissing (Munsee), 1742–72.

mostly as opportunities for visiting friends and relatives, a venue for trade, and a way to survive.

The Rise and Fall of the Munsee Papunhank in Pennsylvania

During the French and Indian War (1754–58), the majority of the Munsee fought against the British. Warrior parties from Assinink even attacked and killed several Moravian missionaries at Gnadenhütten and later took an active role during Pontiac's Rebellion.

The Munsee leader Papunhank was a rare exception to the predominantly anti-British sentiment of his people. This might have had something to do with his being a member of the Turkey phratry, which tended to be more ambivalent than the Wolves toward colonial intrusions. During the war, Papunhank and his followers remained neutral toward the colony of Pennsylvania. When hostilities calmed down in 1758, he returned to the almost deserted upper Susquehanna River and founded the village of Wyalusing. Not accidentally, the beginnings of his new settlement coincided with the surrender of the last Munsee homelands in New Jersey at the Treaty of Easton. While most bands had already relocated further to the north and west, Papunhank's town became a desperate last effort to establish an eastern stronghold of the Munsee tribe.[38]

Papunhank observed that the first Delaware and Mahican converts in the Moravian mission villages along the Lehigh Valley had been able to stay longer on their original homelands than any other local group after the Walking Purchase Treaty. The Munsee who had retreated to the upper Susquehanna River knew that the Haudenosaunee would sooner or later be forced to surrender this area to the British. In order to save Wyalusing, Papunhank traveled to Philadelphia and met with delegates of various Christian denominations, including the Quakers and the Moravians. Papunhank's diplomatic strategy was to propose that all people shared a common belief in one heaven. His spiritual metaphor of being side by side with white colonists in heaven reflected his efforts to cooperate on earth as well.[39]

During Papunhank's attempt to interact with missionaries—atypical of the Munsee—the core of the population removed further, to the Allegheny River.

---

38. Samuel Smith, *The History of the Colony of Nova-Caesaria, or New Jersey* (Burlington: James Parker, 1765), 473.

39. "Account of Conversation with Papunung a religious Indian (1760–1761)," Materials Relating to John Papunhank (Papunung), Westtown School Archives, Westtown, Pennsylvania.

As a consequence of their support for Pontiac's Rebellion in 1763, the Munsee Captain Pipe, Squash Cutter, and Custaloga, all of the Wolf phratry, were forced to sign a peace resolution with the British and enter into negotiations regarding a westward shifting of the frontier. At the same time, the Munsee deserted their remaining eastern towns of Assinink, Pasigachgünk, Tioga, and Oquaga along the river valleys of the Chemung and Canisteo.[40]

In 1765 Papunhank finally succeeded in using the Moravians as a buffer against further removal. He invited the missionaries and their 170 multitribal converts from former missions to move to Wyalusing. With this transaction, he was also able to transfer some of his relatives who had formerly lived at Bethlehem and Gnadenhütten. Wyalusing was renamed Friedenshütten and over time attracted more Munsee remaining in the vicinity.

Yet, despite promising overtures, Papunhank was not able to secure a lasting legal title to Wyalusing. In 1768 representatives of the Haudenosaunee surrendered the upper Susquehanna Valley in the Fort Stanwix Treaty. This agreement between the Iroquois and the British deprived the Munsee of their last eastern settlement. Denied by a "No!" drawing in the Moravians' daily "lot," the villagers of Friedenshütten were discouraged from joining the treaty negotiations. Although the political influence and support of the Moravians would have been crucial, the missionaries decided against the converts and their efforts to keep the land.

At this point the Munsee began to feel the consequences of Moravian pacifism and their ambiguous standing as a Pietist German group in a British colonial setting. The Elders' Conference at Bethlehem had already made plans to remove the congregation to a more remote location on the western frontier. Papunhank's appeals to William Johnson to establish Wyalusing/Friedenshütten as a reservation failed. In addition, Papunhank's own people now blamed him for his cooperation with the Moravians. In a witchcraft trial in 1771, Schmick described how members of the Wolf phratry, represented by a spiritualist named Oniem, openly chastised Papunhank. He accused him of secretly using *Máchtapasseèk*, a poison, and thereby exerting too much negative power over the community.[41]

---

40. "Treaty of Peace Concluded with the Delawares by Sir William Johnson," in *Documents Relative to the Colonial History of the State of New York*, ed. Edmund Bailey O'Callaghan and Berthold Fernow, 15 vols. (Albany: Weed, Parsons, and Co., 1853–87), 7:738–41; Deardorff, *Zeisberger's Allegheny River Indian Towns*, 1.

41. "John Papunhank and Joshua, 1769," MAB, reel 7, box 131, folder 11, item 7; "Friedenshütten Diary, 23. September 1771," MAB, reel 7, box 131, folder 8.

The strategy of the Turkey clan member Papunhank and his efforts to cooperate with the colonialists undermined the interests of the old Munsee Wolf alliance formed in Minisink. Witchcraft language targeted Papunhank for his failure to restore a land base in ceded territory with the help of the Moravians and for having surrendered to their social and political control. Papunhank was not executed but, as his efforts had been in vain, his reputation deteriorated so much that he mostly disappeared from the diaries in subsequent years.

The Ohio Valley Missions

After 1765 the settlements of the western Munsee Wolves were located along the Allegheny River, the crossroads between the British colonies to the east, the Iroquois to the north, and the Great Lakes Algonquian to the west. Together with their neighbors, the Genesee-Seneca, Fox, Nanticoke, and Mississauga, the Munsee now guarded the Fort Stanwix Treaty line in western Pennsylvania against intruding European settlers.[42]

In 1768 missionary pioneer David Zeisberger made his first advances to this region. He hoped to find an alternative to the failing Friedenshütten project and to establish a new western mission field among the Munsee. At their most prominent settlement, Goschgoschünk ("place of hogs"), on the Allegheny River near present-day West Hickory, Forest County, Pennsylvania, Zeisberger met Benjamin Selekis, son of Hendrick Michael, who in 1742 was the first Munsee to be baptized by Moravians. These personal acquaintances helped the missionary gain at least a few listeners. The villagers pondered inviting the Moravians in, and debated whether this would trigger the removal of their relatives at Friedenshütten to the Allegheny region. The majority viewed a missionary as the herald of European intrusion. Accepting a mission post in their midst would contradict the Wolf strategy of fortifying the borderland. The spiritual leader of the village, Wangomen, told Zeisberger of the two heavens for whites and Native Americans. Since each group had a separate heaven, there was no need to reach out and persuade the other. Unlike Papunhank before him, Wangomen made clear that no missionary was needed at Goschgoschünk.[43]

---

42. Michael N. McConnell, *A Country Between: The Upper Ohio Valley and Its Peoples, 1724–1774* (Lincoln: University of Nebraska Press, 1992), 226–28; 260–61.

43. "Zeisberger Travel Diary, October 17–22, 1767," Pennsylvania Historical and Museum Commission (hereafter PHMC), Merle Deardorff Collection, Diaries of David Zeisberger.

The neighboring Seneca likewise opposed the presence of a white man in their midst. They were concerned that Zeisberger, upon returning to Bethlehem, would report details of settlement patterns and topographic descriptions of the Allegheny River to the British colonial government. To settle the conflict but also to maintain control over the missionary, the Seneca in 1770 ordered Zeisberger and his small party of followers to remove from Goschgoschünk to Kuskuski on the Beaver River. This village served as the new council seat of the Munsee Wolves. The most prominent speaker of this community was Custaloga, whom the French called "Casteogain, chief of the Loups on the said river." British sources likewise described him as "chief of the wolf tribe."[44]

Kuskuski had been founded in a region claimed by the Seneca. By moving there, the Munsee showed diplomatic support for the Seneca in their efforts to create a western buffer zone against new settlers. That same year, representatives of the Munsee Wolf and Turkey phratries had participated in a meeting with British authorities at Easton, Pennsylvania. Mytakawkwha ("walking on foot"), speaker of the Wolves, and Kakwah (*káhkhew,* meaning "scrape" or "standing by a tree"), speaker of the Turkeys, both confirmed their loyalty to the Seneca, the Cayuga, and the British.[45] Within this diplomatic network, Custaloga intended to establish a territory for his own people along the Beaver River.[46] The Munsee leader did not favor the presence of missionaries, as they would create factions within the community. Conflicts immediately escalated when his councilor, Glikhikan, converted to Christianity. The Wolves were criticized by the Munsee Anindamonwoágan of the upper town: "You are all led astray and the servants of the white people."[47] To solve the conflict and keep the newly converted from moving away, the Wolves took an unusual step. They adopted Zeisberger into one of their clans in the hope that the German missionary would henceforth act according to Wolf policies. The spiritual leader Wangomen, who had been reluctant to welcome the Moravians earlier, now proposed to incorporate the missionaries. He addressed the villagers: "As you have asked the brethren to live with you, you shall not at any time threaten their lives, and if there should be a war you shall not regard them as other

---

44. Kaiser, "Munsee," 83, 198–200; C. A. Weslager, *The Delaware Indians: A History* (New Brunswick: Rutgers University Press, 1972), 250.
45. Edward E. Ayer Collection, MS 426, Mark Peters Claims Research Papers, Muncie-Delaware First Nation, Munceytown, Ontario.
46. McConnell, *A Country Between,* 226–28, 260.
47. "Zeisberger Diary, October 11, 1771," PHMC, Merle Deardorff Collection, Diaries of David Zeisberger.

white people and kill them, but they shall be your 'adopted' friends and the young people ought to be threatened with severe punishment to prevent them from doing any harm to the brethren."[48]

Nevertheless, the colonial situation along the Beaver River grew worse after 1770. More and more squatters and rum traders poured into the region, increasing starvation and disease. Many non-Christian Munsee, Delaware, and Seneca relocated further west to settlements such as the one nicknamed "Hell Town" (1770–82) in present-day Ohio. Intertribal villages were also common; one was the village "Mohican Johns" (1770–78), founded by Munsee and Mahican.[49]

Meanwhile, the Wolf phratry along the Beaver River in western Pennsylvania intensified diplomatic relations with the Delaware and other Algonquians in the Muskingum Valley in Ohio. The Grand Council of the Muskingum Valley Delaware had likewise relocated to Ohio, to the new capital of Gekelemukpechünk. At Kuskuski, in spite of adopting Zeisberger, bitter factionalism between the Christian and non-Christian parties still poisoned the atmosphere. To discuss these problems in their village with a wider circle of relatives, the Munsee Wolves sent Anindamonwoágan, Glikhikan, and Custaloga as a delegation to Gekelemukpechünk. Custaloga wanted to keep the Munsee converts but was still opposed to a new Christian center in the heart of Wolf country.[50]

At the Grand Council meetings, the Turtles and Turkeys had emerged as the strongest party. The two phratries, composed predominantly of Delaware, developed their own strategy for dealing with the European intrusion. With the consent of the participating Munsee Wolf faction, they planned to resettle all Munsee, Mahican, and Delaware in one region to demonstrate a more compact settlement pattern against European intrusion into the Muskingum River valley. In regard to the Munsee, the Grand Council was worried about the witchcraft trial of Papunhank that had taken place at Friedenshütten a month earlier and wondered if friction over the presence of missionaries could be better resolved if the converts in Pennsylvania were to be relocated. It was decided to invite them to "neutral" Turtle territory in the Muskingum Valley instead of the Wolf

---

48. "Zeisberger Diary, July 14, 1770", ibid.; Edmund De Schweinitz *The Life and Times of David Zeisberger, the Western Pioneer and Apostle of the Indians* (Philadelphia: J. B. Lippincott & Co., 1870; reprint, New York: Arno Press, 1971), 363–65.

49. Francis Paul Jennings, ed., *The History and Culture of Iroquois Diplomacy: An Interdisciplinary Guide to the Treaties of the Six Nations and Their League* (Syracuse: Syracuse University Press, 1985), 216; see Wellenreuther and Wessel's introduction to Zeisberger, *Herrnhuter Indianermission*, 21, map (no page number).

50. "Zeisberger Diary, March 13 and October 9, 1771," PHMC, Merle Deardorff Collection, Diaries of David Zeisberger.

capital at Kuskuski. It is interesting to observe that—despite the mutual agreement at the Grand Council to direct these converts—the invitation to the inhabitants of Friedenshütten came from the clan relations, demonstrating that each phratry remained sovereign in its own matters. The council voted that all Christian converts from the Wolf capital Kuskuski should likewise relocate into the domain of the Turtles and Turkeys. Welhik-Tupeek/Schönbrunn on the Tuscarawas River was to become the new home of converted Munsee and Delaware, while the Christian Mahican would inhabit the nearby new Gnadenhütten settlement. With these shifts in location, it is no surprise that in 1772 the number of Munsee baptisms had jumped to 101, in comparison to only seven before 1754.[51]

When Lord Dunmore's War broke out in 1774, the Grand Council, dominated by the Turkey White Eyes, opted for neutrality in the conflict between the Shawnee and the British. In contrast to the Turkeys and Turtles, the non-Christian Munsee of the Wolf phratry became heavily involved in the Shawnee defense of their homeland. Considering them their "younger brother," many Munsee resettled at Mochwesüng and Little Shawnee Town near the Shawnee capital of Wakatomika. It was during this war that the long-standing alliances of the Munsee Wolves could once more be observed. Participating in a social network foreign to the Moravians, a faction of converted Munsee decided to leave the mission sphere at Schönbrunn. Upon their exodus in July 1774, Allemewi, clan elder of former Goschgoschünk, reasoned that the Moravian missions had become an extremely dangerous location. They were too exposed to the "Virginians," as he called the British enemies of the Shawnee.[52]

During the Revolutionary War, it became clear that the Moravians' interests could not serve Munsee survival strategies. Now Zeisberger took an almost patriotic stand for the American cause. But when he spoke in the name of all four hundred converts at the Grand Council meetings at Gekelemukpechünk, he was destined to fail. In the eyes of the Munsee and Delaware, the German's authority was limited by his phratry membership, and they refused his attempt to speak for all of the Wolves, Turkeys, and Turtles living in his mission settlements. By promoting possible peaceful cooperation with the Americans, he also undermined the interests of the predominantly anti-American Wolves, who

---

51. Kaiser, *Delaware und die Herrnhuter Brüdergemeine*, 176, "Liste der getauften Delaware und Mennissing (Munsee), 1742–1772"; Kaiser, "Munsee," 200–202; "Zeisberger Diary, October 9, 1771," PHMC, Merle Deardorff Collection, Diaries of David Zeisberger; "Friedenshütten Diary, 29. April 1771," MAB, reel 7, box 131, folder 8.

52. Zeisberger, *Herrnhuter Indianermission*, 216, 287–88.

considered him a relative and expected him to support their tactics. Zeisberger's diplomatic efforts at this crucial juncture reveal that his adoption by the Munsee Wolves had neither furthered his consciousness of their social structure nor altered his unexpected political intentions.

By 1777 only a small faction of Munsee were still present at the Grand Council, which struggled to maintain a neutral position in the colonial conflict.[53] Most Munsee had sided with the Wyandot. Their Wolf phratry had adopted the Munsee Wolves upon their arrival in Ohio and now likewise opted to fight against the Americans. According to Heckewelder, most Munsee "made this a pretence of withdrawing themselves from the councils of the Turtle tribe and joining themselves to the Wolf tribe," who were known for their anti-American stance. To support the Wyandot, a second party of at least fifty Munsee, led by Newallike, left Schönbrunn. They also joined the opposition party to the Moravians under the leadership of the Munsee Pelewiechünk.[54] The missionaries had become an obstacle for the Munsee by mingling with the affairs of the Grand Council. Even their once devout convert Glikhikan finally declared his renunciation of the council's and the Moravians' politics. To the disappointment of his startled teachers, he announced, "wir haben ausgeglaubt" (we quit believing), and began preparations to abandon Schönbrunn with twenty of his followers.[55]

The newly established U.S. Middle Department, established by the Continental Congress to handle Indian Affairs along the frontier, soon reacted to this decision of the Munsee Wolf phratry. Fearing their possible alliance with the pro-British Wyandot, American troops were sent to destroy villages and food stores along the frontier and thereby killed numerous Munsee, predominately women and children. These "preventive" massacres in 1778 and 1779 against pro-British Indians became known as the Squaw Campaign and the Sullivan Campaign.[56]

While the majority of the Munsee rejected Zeisberger's pro-American diplomacy, the missionaries tried to keep as many Delaware and Mahican

53. "Schönbrunn Diary, 14. Februar 1777," MAB, reel 8, box 141, folder 9; De Schweinitz, *Life and Times of Zeisberger*, 446.
54. De Schweinitz, *Life and Times of Zeisberger*, 449–50; Kaiser, "Munsee," 205–16; Weslager, *Delaware Indians*, 302; Zeisberger, *Herrnhuter Indianermission*, 363–64.
55. "Schönbrunn Diary, 20. und 24. März 1777," MAB, reel 8, box 141, folder 9.
56. "Edward Hand, Fort Pitt to Jasper Ewing, March 7, 1778," in Reuben Gold Thwaites and Louise Phelps Kellogg, eds., *Frontier Defense on the Upper Ohio, 1777–1778* (Madison: State Historical Society of Wisconsin, 1912), 215–20; "Daniel Brodhead, Fort Pitt, to John Sullivan, August 3, 1779," in Louise Phelps Kellogg, ed., *Frontier Retreat on the Upper Ohio, 1779–1781*, vol. 24 of *Collections of the State Historical Society of Wisconsin* (Madison: The Society, 1917), 43–44.

families as possible in their mission settlements and under the guidance of the Turkeys and Turtles of the Grand Council. The non-Christian Munsee, upon hearing of the loss of their relatives in systematic American manhunts, now became desperate to withdraw their relatives still remaining at Schönbrunn. To rescue them from the advance of American militia, they killed their cattle and urged them forcefully to leave their homes.[57] Zeisberger, obviously not understanding their urgency, denounced them as "der Schaum von allem schlechten Volck" (the dregs of all bad people).[58] He criticized the Munsee for their pro-British partisanship without considering that their stepped-up withdrawal was the result of White Eyes' murder by Americans and additional dreadful events such as the Squaw Campaign. As the war continued, the Munsee's worst fears became a sad reality. In the infamous Gnadenhütten Massacre, American militia killed eighty-six of the Munsee, Mahican, and Delaware converts still associated with the missionaries.[59]

The Revolutionary War marked the birth of the American nation, while the political sovereignty of the Algonquian deteriorated rapidly. Showing his first signs of resignation, Zeisberger wrote of the Ohio River valley tribes, "The world is already too narrow [for them]."[60] During the treaty era that followed, the Munsee held on to their social network and moved in with related clans of more numerous tribes. Some resettled on Chippewa lands in Munceytown, Ontario, and eventually joined the Cayuga on the Brantford Reserve in Canada or the Seneca of upstate New York. Others merged with the Stockbridge-Mahican and found a permanent home in Wisconsin.

Ethnohistorically, the Munsee had never chosen to interact with the Moravians. The Wolf phratry kept especially aloof from the mission advances. Being part of an intertribal social network defined by clan membership, Wolves were looked upon as spiritual providers and protectors of traditional values, whereas missionaries with competing concepts would naturally be perceived as intruders. They shared responsibilities with the Turkey phratry, who were viewed as good negotiators. Papunhank's case provides a prime example of the Turkey strategy of using the Moravian presence to support its own political maneuvers. During the early colonial era, the power of phratry alliances helped the Munsee, who had never been very numerous, to survive colonial encounters and exile from

---

57. Zeisberger, *Herrnhuter Indianermission*, 436, 466.
58. Ibid., 451.
59. Weslager, *Delaware Indians*, 314–17.
60. "David Zeisberger on his Journey to Detroit, April 8, 1782," in Zeisberger, *Diary of David Zeisberger*, 1:86.

their homelands. The sovereignty of intertribal alliances enabled the Wolf phratry to remain politically independent of missionary intervention.

In order to stay in their location, some Munsee eventually chose to cooperate with Moravian missionaries. For a while, conversion to Christianity was seen as a safeguard against losing their land base. Even if the Moravians were aware of Munsee social organization, they did not incorporate the concepts of clan association into their own moral and social structure. While Munsee clan structure aimed to incorporate as many relatives as possible during times of starvation, the Moravians focused on the exclusion of individuals who were not able to live up to the expectations of the Bible. The missionaries controlled the membership lists of the community and thereby personally decided who was eligible for annuities and land control and who had to seek support elsewhere.[61]

The Moravians were successful in their contact with the Munsee only in times of serious social crisis. Their chances for success were higher after the eastern homeland of the Munsee was sold and intertribal phratries had lost their incorporating power. The church never really engaged in the distribution of annuities or legal support for Munsee tribal interests. By the end of the removal period, the various Munsee bands lived in different parts of the United States and Canada. Their situation had become critical as their tribal allies and mentors were forced into the treaty process. Most government arrangements did not take into consideration that the Munsee were adopted by their clan relatives in the various neighboring tribes, and federal agents thus did not regard them as members of the tribes they had joined.

In a desperate effort to establish a reservation of their own, a mixed band of Munsee, Mahican, and Delaware decided in 1837 to move from the Great Lakes area to the newly designed Indian territory of present-day Kansas. Once more, the Munsee looked for support from the Moravians, who were eager to accompany the emigrants, as they expected to present their converts to the other tribes of the region as a shining example of the merits and benefits of Christianity. They joined in the painful removal of the Munsee from various locations in Ontario, Canada, to the banks of the Kansas River. Today, descendents of these families maintain an old Moravian Church graveyard in the Chippewa Hills near Pomona, Kansas, where the Chippewa-Munsee Reservation had existed until its termination in 1900. Even after the last of the missionaries, Joseph

---

61. This policy can be observed in a dispute in 1851 between the Moravian missionaries, the "Munsee and Christian Indians" of Westfield, Kansas, and members of the nearby Munsee settlement, in which the missionaries opted to prevent their converts from sharing annuities with non-Christian relatives. Kaiser "Munsee," 321–27.

Romig, had left, the cemetery still remained in the possession of the church. In 1961 the Kansas Munsee began to inquire at the Moravian Church archives in Bethlehem about regaining legal rights over the remains of their ancestors. Forty-four years later, in January 2005, after numerous requests by the families and their supporters, the Society for Propagating the Gospel, acting as the land trustees of the Moravian Church, promised to transfer the deed to the Munsee community.[62] After a long history of diminishing hope that the Moravians might be useful in maintaining a land base for the Munsee, this cemetery remains as a metaphor for an ambiguous relationship and, at the same time, will be one of the very few parcels of North American land left to the Munsee people.

---

62. "David L. Wickmann, President of the Society for Promoting the Gospel, Bethlehem, PA, to Clio M. Caleb Church, Pomona, KS, January 12, 2005," Clio Church Papers, Private Collection of Clio M. Caleb Church, Pomona, Kansas.

The Gender Frontier Revisited:

Native American Women in the Age of Revolution

JANE T. MERRITT

Several years ago I wrote a piece about encounters between Mahican, Delaware, and German women in eastern Pennsylvania, exploring what Kathleen Brown dubbed "gender frontiers"—women's roles in the creation of diplomatic, economic, and social alliances between Native American and Euro-American peoples in the eighteenth century and the gendered response to those encounters. Tracing the lives of native women who lived near or became part of the Moravian mission communities in eastern Pennsylvania before the Seven Years' War, I found that Mahican and Delaware women exercised an "adaptive capacity" as they made daily decisions concerning their household organization, production, and consumption.[1] Rather than simply resist or assimilate profound cultural change, women adapted new habits within a familiar framework of Native American family traditions. Faced with the rapid changes brought on by European migration and the introduction of new diseases and technologies, native women bridged gaps between cultures, became facilitators for these encounters, yet still put the needs of their children and families first and foremost—a pattern that repeated itself on a variety of frontiers from the Great Lakes to the American southeast.[2]

---

1. Jane T. Merritt, "Cultural Encounters Along a Gender Frontier: Mahican, Delaware, and German Women in Eighteenth-Century Pennsylvania," *Pennsylvania History* 67 (autumn 2000): 505; Kathleen Brown, "Brave New Worlds: Women's and Gender History," *William and Mary Quarterly*, 3d ser., 50 (April 1993): 316–21; Kathleen Brown, "The Anglo-Algonquian Gender Frontier," in *Negotiators of Change: Historical Perspective on Native American Women*, ed. Nancy Shoemaker (New York: Routledge, 1995), 30.

2. Lucy Eldersveld Murphy, "To Live Among Us: Accommodation, Gender, and Conflict in the Western Great Lakes Region, 1760–1832," in *Contact Points: American Frontiers from the Mohawk Valley to the Mississippi, 1750–1830*, ed. Andrew R. L. Cayton and Fredrika J. Teute (Chapel Hill: University of North Carolina Press, 1998), 270–303; Theda Perdue, *Cherokee Women: Gender and Culture Change, 1700–1835* (Lincoln: University of Nebraska Press, 1998); Alison Duncan Hirsch, "Indian, Metis, and Euro-American Women on Multiple Frontiers," in *Friends and Enemies in Penn's Woods:*

The introduction of the German version and now the English translation of David Zeisberger's missionary journals from the 1770s and 1780s in the Ohio Valley provides a means to further test the response of native women to the presence of Euro-American neighbors and Moravian missionaries in a new frontier region. In particular, the journals illuminate the lives of Delaware women and their communities during the volatile era of the American Revolution. There are, of course, limits to these sources as windows on gender. Not only do we face the problems inherent in transcultural translation and its transcription onto the Moravian page, but we also need to decode the gender biases that might color Zeisberger's descriptions of his encounters with the native world. Certainly the death in 1760 of Count Zinzendorf, who had established church-sanctioned avenues for both female piety and women's authority within the Moravian congregations, lessened women's role in the lay ministry of the Moravian mission communities. Zinzendorf's successor, August Gottlieb Spangenberg, drew on the founder's sometimes ambivalent writings about female public activities to suppress the ordination of women, but also, more important, to eradicate the female imagery Moravians had used to describe the Holy Ghost and Virgin Mary.[3] David Zeisberger's attitude toward native women sometimes reflected this new policy. As chief missionary to the Ohio Valley Delawares in the 1760s and 1770s, Zeisberger found Indian women in the west far more hostile to Christianity than native men. Conversely, he thought them far less important to his initial efforts to make contact with native communities. In

---

Indians, Colonies, and the Racial Construction of Pennsylvania, ed. William A. Pencak and Daniel K. Richter (University Park: Pennsylvania State University Press, 2004), 63–84.

3. Merritt, "Cultural Encounters," 531; Beverly P. Smaby, "Female Piety Among Eighteenth Century Moravians," *Pennsylvania History* 64 (summer 1997): 154 (special issue entitled *Empire, Society, and Labor: Essays in Honor of Richard S. Dunn*, ed. Nicholas Canny, Joseph E. Illick, Gary B. Nash, and William Pencak). Professor Smaby generously shared several new essays; one, to appear in *Backcountry Crucibles: From Settlement to Steel*, ed. Jean Soderlund and Catherine S. Parzinski (Bethlehem, Pa.: Lehigh University Press, forthcoming), concerns Zinzendorf's intellectual conceptions of women's place in society, and another, "'No one should lust for power . . . women least of all': Dismantling Female Leadership Among 18th-Century Moravians," in *Pious Pursuits: German Moravians in the Atlantic World*, ed. Michele Gillespie and Robert Beachy (forthcoming), details the demise of female leadership structures after Zinzendorf's death. Language that referred to the Holy Spirit as "Mother" or other female terms decreased after Count Zinzendorf's death, and although David Zeisberger occasionally used this language—for instance when he noted, on June 7, 1772, "We asked our dear Mother for merciful *Absolution* for all the ways we so often cause her sorrow and for not listening to her voice adequately"—more often the term was replaced by "Holy Spirit" as the journals made their way to the European Brethren for circulation. David Zeisberger, *The Moravian Mission Diaries of David Zeisberger, 1772–1781*, ed. Herman Wellenreuther and Carola Wessel, trans. Julie Tomerlin Weber (University Park: Pennsylvania State University Press, 2005), 97 (hereafter cited parenthetically in the text by page number).

1767, upon visiting Indian villages on the upper Susquehanna River, Zeisberger wrote, "Inasmuch as the men of the place were all away, engaged in the chase, and there were only the women at home, I saw that there was nothing for us to do here and we continued our journey."[4] Even after he had established Schönbrunn and settled into its daily spiritual and social life, Zeisberger was far more suspicious of women's influence on the godliness and peace of the community. At a conference in August 1773, Zeisberger wondered, "Why is it that once couples are married, the wives start to criticize their husbands and demand things from them they before would never have dreamed of, as for example that they demand that they work on their plantations and elsewhere, work that originally was the wives' concerns." Although acknowledging native women's ownership of agricultural resources, in essence, Zeisberger thought, "they want to turn their husbands into servants" (562).[5]

We might speculate that his distrust of or lack of interest in the lives of female converts and potential converts stemmed from Zeisberger's own marital status. Without a wife to point out the concerns of the household, which affected both women and men in the mission towns, his journals lean heavily toward political and spiritual activities and deal far less with domestic activities of the community. Anna Mack, Maria Spangenberg, and Johanna Schmick, along with their husbands, were all actively involved in the missionary work at Shekomeko in the 1740s and then at Gnadenhütten and Meniolagomekah in eastern Pennsylvania in the late 1740s and 1750s. As strong figures of authority in their own right (especially because of their language skills), they actively engaged native women in a leadership capacity as well. By contrast, in the Ohio Valley of the 1770s, few Moravian women participated in native missionary activities. Although Zeisberger notes that native women were periodically appointed to the Indians' Helpers' Conference in Schönbrunn and Lichtenau and that they spoke "with various members of their sex" (484), we hear next to nothing about the content of those conversations.[6] With fewer explicit descriptions

---

4. Archer Butler Hulbert and William Nathaniel Schwarze, eds., "The Moravian Records, Volume Two," *Ohio Archaeological and Historical Quarterly* 21 (January 1912): 10.

5. In his later *History of the Northern American Indians,* Zeisberger was more forthcoming in his observations on women's roles and economic activities. He detailed women's corn cultivation and preparation of corn meal, bread, etc. Archer Butler Hulbert and William Nathaniel Schwarze, eds., *David Zeisberger's History of the Northern American Indians* (Columbus, Ohio: F. J. Heer, 1910), 13, 16. See Amy C. Schutt, "Female Relationships and Intercultural Bonds in Moravian Indian Missions," in Pencak and Richter, *Friends and Enemies in Penn's Woods,* 92–94.

6. See also Zeisberger, *Moravian Mission Diaries,* 286 (September 21, 1775); Schutt, "Female Relationships and Intercultural Bonds," 102. Two works by Earl P. Olmstead, *Blackcoats Among the*

of female activity, we have to dig more deeply into Zeisberger's diaries to find native women, their motives, and their lives.

Many of the Indian groups who lived in the Ohio Valley were no strangers to the Moravian presence. Indeed, some of the Mahicans and Delawares had participated in mission life for decades and had followed the missionaries from the Lehigh Valley or Susquehanna River valley. However, key differences in their general circumstances affected female response to the native religious communities by the 1770s. As the British and American colonists slipped closer to war, Native Americans were also experiencing a revolution of sorts; migration of native and white groups into the Ohio Valley after the Seven Years' War caused the severe dislocation of Indian communities, food shortages, depopulation, and intertribal tensions. Shawnees and Mingos, while constantly fighting "Virginians," also vied to gain the allegiance of various Delaware clans. Although the Six Nations claimed control over them, during the Revolution Delawares, under the leadership of White Eyes, attempted to eke out some form of independence. First allied with the Wyandots, and even seeking acknowledgment of land ownership from white Americans, Delawares waged internal battles to determine political control over the life of their clans. Captain Pipe and the Wolf clan resisted the Moravian presence, while Captain White Eyes and the Turtle and Turkey clans supported it. Meanwhile, most Delaware clans tried to maintain a neutral distance from the British and American troops vying for their military support.[7] Stepping gingerly through this volatile political landscape, women brought their own strengths as cultural brokers to bear in this relationship between natives and Moravians, but only to the extent that it served the best interests of their families. They turned to the Moravian mission towns for personal reasons, whether political or religious, but the security and health of their children remained the key to their actions. Among Delawares in particular, Moravian communities provided relative stability and protection. Yet by the early 1780s, when larger events, such as the American massacre of

---

Delaware: David Zeisberger on the Ohio Frontier (Kent: Kent State University Press, 1991), and *David Zeisberger: A Life Among the Indians* (Kent: Kent State University Press, 1997), are also oddly devoid of any discussion of women.

7. Hermann Wellenreuther, "White Eyes and the Delawares' Vision of an Indian State," *Pennsylvania History* 68 (spring 2001): 142, 160; Colin G. Calloway, *The American Revolution in Indian Country: Crisis and Diversity in Native American Communities* (Cambridge: Cambridge University Press, 1995), 8–9, 36–40, 53–64; Wellenreuther and Wessel's introduction to Zeisberger's *Moravian Mission Diaries*, 21–37. Part of the internal conflicts came not from the presence of Moravians but from the divided Delaware loyalties to British and American neighbors.

women and children in Gnadenhütten, Ohio, shattered the neutrality of the Delaware clans, the Moravian missions proved equally vulnerable.

Native women were drawn to the Ohio Moravian communities for a variety of reasons. Some came to the missions from a distance, acting on rumors or stories passed from town to town. In February 1778 a woman arrived from Detroit and "told a Sister that the *Wyandot* talk about us a lot and praise us. . . . Therefore she wanted to come here in the spring and hear the Brothers" (434). Some women came to the mission community with the help or at the insistence of relatives, joining family members already at Schönbrunn or following their husbands' instructions. Lucia, who had come to Bethlehem, Pennsylvania, with her husband in 1756, was admonished to stay with the Brethren before he died. She moved with the Moravians to Schönbrunn in Ohio and spent ten years as a widow with the community until her death in August 1773 (155–56).[8] At times, women made independent decisions and stayed with the mission *despite* their husbands. Rachel, the baptized wife of a local Delaware leader, Welapachtschiechen, "had doubts about whether he would remain with the congregation [at Schönbrunn]. She had often said, If my husband leaves the congregation, I cannot possibly go with him. I would not be able to endure it" (390). Even in the face of reproaches from white missionaries, native women demanded to remain part of the community. In May 1775 a Delaware convert's daughter requested permission to live at Schönbrunn but was advised to stay away "because it might not suit her to live with us." She, in turn, deftly answered "all our objections" and was allowed to stay "on the *condition* that she behave according to our rules. We have done the same with many young widows who did not receive full permission to live with us until they had been baptized and received their inheritance and privileges with God's house and people" (269).

We can assume that many women chose to become part of the Moravian mission community because of the spiritual message the Moravians emphasized. In June 1776 the Delaware Captain Killbuck's wife spoke with the baptized Indian women at Lichtenau and "said she really wants to live in the congregation. She also wanted to live for the Savior, and in her heart she always felt she should come to us" (325). Later that year, another chief's wife mentioned that her children really wanted to go to "the Brothers, where we can hear about the

---

8. Lucas's sister "felt that she would not become well until she came to our place, so she asked her husband to bring her here and he did so." Zeisberger, *Moravian Mission Diaries*, 99 (June 30, 1772).

Savior, because we really want to live like the believers" (338–39). Although it is tempting to interpret these passages as Zeisberger's missionary zeal and wishful thinking, we cannot downplay Native Americans' capacity for reasoning and agency. Native women would be hard pressed to ignore the frequent services, prayers, community meetings, and religious conversations that permeated the daily life of the missions. On some level, those who came and stayed made a conscious decision to participate in religious life.

Following a pattern similar to that of the Moravian communities in the east, more women than men chose to be baptized at the Ohio mission towns. Between 1774 and 1781, 261 women, but only 223 men, became baptized members of the mission congregations (573–611).[9] Older women, widows in particular, entered the communities of Schönbrunn and Gnadenhütten in record numbers, often coming from nearby Delaware towns, even from the households of well-known Delaware leaders. In November 1776 Zeisberger noted that Netawatwees's (or Newcomer's) "widowed wife who has diligently attended our services, moved in with us permanently today. She is already quite old and is planning to spend the rest of her life here" (343).[10] Nearly every month Zeisberger would note that "a widow with 2 children . . . had come here before the holidays for a visit and has now decided and requested to live with us" (179). Or "a widow from *Kaskaskunk* and her son received permission to live with us" (182).[11] Or that "2 widows, *Eva* and her daughter *Anna Margretha*, came here from *Lichtenau* to stay" (515).[12] The phenomenon became so common that in 1780 Zeisberger simply noted: "Some more widows came here to live, as did *Rachel*" (525). Not surprisingly, widows made up a significant portion of the mission population. In early 1774 seventeen widows lived in Schönbrunn. By the end of 1775 twenty-two widows resided in the town (only two widowers). At the end of 1778 the relocated mission, now at Lichtenau, was home to 108 married Brothers and Sisters, 11 single Brothers, 6 single Sisters, 9 widowers, 163 children, and 31 widows, who made up nearly 10 percent of the total population of 328 (181, 487–88). Only after 1780 did the congregation, and the numbers of women, begin to shrink (547).

---

9. Schutt, "Female Relationships and Intercultural Bonds," 102, puts the number at far fewer, but she uses the Fleigel catalog to calculate her figures instead of the Zeisberger Diary Register. Between 1742 and 1764, 276 Delaware and Mahican women and girls were baptized in eastern Pennsylvania Moravian mission towns, while 229 men and boys were baptized. Jane T. Merritt, *At the Crossroads: Indians and Empires on a Mid-Atlantic Frontier, 1700–1763* (Chapel Hill: University of North Carolina Press, 2003), 102–3, chart 105.

10. See also Zeisberger, *Moravian Mission Diaries*, 325 (June 16, 1776), and 437 (March 3, 1778).

11. See also ibid., 185 (April 9, 1774); 433 (January 25, 1778); 503 (April 4, 1779).

12. See also ibid., 428 (January 5, 1778).

Whether arriving from Delaware towns in the west or following the Moravians from the east, whether unbaptized or Christian converts, native women found that the Moravian mission towns offered an array of services for their families that native communities, torn by internal divisions and external conflict, could no longer provide in the 1770s. Amy Schutt has illustrated in her work on mission towns in Ohio that "Indians' desires for their children influenced their decision to join Moravian missions in sizable numbers."[13] Indeed, the Moravians' focus on child care and spiritual services sometimes persuaded even the most suspicious mother to ask permission to stay. In March 1775 a native woman visiting the mission town, who "had always said that what was preached here was all lies," attended the children's service for a baptism and "could not stop crying, and afterward she said that from now on she would not say we were preaching lies anymore. She was now convinced otherwise and actually wanted to become a believer" (262–63).

Although many women appeared to be spiritually motivated, pragmatism also drove their decisions. For instance, they often sought access to better health care for themselves and their children, to give them a chance for survival. Native women saw the mission town as a healthy place, or at least as a place where they might find medical attention. In December 1774 Zeisberger noted that "an Indian woman who was a stranger came here a few days ago to give birth. This took place successfully today. We have already had many cases like this, when Indians in this same situation, in illness, or in danger of their lives, have fled to the Brothers" (248). Some women arrived ill and sought medicine, but also the healing powers of baptism, often recovering after supplication to Jesus and extensive prayer. In February 1776 Zeisberger remarked that Sister Lazara "had been so sick and emaciated for a long time that no one believed she could live. . . . She asked her father very fervently to take her to the Brothers so that she could hear about the Savior again before her end. . . . She was baptized into Jesus' death at her urgent request. From that moment on she improved so much that within a short time she was healthier than she had ever been in her life" (298–99).[14] Perhaps Zeisberger exaggerated the health benefits of Christianity; where he saw spiritual hunger, the women may have experienced bodily hunger. "Sick and emaciated," Lazara's recovery was probably less miraculous than the result of a few good meals.[15]

---

13. Amy C. Schutt, "'What Will Become of Our Young People?' Goals for Indian Children in Moravian Missions," *History of Education Quarterly* 38, no. 3 (1998): 271.

14. See also Zeisberger, *Moravian Mission Diaries*, 261–62 (March 13, 1775); 458–59 (July 26, 1778).

15. See also the story of White Eyes' brother and his wife's sick daughter, whom they brought to Schönbrunn in late summer 1776. "She had continued asking her parents to bring her here to us

Still, if baptism was not a panacea for all ills, native women may have seen it as a means to an end for themselves and their families. Joining Moravians provided new kin networks and support systems. Kinship in native communities included people born or married into a family, but Indians also recognized the importance of turning strangers into "either actual or symbolic kinspeople" to strengthen political alliances or increase access to available resources.[16] Delaware women, raised in matrilineal societies, created new kinship ties with other women in the mission communities, turning to them for support. Women knew that if they were incapacitated or died, others would take care of their children. Paulina, a national helper in the Moravian congregation for nearly ten years, died in childbirth in December 1777, leaving eight children (422–23). A native convert from Gnadenhütten, Ohio, Anna Johanna, adopted her youngest boy, Daniel, while the members of Schönbrunn cared for the others (424–25). Despite the absence of Moravian women as models of community authority, the Moravian practice of sex segregation reinforced the female bond between native "sisters," mirroring the long tradition of Delaware matrilineal clans.

More than anything else, native women coveted the perceived security that Moravian communities provided for their families, especially during the tumultuous revolutionary era. Not surprisingly, nearby white settlers, more often than soldiers engaged in battle, threatened their safety. In August 1774 Schönbrunn received news from the nearby Delaware village of Gekelemukpechünk "that White people had been seen in the bush near the *Ohio*. Because of this, some Indians fled here with all their possessions. *White Eye's* wife also came here from *Gekelemukpechünk* with her children" (221). Still, by the mid- and late 1770s, revolutionary battles reached far into the frontier regions of the Ohio Valley and Great Lakes, testing the patience of neutral Delawares and putting women and children at the greatest risk. It is hardly surprising that American troops under General Hand in February 1778 were unable to distinguish Delaware women from their warrior husbands when they attacked and killed several on the Ohio River during the so-called Squaw Campaign. While an embarrassment to the soldiers, their actions gave sanction to many white Americans on the frontier

---

until they did so and she said, Perhaps I will die, and I want to die with the Brothers. Perhaps I can be baptized first and then I will go to the Savior. [She came to a service] . . . and then she rested and slept better than she has in a long time, and in a short time she became completely well. This was a great miracle for her parents and they thought about this a lot." Ibid., 331 (August 13, 1776).

16. Richard White, *The Middle Ground: Indians, Empires, and Republics in the Great Lakes Region, 1650–1815* (New York: Cambridge University Press, 1991), 15; Schutt, "Female Relationships and Intercultural Bonds," 87–103.

to follow suit, and more Indians sought refuge with the Moravians.[17] One Moravian convert had often told his sister, "Stay here [at Lichtenau] and do not let yourself be turned against them. You will not be better off anywhere else" (473). The wife of Job Chelloway, a longtime friend and liaison to the Moravians, arrived in Lichtenau in August 1778 "from *Great Island* on the *West Branch* of the *Susquehanna*. She said she had fled to save her life because the White people had killed all the Indians there, including her husband and her children" (461). But, at the tail end of the Revolution, the mission towns could not secure natives from the fury of Americans who equated British and Indian actions and did not bother to distinguish between neutral and hostile Delawares, let alone recognize Christian Indians. These blind hostilities culminated with the March 1782 massacre at Gnadenhütten, Ohio, when Pennsylvania militiamen deliberately executed the mostly Moravian Delaware converts they had captured on the suspicion that they had harbored hostile native war parties.

Although some Delaware women turned to baptism in the Moravian faith to take advantage of the mission resources and help their families, I do not mean to imply that native women gave up traditional beliefs and practices completely. Indeed, some did not conform to the rules and regulations of the mission towns and were asked to leave. In October 1773 Zeisberger "had to inform *Abigail, Peter's* wife, our *Abraham's* daughter, that she could no longer stay here because of her bad behavior" (163). Two years later "*Margreth* and her daughter" insisted on leaving the congregation since "they have not been able to shape up and all the efforts we made were in vain" (267). Women even played active roles in undermining the Moravian mission efforts. In July 1777, after twenty Native American warriors came to town and started to harass the members working in the nearby fields, the Moravians assumed that "a woman who lives outside of *Goschachgünk* had directed [them] to our fields, gone with them part of the way, and told them that we worked there every day" (386).[18] Still, in general, the mission provided resources that resourceful women could use, adapting to new circumstances, incorporating new peoples into their traditional networks of support, but always with the past in mind. After Debora, a widow, died in 1780, Zeisberger found among her things "a very small heathen idol, that is a *Beson* such as old women who live among the savages usually have." Native women believed that the relic would keep them from suffering, especially "in

---

17. Calloway, *American Revolution in Indian Country*, 37.
18. See also Zeisberger, *Moravian Mission Diaries*, 255 (January 17, 1775).

their old age." Even though Debora had been a faithful member of the congregation for nearly a decade, poor Zeisberger brooded that they would "never really know if she put any hope in [the idol] or if she had" simply forgotten that she still had it (541). The answer probably would not have mattered to most Delaware women; if the Moravians and their god did not provide, they could always try Plan B.

Debating Missionary Presence at Buffalo Creek:

Haudenosaunee Perspectives on Land Cessions, Government Relations, and Christianity

ALYSSA MT. PLEASANT

In mid-October 1800 Farmer's Brother, a prominent Seneca man at the Buffalo Creek reservation in western New York, received a visit from the Reverend Elkanah Holmes. Holmes, a Baptist minister in the employ of the New-York Missionary Society, "desired the favor of him, and the chiefs of the nation, to meet me in council."[1] Several days later the Senecas granted Holmes's request, and the missionary arrived at the council house to find an overflow crowd of 150 people assembled to hear his talk. The Seneca orator Red Jacket opened the proceedings, welcoming Holmes and inviting him to speak. Holmes proceeded to deliver remarks from the missionary society, as well as a message from the Oneidas and Mahicans whom he had visited on his way to Buffalo Creek. He also expressed interest in preaching to the people of Buffalo Creek about the Great Spirit and Jesus Christ. After some consultation, Red Jacket announced that the assembled chiefs considered Holmes honest and therefore invited him to preach the next day.

Holmes was not the first minister to visit Buffalo Creek. Indeed, Haudenosaunee people in western New York had a long history of interaction with Christian missionaries. Jesuit missionaries traveled to the region in the mid-seventeenth century, establishing three short-lived missions among the

---

Earlier versions of this essay were presented at the annual meeting of the American Society of Ethnohistory in Riverside, California, in October 2003, and at Buffalo State College, Buffalo, New York, February 13, 2004. I wish to thank the commentators and audience at those events, as well as the participants in the David Zeisberger conference at Penn State, for their thoughtful responses to my research. Additionally, I thank Jon W. Parmenter for his comments on the dissertation chapter from which this essay is drawn.

1. Elkanah Holmes, "Letters of Rev. Elkanah Holmes from Fort Niagara in 1800," *Buffalo Historical Society Publications* 6, no. 8 (1903): 194–95.

Senecas.[2] Samuel Kirkland, a Protestant missionary who devoted his life to working with Haudenosaunee people, toured the Seneca homelands in 1765–66 and found the communities uninterested in Christianity. When he traveled to Buffalo Creek twice in 1788, Kirkland's trips combined treaty negotiations and religious matters. While the missionary successfully fulfilled his responsibilities as the representative of the states of Massachusetts and New York, his second attempt to establish a mission in Seneca territory failed.[3] Holmes and the missionary organization that sponsored his work were the next to pursue the idea of establishing a presence at Buffalo Creek. Inspired by the evangelism of the Second Great Awakening, the Presbyterian, Baptist, and Dutch Reformed churches combined to form the New-York Missionary Society in 1796. This organization and others like it dedicated themselves to promoting the gospel and "civilization," as exemplified by Euro-American-style agriculture and household management, among American Indians.[4]

At the turn of the nineteenth century, Haudenosaunee people at Buffalo Creek began an extended period of negotiation with these missionaries. By 1820, some residents of Buffalo Creek had signed a covenant with the New-York Missionary Society that permitted the missionaries to proselytize on the reservation. In the 1960s and 1970s scholars identified the years between 1817 and 1819 as the period of a crucial "Christian-Pagan split" for Haudenosaunee people.[5] Despite the significance of this period in modern Haudenosaunee

---

2. Thomas S. Abler and Elisabeth Tooker, "Seneca," in *Handbook of North American Indians*, ed. William C. Sturtevant, vol. 15, *Northeast*, ed. Bruce G. Trigger (Washington, D.C.: Smithsonian Institution, 1978), 505–6; William Engelbrecht, *Iroquoia: The Development of a Native World* (Syracuse: Syracuse University Press, 2003), 149n6.

3. Walter Pilkington, ed., *The Journals of Samuel Kirkland: 18th Century Missionary to the Iroquois, Government Agent, Father of Hamilton College* (Clinton, N.Y.: Hamilton College, 1980), 137–54; Samuel Kirkland, "Journal of S. Kirkland Missy to the Five Nations, from Septem' 23rd to Decem', with Some Account of Their Present State and Disposition Toward the Government of New York, 1788," Buffalo and Erie County Historical Society Archives, Buffalo, New York, A00-348, box 17; Christine S. Patrick, "The Life and Times of Samuel Kirkland, 1741–1808: Missionary to the Oneida Indians, American Patriot, and Founder of Hamilton College" (Ph.D. diss., State University of New York at Buffalo, 1993), 402–15, 421–25; Laurence M. Hauptman, *Conspiracy of Interests: Iroquois Dispossession and the Rise of New York State* (Syracuse: Syracuse University Press, 1999), 71.

4. For further discussion regarding the connection between "civilization" programs and Protestant missionaries, as well as the federal government's support of these efforts, see Robert F. Berkhofer Jr., *Salvation and the Savage: An Analysis of Protestant Missions and American Indian Response, 1787–1862* (Lexington: University Press of Kentucky, 1965), and Francis Paul Prucha, *The Great Father: The United States Government and the American Indians*, 2 vols. (Lincoln: University of Nebraska Press, 1984), 1:135–58.

5. Anthony F. C. Wallace, *The Death and Rebirth of the Seneca* (New York: Knopf, 1970; reprint, New York: Vintage Books, 1972); Robert F. Berkhofer Jr., "Faith and Factionalism Among the Senecas: Theory and Ethnohistory," *Ethnohistory* 12 (1965): 99–112; Berkhofer, *Salvation and the Savage*.

history, there has been no in-depth scholarly analysis of the key events that produced this important cleavage in Haudenosaunee polity. This essay examines some of the councils and conversations that occurred in the western part of the Haudenosaunee homelands during the critical period from 1817 to 1819. It focuses on events at Buffalo Creek and places them in the larger context of Haudenosaunee-missionary relations at the reservation during the first two decades of the nineteenth century. In taking a longer view of Haudenosaunee-missionary relations at the Buffalo Creek reservation, this essay demonstrates that there was an extended series of discussions about the role of missionaries on the reservation. Councils with missionaries reveal shifting attitudes about Christianity, at which Haudenosaunee people reiterated time-honored understandings of Haudenosaunee–Euro-American relations as embodied in Guswenta, and carefully considered whether a policy of "gradual compliance" with Christianity would be useful to them in their determined resistance to land cessions. In addition, close examination of the historical record reveals that issues surrounding land cessions provoked the intense debates of the critical period referred to as the "Christian-Pagan split."

Articulating a Policy of "Gradual Compliance" in Light of Guswenta

When the Seneca orator Red Jacket responded to Reverend Holmes's speech in 1800, he drew a clear distinction between Haudenosaunee beliefs and those of Christians: "the Great Spirit has given to you white people the ways you follow to serve him, and to get your living . . . he has given to us Indians the customs that we follow to serve him."[6] In choosing to speak of the distinct ways of life practiced by Haudenosaunee people and Euro-Americans, Red Jacket invoked a long-standing principle of Haudenosaunee–Euro-American relations. This principle, recorded in the wampum belt known as Guswenta, acknowledged equality between the Haudenosaunee and Euro-Americans and established peace and friendship on the basis of noninterference by either party in the other's government, religion, or way of life.[7] After reminding Holmes of this

6. Holmes, "Letters of Rev. Elkanah Holmes from Fort Niagara," 199.
7. Guswenta, also known as the Two Row Wampum, is a belt of white and purple beads. The purple beads are strung on two parallel rows and are described metaphorically as boats, one a canoe representing the Haudenosaunee people and the other a sailboat representing Europeans. These two rows of purple beads are separated by three rows of white beads, which hold the respective meanings peace, friendship, and forever. For further discussion of Guswenta, see Chief Irving

principle, Red Jacket gently teased the missionary about Americans' fondness for furs. These furs, Red Jacket noted, were a product of Haudenosaunee lifeways, and their continued availability was a testament to the Great Spirit's generous preservation of game animals for Haudenosaunee people. With a bit of well-placed humor, Red Jacket's speech suggested that following the principles of Guswenta benefited both Haudenosaunee people and Euro-Americans.

In addition to humor, Red Jacket incorporated flattery into his speech. Land cessions were an issue Haudenosaunee people had struggled with since their first encounters with Europeans, and Red Jacket complimented the missionary when he suggested that the advice of "such good people as you and your Society" might have prevented deception and the loss of land. At the same time, however, Red Jacket expressed wariness of Christian missionaries and the education they proffered. He narrated a brief history of Euro-American-style education among Indians: "when learning was first introduced among Indians, they became small, and two or three nations have become extinct . . . it was also introduced to our eldest brothers the Mohawks; we immediately observed that their seats began to be small; which was likewise the case with our brothers the Oneidas." Through these comments, Red Jacket associated Euro-American-style education with native peoples' death and the dispossession of their lands. Red Jacket did not anticipate massive population loss in the western part of the Haudenosaunee homelands, but he did fear that formal education "might be the means of our fairing [sic] the same misfortunes of our brothers [the Mohawks and the Oneidas]; our seat is but small now; and if we were to leave this place, we would not know where to find another."[8]

Haudenosaunee people living in the western part of their homelands had recently ceded a tremendous area of land in the 1797 Treaty of Big Tree, reserving only eleven reservations (or "seats") for their population. With this treaty and its associated land cessions fresh in their minds, Haudenosaunee people could not contemplate taking any action that might risk further loss of land.[9] For this reason, Red Jacket explained, "we here cannot see that learning would be of

---

Powless, "Treaty Making," in *Treaty of Canandaigua, 1794: 200 Years of Treaty Relations Between the Iroquois and the United States,* ed. Anna M. Schein (Santa Fe: Clear Light Publishers, 2000), 23.

8. Holmes, "Letters of Rev. Elkanah Holmes from Fort Niagara," 199–200.

9. In September 1797, at the Treaty of Big Tree, the Senecas sold several million acres of land to the Holland Land Company, reserving for themselves eleven parcels totaling approximately two hundred thousand acres. For the text of the treaty, see Walter Lowrie and Matthew St. Clair Clarke, eds., *American State Papers, Indian Affairs,* 2 vols. (Washington: Gales and Seaton, 1832), 1:627. Detailed discussion of land speculators' motivations at this treaty can be found in Hauptman, *Conspiracy of Interests.*

any service to us." After rejecting the missionary's proposals, Red Jacket again employed flattery: he encouraged Holmes and his missionary organization to "make your minds perfectly easy," or take these remarks in stride, because the Haudenosaunee "are convinced your intentions are good."[10]

The position taken by Red Jacket was not, however, the sole view of Christian education held by Haudenosaunee people at Buffalo Creek. On October 21, 1800, Farmer's Brother paid a visit to Holmes. The war chief explained that his people had not had the chance to express all their thoughts the last time they had met with the missionary. Farmer's Brother proceeded to request that the missionary take responsibility for educating a member of the younger generation, a grandson of Farmer's Brother.[11] In this he took advantage of an opening in Red Jacket's speech that allowed for "others who come after us, to judge for themselves" the risks and benefits of Euro-American-style education. Although Farmer's Brother expressed strong reservations about Christian education, explaining that another grandson had begun drinking, gambling, and frequenting brothels while in the care of the Quakers, he was willing to give the Christians another chance. Because of the "good words" from Holmes and the "good talk sent to us by your good Society," he had great hopes that the education this young man would receive among them would make him "of great use to us Indians."[12]

For Farmer's Brother and the people of Buffalo Creek, this decision represented a substantial risk. Previous experience had shown that a young man could easily become corrupted while in the care of missionaries. As Farmer's Brother explained, this corruption was dangerous to the community as well as the individual: "if we should send more of our boys, and they should learn such bad ways as he had, that [sic] our land would be cut into small pieces, and

---

10. Holmes, "Letters of Rev. Elkanah Holmes from Fort Niagara," 200.

11. It is possible that this young man was not a direct lineal descendant of Farmer's Brother but rather the son of his niece. William Johnston, a former British officer who served in the Indian Department at Fort Niagara, married a niece of Farmer's Brother, with whom he had a son named John Johnston. According to Ketchum, "much pains [were] taken" with John Johnston's education, which he received at Yale College. William Ketchum, *An Authentic and Comprehensive History of Buffalo*, 2 vols. (Buffalo, N.Y.: Rockwell, Baker & Hill, 1865; reprint, Bowie, Md.: Heritage Books, 2002.), 1:60–61, 141–42. The 1802 annual report of the New-York Missionary Society contains a reference to a young Seneca chief named John Johnston. This man traveled to New York with Reverend Elkanah Holmes in April 1802 and is described as "entrusted to the Society for his education." In all likelihood, the grandson described by Farmer's Brother is this same person. See New-York Missionary Society, *A Sermon Delivered Before the New-York Missionary Society, to Which Are Added the Annual Report of the Board of Directors and Other Papers Relating to American Missions* (New York: New-York Missionary Society, 1802), 65.

12. Holmes, "Letters of Rev. Elkanah Holmes from Fort Niagara," 200, 202.

our nation dispersed and ruined."[13] The people of Buffalo Creek understood that formal education might lead to destructive habits and poor decisions that could threaten the existence of the Seneca Nation. Their greatest fear was loss of land, which they had seen occur among the Mohawks and Oneidas following the introduction of Euro-American-style education. At the same time, the community, or some portion of it, believed that knowledge of "the good customs of the white people" could benefit the community and the nation. The people of Buffalo Creek thus decided to resume the experiment in formal education they had begun years earlier, although this time they entrusted one of their young men to the care of Holmes's organization rather than the Quakers.

This series of conversations in the fall of 1800 demonstrates the Haudenosaunee people's vacillating views of Euro-American education and Christian missionaries. The people of Buffalo Creek were determined to maintain their land and life-ways. There were divergent opinions, however, about the best means to this end. The principles outlined in Guswenta had long served the Haudenosaunee well, yet there were growing concerns about the importance of literacy and numeracy transmitted by the Euro-Americans. Several years later, during another series of conversations with Holmes, the people of Buffalo Creek explored the possibility of balancing the competing desires to maintain their land and life-ways and to take advantage of the potential promise of education for resisting land cessions.

Red Jacket explained the community's position to Holmes in a speech he made in September 1803. Reminding the missionary that "your customs are different from ours," Red Jacket went on to say, "we agree to yours; but are not content to forget some of our own customs, which have been handed down to us by our forefathers."[14] As the orator articulated stipulations to the agreement, he explained the community's reasoning in accepting instruction from the missionaries. "From want of education and a knowledge of your customs" he explained, Delawares, Tuscaroras, and others became victims of deception and fraud and were reduced to the status of menial laborers. Red Jacket concluded with the reproach that "if they had followed the customs of their forefathers, they would have known better." These statements suggest the tension between perceptions that knowledge of American ways was both useful and necessary to the Haudenosaunee and concern that acquiring this knowledge might lead to the abandonment of time-honored indigenous traditions, beliefs, and practices. After careful consideration, Red Jacket explained, the community had agreed

---

13. Ibid., 202.
14. J. W. Sanborn, ed., *A Long-Lost Speech of Red Jacket* (Friendship, N.Y., 1912).

that it would "gradually comply with what the Missionary Society has recommended to us, that we may not be deceived and taken advantage of."[15] The decision to "gradually comply" with the missionary society's request to build a school and church reflects a compromise worked out through lengthy deliberations among the Haudenosaunee.

The community's interest in compromise and "gradual compliance" was undoubtedly encouraged by their knowledge that the young man whom they had entrusted to the missionary society in 1800 was making progress in his education; Red Jacket cited the "great hopes" that news of the young man's progress had inspired in the people of Buffalo Creek. Conversations with political leaders of the United States also influenced the community's decision; Red Jacket recalled George Washington's recommendation that the Haudenosaunee and the United States "should be united as friends and brothers."[16] Unmentioned, but likely to have figured in the discussions, was a more recent conversation with another U.S. president, Thomas Jefferson.

In February 1803 Jefferson had addressed a delegation of Seneca, Oneida, and Onondaga people. Responding to the delegation's concerns about their treaties with the United States, Jefferson renewed the chain of friendship, confirmed Haudenosaunee title to Buffalo Creek, Allegany, and all other reservations, and reiterated the nation-to-nation relationship between the United States and the Haudenosaunee. In his closing remarks the president voiced the United States' desire to see Haudenosaunee people "advance in the cultivation of the earth, in manufacturing clothes, and in whatever may contribute to feed & clothe your people."[17] By linking his affirmations of land tenure and peaceful relations to a discussion of the developing "civilization" policy of the United States, Jefferson impressed upon Haudenosaunee diplomats the importance of accepting elements of Euro-American culture in their lives.[18] From Jefferson's perspective, in order

---

15. Deidamia Covell Brown, *Memoir of the Late Rev. Lemuel Covell, Missionary to the Tuscarora Indians and the Province of Upper Canada, Comprising a History of the Origin and Progress of Missionary Operations in the Shaftsbury Baptist Association, up to the Time of Mr. Covell's Decease in 1806* (Brandon, Vt.: Telegraph, 1839), 99–100.

16. Ibid., 100.

17. For the full text of Jefferson's response, see Thomas Jefferson, "Brothers of the Seneca, Oneida & Onondagua Nations, February 14, 1803," Jasper Parrish Papers, Special Collections, folder 68, Vassar College Library, Poughkeepsie, New York. This speech was also transcribed and annotated in Dorothy May Fairbanks, "Letters and Documents Relating to the Government Service of Jasper Parrish Among the Indians of New York State, 1790 to 1831" (honors thesis, Vassar College, 1940), 95–100. Fairbanks's interpretation of the document focuses on Jefferson's discussion of jurisdictional issues brought to the fore by the Stiff-Armed George case, a subject taken up in chapter 3 of this dissertation.

18. For discussion of "civilization" policy and Jefferson's role in its development, see Prucha, *Great Father*, 135–40.

to unite with the United States as "friends and brothers," the Haudenosaunee would have to change some of their practices.

While the United States' emerging "civilization" program for American Indians offered an expansive view of the transformations that would occur as a result, the people of Buffalo Creek defined the meaning of "gradual compliance" very narrowly. Residents of the reservation sought to strike a delicate balance between knowledge of American customs, which they hoped would protect them from deception and exploitation, and preservation of the customs of their forebears. As Red Jacket put it, "We, the chiefs of the Seneca, Onondaga, and Cayuga nations, have agreed to listen to what has been recommended to us:—not that we say all will listen; but that the greater part have agreed to hearken to what our fathers, the Missionaries, have said to us." Members of the three Haudenosaunee nations residing at Buffalo Creek would tolerate the presence of missionaries, but they might not embrace all of their suggestions. This statement, when considered alongside Red Jacket's comments about the young chief, shows that the feeling of good will toward the missionaries was not unanimous. Red Jacket illuminated some pockets of resistance when he told Holmes, "Look around the room, and you will see a number of us with the appearance of old age upon our countenances, who have no idea of leaving off some of our ancient customs." Although Red Jacket acknowledged that the young people of the community might "judge for themselves" the missionaries and their project, he insisted that reservation residents would continue to observe their "customary worship" during the annual midwinter and green corn celebrations of the Haudenosaunee spiritual cycle.[19]

Red Jacket's 1803 speech defined "gradual compliance" in a way that created a very narrow opening for Christian missionaries. It also illuminated entrenched resistance to their innovations, resistance that held significant sway during Holmes's 1800 visit to the reservation and would continue to influence Haudenosaunee views on the appropriate role of missionary organizations and their representatives at the Buffalo Creek reservation. At the same time, the words of Farmer's Brother and Red Jacket's nod to "gradual compliance" demonstrated the Haudenosaunee people's real interest in these changes. As the nineteenth century

---

19. Sanborn, *Long-Lost Speech*. In mentioning the three Haudenosaunee nations that had established villages at Buffalo Creek, Red Jacket indicates that the leaders of the three nations came together to determine the community's position regarding Holmes and the New-York Missionary Society. This suggests that although the reservation was located within Seneca territory, the governance of Buffalo Creek was sometimes a multinational affair.

progressed, opinions at Buffalo Creek continued to vacillate between the desire for Euro-American-style education and commitment to the principles of Guswenta.

Defining "Gradual Compliance" Through Haudenosaunee Practice

Despite the community's interest in Euro-American-style education expressed during Holmes's 1803 visit, it was not until 1811 that Jabez Hyde, a catechist affiliated with the New-York Missionary Society, was permitted to establish a school at Buffalo Creek. In 1820 Hyde reflected on his experience as a schoolteacher there. The school was troubled from the outset, and his nine years of service had been frustrating. Lessons were interrupted several times as the War of 1812 disrupted life at the reservation, and even during peacetime students attended intermittently. Hyde was discouraged by the shortage of students, but even more troubling was the community's prohibition of religious instruction. He was "led to despair," he wrote, "of doing anything for them while they refused to listen to the Gospel."[20] Hyde's appeals for permission to proselytize were met with statements such as "Educate our children and they will probably embrace your religion, and future generations of Indians will doubtless become Christian."[21] These polite refusals, echoed in other American Indian communities' responses to missionaries, enabled Buffalo Creek residents to evade the ministrations of evangelists while securing the continued service of white teachers. This form of resistance is part of a pattern of "grudging accommodation" that Carol Devens, in her study of Indian-missionary interactions in the Great Lakes region, has identified in areas where the pressures of nearby white settler societies demanded that communities negotiate with colonizers.[22]

Hyde's frustration stemmed from the limited form of accommodation practiced at the reservation. When Red Jacket first defined "gradual compliance" in 1803, he indicated that the community would tolerate a small degree of innovation. Eight years later, when Hyde was finally permitted to set up shop at Buffalo Creek, the missionary society and its representative began to

---

20. Jabez Backus Hyde, "A Teacher Among the Senecas: Narrative of Rev. Jabez Backus Hyde, 1811–1820," *Buffalo Historical Society Publications* 6, no. 8 (1903): 256.
21. Ibid., 9.
22. Carol Devens, *Countering Colonization: Native American Women and Great Lakes Missions, 1630–1900* (Berkeley and Los Angeles: University of California Press, 1992), 45–68. This work identifies communities where residents permitted a missionary to instruct their children, while adults "insisted that they themselves were 'too old and too ignorant' for his preaching" (58–59).

appreciate the true meaning of the phrase. Hyde, a trained catechist who longed for the opportunity to provide religious instruction to the Indians, chafed at its prohibition. In addition, although the Buffalo Creek residents permitted literacy instruction, Hyde was wholly dissatisfied with the limited progress his few students made. He was disillusioned by the poor attendance at his school and began to question the missionary society's program of "civilizing" Indians before introducing religious instruction. Although Hyde continued to hold out the hope that he might eventually receive permission to provide religious instruction, he slowly realized that the suggestion that children might eventually embrace Christianity was an evasion.[23]

Distress and Alarm: The Intersection of Land Cessions, Government Policy, and Christianity

Late in 1817, before a council of twenty-one chiefs from several villages, Hyde made a final, desperate attempt to convince the community of the merits of Christianity. He timed his presentation carefully, waiting four months until he believed the situation was right. According to his description of events, the speech Hyde delivered over the course of two days made an impression: the assembled chiefs agreed to allow the missionary-instructor to deliver sermons, and for two months, he noted, "there appeared evidently a great alteration for the better." This brief period of Christian instruction was followed by what Hyde described as "so dark a season [that] it appeared as though the abyss had opened upon us."[24] The remarkable change in the community's position regarding Christianity, as well Hyde's cryptic comment a few months later, can be explained through careful consideration of tensions surrounding land cessions in the 1810s.

Since the beginning of the decade, when David Ogden established the Ogden Land Company and purchased the preemptive right to Seneca lands from the Holland Land Company (which held this right under the Treaty of Big Tree), there had been renewed interest in dispossessing the Seneca people of the remaining reservations in their homeland.[25] By 1814 members of the Ogden Land Company were advocating the removal of Haudenosaunee people from

---

23. Hyde, "Teacher Among the Senecas," 256.
24. Ibid., 257.
25. For an extended examination of the Ogden Land Company's role in Seneca dispossession, see Mary H. Conable, "A Steady Enemy: The Ogden Land Company and the Seneca Indians" (Ph.D. diss., University of Rochester, 1995).

western New York.[26] Within a year Erastus Granger, the federal Indian agent to the Haudenosaunee, proposed that the Indians consider removing to the west. Also in 1815, the state of New York succeeded in acquiring Seneca-owned islands in the Niagara River, a purchase it had been trying to effect since 1810.[27] Increasing pressure for land cessions and removal coincided with incidents of trespass and timber stripping at Buffalo Creek.[28] While the Haudenosaunee protested these developments and reiterated their refusal to sell land, pressure from land speculators and state and federal officials only increased. As Laurence Hauptman has shown, developing federal removal policy, New York politicians' investment in the Erie Canal, and land speculation fueled by this new thoroughfare combined to exert a powerful force bent on Haudenosaunee dispossession.[29]

Hyde had witnessed visits and negotiations by land speculators and was undoubtedly impressed by the Senecas' insistence on retaining their land base. He had also developed an understanding of Haudenosaunee spiritual practices and knew that thanksgiving was a central element of Haudenosaunee beliefs. During the late 1810s he came to believe that Haudenosaunee people's focus on thanksgiving was a liability for them. When land speculators and government agents moved to extinguish Haudenosaunee title to their homelands, crisis rocked Buffalo Creek, and Hyde observed "a kind of delirium, a desperation," among community residents.[30] Hyde believed that spirituality offered a way for the Haudenosaunee to see themselves through this crisis, but he also believed that rites and ceremonies centered on thanksgiving "shut them out from all application to God except the influence they may suppose their religious rites have in moving the Divine Being to be propitious to them." In conversations

26. Thomas L. Ogden, "Remarks to Bishop Hobart, December 14, 1814," David Ogden Papers, Clements Library, University of Michigan, Ann Arbor, Michigan, provides an early articulation of the Ogden Land Company's interest in Haudenosaunee removal.

27. The controversial "treaty" that allowed this purchase is discussed in Hauptman, *Conspiracy of Interests*, 136–39. In August 1993 the Seneca Nation challenged the validity of this sale in a federal lawsuit against the state of New York, arguing that the absence of federal commissioners at the negotiations, as well as Congress's failure to ratify the "treaty," violated the 1790 Trade and Intercourse Act. A recent court decision rejected the Seneca Nation's claim; see *Seneca Nation of Indians v. New York*, 382 F.3d 245 (U.S. Court of Appeals, Second Circuit, 2004).

28. On October 26, 1816, James Strong registered Young King's complaints regarding timber stripping, noting that the Haudenosaunee expected heavy fines to be levied against individuals who violated their territory. James M. Strong, "Letter to Jabez Hyde," Erastus Granger Papers, Marshall Family Collection, Special Collections, Penfield Library, State University of New York at Oswego, New York.

29. Hauptman, *Conspiracy of Interests*, especially chapters 7–12.

30. Jabez Hyde, "Jabez Hyde Letter to Isaac G. Hutton, Seneca Village, June 18" (1818), Papers of the Hutton Family, 1762–1887, University of Virginia Special Collections, Charlottesville, Virginia.

with Hyde, reservation residents conveyed their understanding that personal appeals for comfort or succor "implie[d] dissatisfaction with our condition and irreverent attempt to influence the Divine Being." Rather, Buffalo Creek residents believed that it was their duty, in Hyde's words, "to give thanks to God for his benefits and submit with quietness to the allotment of his providences."[31]

Twentieth-century scholars have explored Haudenosaunee beliefs rooted in the principles of thanksgiving. Wallace L. Chafe has documented the thanksgiving address, noting that it is "the most ubiquitous of all Seneca rituals, for it opens and closes nearly every ceremony." Chafe describes the address as a sixteen-part ritual that conveys "not only the conventionalized amenities of both thanking and greeting, but also a more general feeling of happiness over the existence of something or someone."[32] References to its origin can be found in a 1928 publication by J. N. B. Hewitt, the Tuscarora anthropologist. In the creation tradition recorded by Hewitt, De-hae-hiyawa-kho, or the Earth Grasper, instructed that when people gather together they should "greet one another repeatedly with thanksgiving" and proceed to offer thanks for a series of terrestrial and celestial elements, among them "this Earth here present, whereon we travel about from place to place; for that she will care for all those things which He who finished our bodies has completed."[33] Chafe provides a detailed account of the thanksgiving address in *Seneca Thanksgiving Rituals*, which transcribes and translates Seneca chief Corbett Sundown's 1959 rendition of the address.[34] Both the Hewitt and the Chafe publications are important primary sources that demonstrate the centrality of thanksgiving and the land, including its geographic features, flora, and fauna, to the Haudenosaunee people. These initial instructions underlie Haudenosaunee understandings of their place in the world and inform their practices and beliefs.

In the late 1810s Jabez Hyde recognized that the threat of land cessions had created a situation in which the Haudenosaunee people were deeply dissatisfied and living in "continual dread" of losing their land. He also recognized that the people of Buffalo Creek were grappling with a crisis for which they had limited spiritual coping mechanisms. Rituals conveying thanks for land the Haudenosaunee feared they might lose in the coming weeks or months may

---

31. Hyde, "Teacher Among the Senecas," 245.
32. Wallace L. Chafe, *Seneca Thanksgiving Rituals*, Bureau of American Ethnology Bulletin 183 (Washington, D.C.: U.S. Government Printing Office, 1961), 1.
33. J. N. B. Hewitt, "Iroquoian Cosmology, Second Part," *U.S. Bureau of American Ethnology Annual Reports* 43 (1928): 568.
34. Chafe, *Seneca Thanksgiving Rituals*, 16–45.

have been perceived as inadequate or inappropriate. The despondency Hyde witnessed could have been addressed through the condolence ceremony, had this grief been rooted in the loss of an individual. Unfortunately, while this foundational ceremony of the Haudenosaunee Great Law of Peace provides a process for wiping away the tears, unstopping the ears, and clearing the throats of individuals, families, clans, and nations experiencing grief at the loss of a loved one or leader, it does not address the grief associated with loss of land. In the midst of growing pressures, Hyde delivered a compelling speech that offered the people of Buffalo Creek a new way of processing their situation. Hyde reminded reservation residents of their vulnerability and suggested that "certain inevitable ruin awaited them" unless they embraced Christianity—a form of belief that encouraged personal appeals to a higher power and promised deliverance from distress.[35]

Hyde's speech coincided with a lengthy council at Buffalo Creek, which deliberated on the course of action the Haudenosaunee should take to address their growing concerns about land cessions and white encroachment. After three days of consultation, they determined to lay their concerns before the president of the United States.[36] On January 1, 1818, Hyde served as a witness to their letter to President Monroe. "Distressed and alarmed," they conveyed to Monroe their astonishment at recent actions taken by land speculators and agents of the U.S. government. The letter detailed an extensive list of concerns. David Ogden was exerting pressure on them, claiming that the reservations in western New York actually belonged to his company. Conversations with Jasper Parrish, a federal Indian subagent, revealed the United States' intention to drive the Haudenosaunee people off their reservations in New York. Vague conversations about removal to the west seemed fraught with deception and misrepresentation, as the Haudenosaunee understood that the United States was moving rapidly to extinguish Indian title in that region as well. Finally, any reassurances they hoped to find in their treaty with the United States were destroyed when they discovered that a Buffalo resident had taken the document from an inebriated chief as security for liquor.

The Seneca, Cayuga, and Onondaga chiefs who signed the letter were desperate for reassurance. While they righteously stated "it is our fixed and determined purpose to live and die on our present seats," the Haudenosaunee people clearly believed they were in a precarious situation. Acknowledging the

35. Hyde, "Teacher Among the Senecas," 245, 257.
36. Hyde, "Jabez Hyde Letter to Isaac G. Hutton, Seneca Village, June 18."

military might of the United States, they asserted their "right to choose between being killed right out or a lingering execution of being driven a thousand miles into the Wilderness." The language of the letter suggests that the Haudenosaunee considered death a possible outcome of their situation. They appealed to the president to intervene on their behalf: "You cannot see your red children, with their little ones, driven from their lands by fraud and stealth, dying by families on the way through hardship and privation; leaving the sepulchers of their fathers; leaving their farms, their farming utensils, and their cattle behind; exchanging all their advances toward civilized life and its comforts, for the hardships of a hunting life."[37] President Monroe, they believed, could not fail to respond to this appeal, grounded in the language of "civilization." Previous presidents had suggested that continued coexistence as "friends and brothers" hinged on Haudenosaunee people's acceptance of the government's "civilization" program, and the language of the letter therefore emphasized the Haudenosaunee appropriation of Euro-American-style agriculture.

Once the letter was completed, the council went on to consider other affairs. When the proceedings concluded after twelve days, Hyde observed a general feeling of satisfaction with the course they had taken. It was during the two months that followed this council that Hyde was able to preach and, he felt, make a favorable impression on the residents of Buffalo Creek. As time passed, however, with no response from the president, concerns grew and the fears underlying the appeal to Monroe resurfaced.

While awaiting the president's long-overdue response, the people of Buffalo Creek received a communication in Mohawk. This message claimed that upon receipt of the letter from Buffalo Creek, the president "raved like a mad man" and announced that he would have no more to do with the Haudenosaunee. Further, the Mohawk rumor suggested that if they did not leave the United States in three years, the president "would draw his sword and exterminate them." Several weeks later, the people of Buffalo Creek learned that the Six Nations Agency was to be abolished and that they would no longer have a local intermediary responsible for representing their concerns to the federal government. Jasper Parrish confirmed these changes in June when he arrived to distribute annuities, explaining that upon completion of the task he had no further responsibilities to the Haudenosaunee.[38] In the space of six months, this series of events transformed Haudenosaunee fears into realities.

37. Seneca, Cayuga, and Onondaga Chiefs, "Letter to U.S. President James Monroe, January 1, 1818," Seneca, Indian box 2, Rare Books and Manuscripts Division, New York Public Library, New York.
38. Hyde, "Jabez Hyde Letter to Isaac G. Hutton, Seneca Village, June 18."

Council Fires in a State of Confusion

In the summer of 1818 the Haudenosaunee people faced a spiritual crisis of monumental proportions. Hyde noted that "the minds of the Indians were continually agitated with the subject of religion" during this period.[39] The events of the preceding months led many to question whether their ways pleased the Creator, prompting calls to convene councils, where these concerns continued to be expressed over the course of the summer. One of these councils brought representatives from communities throughout the Haudenosaunee homelands together for twelve days of discussion at the Tonawanda reservation. Although Hyde did not attend the council, Reverend Timothy Alden visited Tonawanda at this time and was invited to sit in on the council meeting during the two days he spent at the village. Alden recorded that "the great object of this council was, to revive the moral instructions formerly received from Goskukkewaunau Konnedieyu [Handsome Lake], the prophet, as he was called ... who died about the year 1815."[40] Many participants advocated continued adherence to these teachings, which were grounded in a series of visions that inspired adaptations to and renewal of Haudenosaunee religious practices at the turn of the nineteenth century.[41]

Returning to Buffalo Creek before the council finished, Alden preached at the council house to a large group of Indians that included Little Billy, Captain Pollard, Young King, Twenty Canoes, and several other chiefs. These men, who played important roles in the reservation community, were not involved in conversations focused on renewing the teachings of Handsome Lake. Red Jacket and a number of other chiefs from the reservation remained at Tonawanda at this time.[42] This series of councils and meetings demonstrate that spiritual and religious differences were emerging on the Buffalo Creek reservation. In August 1818 Hyde became personally involved in the religious debates when five men, "wearied out with being held off until all were agreed," approached him and requested to learn the gospel.[43] With this decision the men abandoned efforts

---

39. Hyde, "Teacher Among the Senecas," 259.
40. Timothy Alden, *An Account of Sundry Missions Performed Among the Senecas and Munsees; in a Series of Letters* (New York: J. Seymour, 1827), 58.
41. The classic work on Haudenosaunee revitalization is Wallace, *Death and Rebirth of the Seneca*.
42. Alden, *Account of Sundry Missions*, 62.
43. Hyde, "Teacher Among the Senecas," 260. Hyde takes pains to note that these young men came from prominent families. Later in the narrative he repeatedly discusses interactions with Red Jacket's sons, Jonathan and William. It is possible that these two men were among the initial group to embrace Christianity.

to achieve consensus in council and provided Hyde with his long-awaited opportunity to preach at Buffalo Creek. In the face of tremendous ridicule, the small group gathered weekly to observe the Sabbath. A month passed before anyone else joined the group, and then, slowly, a few more people began to attend the meetings.[44]

Christian worship continued in spite of opposition to the missionary's efforts to proselytize, which increased throughout the fall. In September 1818, when the New-York Missionary Society sent another missionary to Buffalo Creek, "the Senecas were unwilling to receive him . . . a serious and most unfortunate collision had occurred between Mr. Ely [the missionary] and the Indians, at a public council of the Tribe."[45] Fearing that this turn of events threatened future missionary activities at Buffalo Creek, the missionary society sent two of its board members to investigate the situation. Their inquiries indicated that the missionary had done nothing wrong, which confirmed that a vocal and influential segment of the community vehemently opposed Christianity regardless of the messenger. But the board members also discovered that part of the community remained receptive to missionaries. During their visit, some people asked them to clarify "how far the wishes of the good people extend towards us, in helping us along to the light. We would know to whom you look for your reward for your good feelings and endeavours for us. . . . We would wish a few lines to have it in writing to show that you expect God will reward you hereafter."[46] The missionaries construed this inquiry as a request to draft a formal covenant between the people of Buffalo Creek and the missionary society. Consequently, a covenant of friendship was agreed upon that formalized the missionary society's commitment to send two teachers to Buffalo Creek and permitted these teachers to provide religious instruction. This agreement represented the first time the people at Buffalo Creek formally agreed to allow missionaries to proselytize in their communities.[47]

Opposition to the covenant was quick to follow. A meeting was held at Tonawanda, and supporters of the covenant were informed that they would have to explain themselves at the spring 1819 council. When the council convened in June 1819, those who supported the missionaries were taken to task by other

---

44. Ibid., 260–61.
45. New-York Missionary Society, *Report of the Directors of the New-York Missionary Society Presented at the Annual Meeting Held on April 3, 1819* (New York: New-York Missionary Society, 1819), 4.
46. Ibid., 6.
47. Hyde, "Teacher Among the Senecas," 262.

members of the community. The warriors, who opened the council, underscored community divisions through metaphorical language. They described a council fire in a state of confusion, with brands being pulled in different directions. Some people were likely to get burned, they argued, and all were endangered. The warriors who used this language identified the missionaries' partisans as the source of this confusion and demanded that they explain themselves. Outnumbered six to one, the missionaries' supporters explained their position and read the covenant to the assembled council. Discussion continued the next day in a council house at another village. Speakers from both sides engaged in debate that Hyde characterized as "warm and animated." Those opposed to the missionaries argued that it was foolish to search for any good from white people, whom they considered the source of Indians' corruption and misery. They also described the acceptance of Christianity as an affront to the memory of their ancestors. Such actions, they argued, risked provoking the ire of the Creator, whose benevolence had ensured the Indians' happiness and prosperity before the arrival of the Europeans.[48]

Those open to the missionaries' message responded that they did not share this interpretation of Haudenosaunee history. Instead they believed that their current situation had resulted from the actions of their ancestors as much as from the agency of Euro-Americans. They critiqued Haudenosaunee participation in contests against other Indian nations and criticized decisions to cede land. Ultimately this group argued that actions taken by their forebears had compromised the prosperity and happiness the Haudenosaunee people had once enjoyed. With their former advantages now gone, those sympathetic to the missionaries argued that it was impossible to continue following the example of their ancestors and still escape ruin.

The debate became increasingly heated in the days that followed. Hyde described the tone as "personal and irritating," then as threatening. Only the arrival of U.S. commissioners sent to obtain additional land cessions interrupted the council proceedings. Uniting in opposition to this proposed cession, the Indians nominated Red Jacket to speak on their behalf. The orator not only rejected the proposed treaty but expressed the Indians' determination that no white men, whether missionaries, schoolmasters, or Quakers, should live on their land. Probably carried away by the events of the recent council, Red Jacket made these remarks without authorization. Supporters of the missionaries complained that he did not represent them on the issue of missionaries and

48. Ibid., 263–64.

schoolteachers, but the debate did not resume following the conference with the commissioners. Although there was no resolution to the debate regarding Christianity, Red Jacket had succeeded, for the moment, in having the last word on the subject.

On the Sabbath following the commissioners' departure, a large group gathered at the mission, but without an interpreter Hyde was unable to lead a service. Instead, one of the Indians led a conversation to which Hyde remained a silent witness. This marked the beginning of a series of difficulties that Hyde experienced with his interpreter and the congregation, which eventually prompted him to give up his work at the reservation. Summarizing his experiences in 1820, Hyde insisted that he had had a positive influence at Buffalo Creek. Nonetheless, he discouraged efforts to expand the missionary presence at the reservation, arguing that it "would probably kindle a fire" that would not be extinguished for years.[49]

Despite Jabez Hyde's deep concerns about the divisive effects of continued missionary presence at Buffalo Creek, the New-York Missionary Society and its successors were not deterred. For four years following the 1819 covenant, missionaries persisted in proselytizing at Buffalo Creek and eventually succeeded in establishing the Seneca Mission Church in 1823. Within the reservation community, the ongoing debates following the first Sabbath celebrations at Buffalo Creek extended previous conversations regarding the best ways to preserve Haudenosaunee communities and traditions. Although these debates initially threatened to divide the reservation, by the early 1820s individuals who supported the missionaries managed to cultivate a new form of "gradual compliance," and the people of Buffalo Creek began an experiment in tolerance that allowed reservation residents to embrace Christianity. Together with missionaries Thompson S. Harris and Asher Wright, some Haudenosaunee people worked to build an institution that met their needs during this period of tremendous upheaval. Although missionaries continued to face opposition in the years that followed, the Seneca Mission Church remained a fixture on the reservation until the early 1840s. When the Buffalo Creek reservation was ceded to land speculators following an 1842 treaty, the mission relocated to the nearby Cattaraugus reservation and continued to serve the Haudenosaunee people.

---

49. Ibid., 264–67, 273.

IV.

Conclusion

Translation as a Prism:

Broadening the Spectrum of Eighteenth-Century Identity

JULIE TOMBERLIN WEBER

An ideal translation, according to eighteenth-century Russian author Nikolai Gogol, should be as transparent as a windowpane so that readers can clearly see the original text.[1] In their introduction to the English translation of David Zeisberger's diaries, editors Hermann Wellenreuther and Carola Wessel echo Gogol's lament that this transparency is unobtainable and that no translation can ever live up to an original text.[2] As a translator, I readily concede the limitations of translation as an attempt to replace or re-create an original text. However, if we magnify the ambiguities and distortions a translator produces rather than trying to minimize them, we can experience translation as a prism that broadens and transforms our understanding rather than as a window that distorts it.

When we observe light passing through a prism, what we see and experience depends on whether we focus on the "pure" white light, the prism, or the walls on which a rainbow might become visible. Our experience also depends on how willing we are to manipulate the relative positions of the light, the prism, and any surfaces to be illuminated. Translation involves a similar transformation of a source text into a modern text that illuminates multiple discourses, both contemporary and historical. While the great German translators, including Luther, Lessing, and Goethe, readily acknowledged the limitations of translation, they upheld it as a critical act that could bring new life to contemporary discourses. To my knowledge, none of these translators compared translation to a prism,

---

1. Joachim Störig, ed., *Das Problem des Übersetzens* (Darmstadt: Wissenschaftliche Buchgesellschaft, 1963), xxvii. Frauke Geyken shared Gogol's image in her comments for the session on "Editions, Translations, Cultural Worlds," at the conference.
2. Georges Mounin articulates an even bleaker perspective on translation: "morphologically, syntactically, lexically, . . . languages tend to make all translation impossible, except at a level of approximation where the 'losses' are higher than the 'gains.'" Quoted in Antoine Berman, *The Experience of the Foreign*, trans. S. Heyvaert (New York: State University of New York Press, 1984), 188.

but each described it as a re-articulation that transforms, essentially refracting the living "whole" of an original text through particular linguistic ambiguities.

When Goethe reviewed a translation, he was more concerned with the questions it provoked than the answers it provided. Another contemporary of David Zeisberger, the German author Wilhelm von Humboldt, shared Gogol's view the translation is inherently doomed, writing in 1796, "Any translator must inevitably encounter one of the following obstacles: he will cleave with too much accuracy either to the original, at the expense of his people's language and taste, or to the originality of his people, at the expense of the work to be translated."[3] Goethe, however, argued that these obstacles were not a sad reality but a golden opportunity to articulate new questions. In his 1828 essay *German Romance*, Goethe argued that the introductions and glosses about such ambiguities reveal the purpose, clarity, and quality of translation; these marginalia constitute both a frame for the translated text and a new "original text," produced through the translator's engagement with the original source text.

Goethe identified the translator as "Vermittler dieses allgemein geistigen Handels," a negotiator between cultures who contributes to world peace.[4] In his *Diaries*, David Zeisberger identifies himself as a Christian joined to Luther in an altar of living stones, and he consciously shapes his experience to fit Luther's language. By discussing some of the ambiguities I confronted while translating David Zeisberger's diaries, I hope to clarify Zeisberger's own role as a translator and negotiator in a multicultural world, and to share the questions his diaries provoke about how we construct identity and culture.

Respecting the Untranslatable

Goethe insists that "one must attain the untranslatable and respect it; for it is precisely there that the value and the character of each language lie."[5] This does not excuse producing a stilted or sloppy translation or remaining so faithful to the original text that the translation fails to meet the standards of good writing.

---

3. Quoted in ibid., ix.

4. Johann Wolfgang von Goethe, *Werke: Jubiläumsausgabe*, ed. Friedmar Apel, 6 vols. (Frankfurt am Main: Insel Verlag, 1998), 6:365.

5. Goethe refers to the "Unzulänglichkeit des Übersetzens," in a review of Thomas Carlyle's English translation of selected German fiction. Goethe published this review in his journal *Über Kunst und Altertum* 6, no. 2 (1828). The complete title of Thomas Carlyle's 1827 publication was *German Romance: Specimens of Its Chief Authors; with Biographical Sketches and Critical Notices; by the Translator of Wilhelm Meister and Author of the Life of Schiller*. See Johann Wolfgang von

Respecting the untranslatable might mean using extensive footnotes to explain alternatives considered but not chosen. It might also mean leaving some words in the original language. Many editors and readers find such practices distracting or irritating, but simply glossing over ambiguities denies the reader any signs of the potentially richest sites for further inquiry into the discourse in which both original text and translation participate.[6]

In translating David Zeisberger's diaries, my desire to satisfy English readers led me on endless searches through antiquated and contemporary English, German, Lutheran, Moravian, and Native American sources. A quick glance at my collection of reference materials reveals the multicultural nature of Zeisberger's experience and writings. With the assistance of the Internet I scoured the 62,571 pages of Zedler's *Universal-Lexikon,* published between 1732 and 1754, for an eighteenth-century perspective on Zeisberger's language.[7] I checked Moravian archivist Paul Peucker's *Herrnhuter Wörterbuch* to understand how words were used in the specifically Moravian context, and Daniel Crews's English glossary of *Moravian Meanings* to render peculiarities of eighteenth-century Moravian German in a manner consistent with twenty-first-century Moravian English.[8] I often turned to the German Luther Bible for clues about the many images Zeisberger borrowed from that text.[9] Finally, I consulted scholarly works on Native American cultures for standard usage of Native American terms.

Zeisberger wrote diaries that require even the German reader to engage in limited but repeated acts of translation—for example, when he employed such English words as "Chief," and "Fort," and such Native American words as "Wampum" or "Beson." The multilingual character of Zeisberger's diaries reflects the intercultural character of the eighteenth-century Ohio River valley. His decision to use "foreign" terms like "Fort," "Revier" or "Speech," even when there were perfectly acceptable German equivalents, identifies the sites where

---

Goethe, *Sämtliche Werke, Breife, Tagebücher und Gespräche,* ed. Wilhelm Grosse and Hendrik Birus, 40 vols. (Frankfurt am Main: Deutscher Klassiker Verlag, 1997), 6:364.

6. Robert Leventhal, in *The Disciplines of Interpretation: Lessing, Herder, Schlegel, and Hermeneutics in Germany, 1750–1800* (Berlin: Walter de Gruyter, 1994), emphasizes that interpretation can take place only in a space, "a breach, one could say, between the familiar and the incomprehensible" (5).

7. Johann Heinrich Zedler, ed., *Grosses, vollständiges Universal-Lexicon aller Wissenschaften und Künste,* Münchener Digitalisierunszentrum Bayerische Stadtsbibliotek, March 10, 2004, http://mdz.bib-bvb.de/digbib/lexika/zedler.

8. Paul Peucker, *Herrnhuter Wörterbuch: Kleines Lexikon von Brüderischen Begriffen* (Herrnbut: Unitätsarchiv, 2000); C. Daniel Crews, *Moravian Meanings: A Glossary of Historical Terms of the Moravian Church, Southern Province,* 2d ed. (Winston-Salem, N.C.: Moravian Archives, 1996).

9. Even at their remote mission outposts, eighteenth-century Moravians took time each year to celebrate Reformation Day and to honor "der grosse Reformator" as a founder of their faith.

the relationship between the cultures was under construction, not necessarily where they were unable to communicate.

Editorial Questions

In his "Sendbrief vom Dolmetschen" (1530), Luther explicitly claims ownership of his New Testament translation: "It is my testament and my translation and it should be and remain mine."[10] He also challenges readers to produce their own translations. Luther modeled the translator's responsibility to clarify personal responses to ambiguities within a text, thus maintaining the integrity of the original as well as the translated text. According to Goethe, Luther grasped the unity of the Bible through his struggle to translate a few particularly difficult words, and Luther articulates this in his *Preface to the Old Testament*. Goethe upholds Luther as his ideal translator because he articulated and claimed these personal insights about the Bible as a whole in the marginalia. Goethe develops this model of translation as a process that results in much more than a translated text in a letter to his friend Zelter, in which he outlines plans for a cantata the two men hoped to write in honor of Luther. Goethe suggests that he and Zelter shouldn't actually use Luther's own words in their cantata, because "the excellent man is altogether dogmatic and practical, as is his enthusiasm" (my translation).[11] Rather than praise the accuracy, beauty, or accessibility of Luther's German translation of the Bible, Goethe praises Luther's prefaces and glosses. The measure of the translation is not the actual words of the translation but its participation in a contemporary discourse.[12]

As a translator, I was particularly excited to join an editorial team that included both native German and English speakers, and both Moravians and non-Moravians, as we sought to enable a wider audience to explore David Zeisberger's diaries. I cannot join with Luther in claiming that this translation is mine alone, however, for editorial decisions had to be made where there were differing opinions. As an English-speaking Moravian married to a fourth-

---

10. Martin Luther, *D. Martin Luthers Werke: Kritische Gesamtausgabe*, 68 vols. to date (Weimar: Hermann Böhlaus Nachfolger, 1883–), 4:180. In Luther's words, "Es ist mein Testament und mein Dolmetschung und soll mein bleiben und sein."

11. Max F. Hecker, ed., *Der Briefwechsel zwischen Goethe und Zelter: Im Auftrag des Goethe-und-Schiller-Archivs nach den Handschriften* (Bern: Herbert Lang, 1970), 531.

12. "Setzt man nun, um auf einen höheren Standpunkt zu gelangen, anstatt jener zwei Worte [Gesetz und Evangelium]: 'Notwendigkeit' und 'Freiheit,' ihren Synonymen, mit ihrer Entfernung und Annäherung, so siehst Du deutlich, daß in diesem Kreise alles enthalten ist, was den Menschen

generation Moravian pastor, I would have chosen to leave terms such as "Diener" and "Saal" in German, because English-speaking Moravians still use these terms today. Most contemporary English-speaking Moravians are familiar with other German words that have shaped our tradition, such as "Lebenslauf," which we translated in the published diaries as "memoir," and "Gemeinhaus," rendered as "congregational house." Many Moravians consider our German heritage an essential part of our identity as a church, and we as a community have chosen not to translate some terms but to incorporate the German into our English.

Another editorial decision involved our choice of which English Bible translation to cite for the passages Zeisberger quotes from the Luther Bible. It is true that the English in the King James Bible (1611), which the editors chose to use, is chronologically closer to the German of Luther's Bible (1534) than a more modern English translation, but I would have chosen to use a modern English translation. Luther worked tirelessly to use the idiom of everyday life in his translation, to emphasize the relevance of the sacred scriptures to the individual's personal experience. Although the language of Luther's Bible was more than two hundred years old when Zeisberger wrote his diaries, those diaries reveal the extent to which he interpreted his daily life through the idiom of Luther's Bible. The King James translation is beautiful and poetic, but to most modern readers it sounds removed from everyday language. Furthermore, while Luther intentionally prodded individuals to read the Bible critically by including extensive marginalia, the King James Bible omitted glosses in order to safeguard the incomprehensible, mystical aura of the text.[13] Finally, in translating the bulk of Zeisberger's diaries, we made no attempt to approximate eighteenth-century usage; therefore the use of an antiquated English Bible translation exaggerates the linguistic distance between the Luther Bible and Zeisberger's world.

Ultimately the particular editorial decisions we reached are not as important as acknowledging the options we considered and explaining our choices. I am confident that our collaboration produced a translation that will provoke more critical thought than a translation produced by one individual would have done.

---

interessieren kann" (Goethe *Werke*, 31:531). Goethe writes, "If you replace the two words [law and gospel] with their synonyms 'necessity' and 'freedom,' in order to reach a greater perspective on it through their distance and approach, then you clearly see that these terms define a circle that includes everything of interest to humans" (my translation).

13. In a review of Adam Nicolson's *God's Secretaries: The Making of the King James Bible* (New York: Harper Perennial, 2003), Paul Gleason explains that the King James Bible did not include footnotes because leaders of the church understood the Bible as a mystery beyond rational comprehension. See Gleason, "The Making of the King James Bible by Adam Nicolson," February 15, 2005, www.yalereviewofbooks.com/archive/spring04/review09.

Ambiguous Terms

Two ambiguous terms in Zeisberger's diaries, "Haufe" and "Virginian," illustrate how the process of translation unites Zeisberger, an eighteenth-century German-speaking Moravian missionary, with two German-speaking non-Moravian editors, an English-speaking Moravian translator, and a diverse audience of English-speaking readers in a discourse about how our choice of words shapes our conversation about identity in a multicultural world. David Zeisberger frequently refers to the faith community in which he lives as a "Haufen." While he uses the term in a very consistent and formulaic way, it is not mentioned in the list of distinctly Moravian vocabulary like "Diener" or "Saal." Yet his diaries reveal that the term was central to Zeisberger's identity and his understanding of how God had gathered this particular group of believers together. Zeisberger also records how his contemporaries from various cultures perceive the name "Virginian" as both ambiguous and significant. Modern English speakers who read only excerpts of the diaries might miss the ambiguity of this word, or its life-and-death significance, but the diaries emphasize the confusion surrounding the word. I will discuss "Haufen" as an example of how translation confronts the reader with ambiguity and "Virginian" as an example of how Zeisberger recorded his contemporaries negotiating linguistic ambiguity.

Modern German dictionaries define a "Haufen" as a "pile," such as a pile of money, a pile of stones, or a pile of work. The word can also refer to a "crowd" of people, often carrying the connotation of "the masses." None of these modern meanings seems appropriate for translating this word in David Zeisberger's diary, exemplified in this entry for January 1, 1775: "Then the congregation knelt down and Brother *David* commended the entire *gathering* [Häuflein] to the Savior of the Heathen for his grace, especially the two who had been received and God's entire work among the heathen here. He asked that the light of the wounds might break through the darkness soon and bring warmth and life to cold and dead hearts so that many more might become rewards for his suffering."[14]

Zeisberger's usage suggests that this word includes the children and regular guests, as well as the communicants within the community ("Abendmahlsgeschwister"). Although the word does not appear as a primary entry in Zedler's extensive

14. Zeisberger writes, "die Gemeine niederfiel und Bruder David empfahl das ganze Häuflein, besonders die zwey Aufgenommenen und das ganze Werk Gottes hier dem Heiden Heiland zu Gnaden, daß das Wunden-Licht bald durch die Finsternis hindurch und die kalten und todten Herzen erwärmen und beleben möge, damit noch viele ein Lohn seiner Schmerzen werden mögen."

Universal-Lexikon, it does appear in several distinct discourses relevant to David Zeisberger. "Haufen" also appears in the discourse of Moravian missions, in diaries and letters from other Moravian missions such as Springplace, Georgia, in the 1820s. Hymns published in eighteenth-century Moravian hymnals most frequently use "Haufen" to refer to a crowd or throng of people, which reflects Luther's New Testament usage of the word. An eighteenth-century hymn written by Erdmuth Dorothea von Zinzendorf, first wife of Nikolaus Count von Zinzendorf, links the image of the "Haufen" as a crowd with that of the Shepherd, proclaiming that it does not matter where the crowds come from, as long as they come and are received by believers.[15] This use of "Haufen" for crowds of people is much more appropriate to Erdmuth's experience of receiving repeated waves of religious refugees from Moravia and Bohemia than it would have been to Zeisberger's situation among the Delaware, where there were hardly large crowds running to join the believers.

In 1734 Nikolaus Count von Zinzendorf wrote a hymn that also suggests "flock" as a possible translation for the word "Haufen." This hymn clearly explains how God gathers followers. Although God often accomplishes this through one or two believers, they themselves are not shepherds or leaders; they are merely the "property" (*Eigentum*) of the Shepherd Jesus.[16] In the seventh verse Zinzendorf emphasizes the significant role of sacrifice in his faith, when he proclaims that obedience precedes sacrifice, while disobedience precedes sorcery. The sacrifices that are pleasing to God are an obedient heart and an open ear. The hymn concludes with a prayer that through the baptism of fire and the Spirit, God would make each member of our "Haufen" like the "Schaar" (host or flock) on the glassy seas.

These hymns suggest a relationship between "Haufen" as a flock of sheep, the Jewish sacrificial tradition, and the image of Jesus as the sacrificial Lamb of God, images consistent with Zeisberger's repeated references to his community as a "Haufen" gathered as a reward for God's sufferings. But they do not explain

---

David Zeisberger, *Herrnhuter Indianermission in der Amerikanischen Revolution: Die Tagebücher von David Zeisberger, 1772 bis 1781,* ed. Hermann Wellenreuther and Carola Wessel (Berlin: Akademie Verlag, 1995), 3:255.

15. See Erika Schneider and Helmut Schneider, *Zinzendorf und Freylinghausen: Gesangbücher des 18. Jahrhunderts* (CD-ROM, Bad Bentheim, 2001), for Moravian hymn texts and melodies, including Erdmuth Dorothea von Zinzendorf's "Allmächtiger GOTT Zebaoth! hilf den zerstreuten schafen," hymn 128 in Nicolaus Ludwig Zinzendorf, *Londoner Gesangbuch: Alt und neuer Brüder-Gesang,* ed. Dietrich Meyer and Gerhard Meyer (Hildesheim: G. Olms, 1980).

16. Nikolaus von Zinzendorf, "Du Band, du vestes Liebes-Band / du hast uns endlich doch gefunden." Hymn 36, *Evangelisches Gesangbuch* (1735), ibid.

why he chose this word instead of one more typically associated with a flock of sheep in Luther's Bible or eighteenth-century German—"die Herde" or even "die Gemeinde." If we turn to Luther's Bible for more clues about Zeisberger's use of the word, many references to "Haufe," "Haufen," or "Häuflein," suggest that a "Haufe" consists of anything gathered at God's command or by those who oppose God. These passages record sacrifices and rewards: a pile of stones constructed as an altar for sacrificing (Genesis 31:46, among others), a company of people brought together and blessed by God (Genesis 28:3), and the piles of animals brought by the Israelites to sacrifice (2 Chronicles 31:6), among others. Some passages also use "Haufe" to refer to punishment of those who have been disobedient to God's will: heaps of dead frogs following one of the plagues sent to Pharaoh (Exodus 8:1–10), the heads of the sons of kings (2 Kings 10:8), a people deceived by a false sense of strength (2 Chronicles 13:8). In each of these Old Testament examples, the word "Haufe" refers to discrete objects gathered by a higher power to honor the divinity.

In Luther's Bible the word "Haufe" traces a series of events in which God punishes willful disobedience and accepts and blesses sacrificial obedience. These biblical examples and Zinzendorf's hymn suggest why Zeisberger may have understood his community as living stones being shaped into a sacrificial altar. Luther uses one German word, "Haufen," to describe events that the RSV Bible renders with seven different terms: pile, company, crowd, horde, multitude, men of Israel, and bundle. The Hebrew text of these same Old Testament passages also uses a great variety of words, whereas Luther keeps using the word "Haufe." Although the theme of obedience and sacrifice can be traced through these verses in English and Hebrew, the language of these texts does not link them explicitly, as Luther's Bible does. This illuminates Zeisberger's repeated prayer that God would join more believers to them to serve as a reward for God's own suffering.

Of all the images for believers the Bible offers, Zeisberger repeatedly chooses an image that unites the sacrificial rewards and punishments of the Old Testament with the New Testament image of believers as living stones being formed into a spiritual house (1 Peter 2:5).[17] I have not yet determined whether Luther was the first to unify these Old Testament stories of reward and punishment through the use of the word "Haufe," or whether he borrowed this from an

---

17. "Like living stones, let yourselves be built into a spiritual house, to be a holy priesthood, to offer spiritual sacrifices acceptable to God through Jesus Christ" (NRSV).

earlier German translation. It is clear, however, that Zeisberger's understanding of himself and his community is shaped through Luther's language for sacrifice and rewards, perhaps called to his attention through Zinzendorf's theological language. This unifying function of the word "Haufe," and the deep conviction that God was the agent and Zeisberger and others in the community were being gathered rather than doing the gathering, is lost if the translator does not approach Zeisberger's usage through Luther's German Bible.

Zeisberger's usage of the word "Haufen" reveals to contemporary readers how Luther's biblical language shaped his personal and social identity. His documentation of explicit discussion of the word "Virginian" throughout the diaries also reveals how Zeisberger's contemporary Native Americans, British, and Americans understood the power of one word to reshape their identities. Individuals defined and redefined themselves and their situation in relation to the changing meaning of the word "Virginian." Whether an individual was considered a "Virginian" could be the difference between life and death in certain situations. Although most American readers would not pause to consider what Zeisberger meant by "Virginian" on a given page, a historian might see the word as a red flag; Zeisberger's use of the term reveals that the red flag was already up as he was writing the diaries.

The ambiguity about what a "Virginian" was had nothing to do with Virginia's geographical location; Zeisberger knew precisely where Virginia was on a map. "One *Delaware* Indian came here with a White man who was a prisoner of the *Wyandot*s. They were on their way to the *Fort*. He is a well-to-do man from *Virginia*, where his family lives. He was amazed to see our 3 *Settlement*s and so many Christian Indians and to see that we had maintained our position thus far in the war. He said this is not the work of men, but of God" (1775). In another entry, however, Zeisberger explicitly notes the changing meaning of the word "Virginian" and the significant political implications it carries:

> He told them that the *Virginians* (because all White people are now called this here) were not planning to come across the *Ohio* into Indian country unless they were forced to. They wanted to offer the *Nations* peace once more, but this would be the last time. If they accepted their message now and inclined their ears to suggestions of peace, they could be assured that they had nothing to fear from the *Virginians*, who would like to shake hands with them and live in peace with the *Nations*. Therefore the *Wyandot* disciplined their people in

the presence of the messengers and ordered them to stop carrying out further hostilities against the White people.[18]

The same diary entry then expands the understanding of a "Virginian" as a white man to include anyone who accepts white people and their ministers:

> They promised to come to *Goschgosching* and restore peace with the *Colonies*. May God allow this to happen. However, they offered little response to the message they had sent along about us White Brothers. They said only that people call them *Virginians* because they listened to them, believed what they said, and had *Minister*s living with them. They knew of no other reason for this and it could not be helped. (377–78)

Later in the diaries, a "Virginian" refers to any American: "Last night was the time when people said we were supposed to be attacked because we would not join the hostile Indians and flee with them, since it was now obvious enough that we were on the side of the *Virginians*, as the *Americans* are now being called" (478). Vague threats and promises issued against or on behalf of "Virginians" were often delivered by messengers who were not necessarily reliable, and they often left the recipient unclear about who the players in a given situation were. I do not mean to imply that there was a clear chronological development in the meaning of the word "Virginian." The meaning varied depending on where the speaker was located geographically and culturally relative to particular events of which another speaker might have no knowledge.

Marginalia to the English Translation

In *The Archaeology of Knowledge* Michel Foucault writes that each text constitutes an artifact "beyond its internal configuration and its autonomous form, [and that every text] is caught up in a system of references to other books, other texts, other sentences: it is a node within a network."[19] If we accept this claim, we can then consider how particular words within a text shape our critical inquiry as well as how they express or reflect a world that preceded the text. Like a parody,

---

18. David Zeisberger, *The Moravian Mission Diaries of David Zeisberger, 1772–1781*, ed. Herman Wellenreuther and Carola Wessel, trans. Julie Tomberlin Weber (University Park.: Pennsylvania State University Press, 2005), 377 (hereafter cited parenthetically in the text by page number).

19. Trans. A. M. Sheridan Smith (New York: Pantheon Books, 1972), 23.

revision, or interpretation of any text, a translation compels the reader to confront the language of a text and to focus on the linguistic ambiguities that in fact exist within every language and within every text. Translating David Zeisberger's diaries into English provokes the translator to consult other discourses about biblical translation, Moravian history and faith, and Native American studies. Rather than simply borrow words and meanings from these discourses, however, the translator may stumble upon ambiguities within those discourses and bring the various discourses together.

The interdisciplinary conference and the publication of this volume of essays exemplify the critical marginalia that Goethe considered the true fruit of the translation process. The quality of this discourse, according to Goethe, is the best indicator of how successful the translation process has been. In other essays in this volume, scholars have discussed the questions they explored in and through Zeisberger's diaries: "What is a Delaware?" "What is an Iroquois?" "What was the relationship between various Native American groups and Moravian missions?" At the conference, research questions designed to explore specific intercultural relationships among Europeans and First Peoples of North America provoked broader questions about the assumptions and values of scholars from various contemporary cultures and disciplines.

One scholar at the conference questioned the wisdom of spending scarce resources on translating a diary that had been translated in the nineteenth century. This question hearkens back to Gogol's image of a translation as a windowpane, and it assumes that a modern translation is justified only if the previous one was inadequate. Retranslation, however, has a long and respected tradition in Germany in particular, which reflects Goethe's conviction that the process of translation provokes discourse more valuable than the translated text itself.[20]

Another scholar questioned the value of publishing what some scholars consider yet one more example of the "European perspective" on "the Native American experience." But Zeisberger does not refer to himself as a European, and so conference participants were challenged to consider their own use of the term "European" as carefully as we have considered Zeisberger's use of the terms "Haufen" and "Virginian." Zeisberger uses the word "European" only once in these diaries, in reference to a packet of letters that had arrived from Europe. Zeisberger's diaries rarely identify people in relation to Europe, Germany, or the American colonies, except in the few references to "Virginians." Nor did

---

20. Antoine Berman discusses the twentieth-century German "will to reopen access" to texts in *Experience of the Foreign*. German authors retranslated many classic texts that had been "obscured by too much clarity" in some translations and "exhausted by too much radiance" in others (176).

Zeisberger identify himself primarily as a Moravian Brother, and he could hardly be upheld as a "typical Moravian" missionary. He served for years as an unmarried missionary, which was quite unusual. He was a "professionally educated missionary" who did not learn a trade, equally unusual among Moravians, who generally expected missionaries to support themselves. Zeisberger did not refer to himself as European, or German, or white, or American.

He had lived as a religious refugee with his natural parents in Europe; after being adopted into a Native American family as an adult he again lived as a religious refugee. He did not view himself as a rolling stone, or as a cornerstone, but as part of a collection of stones gathered for a greater purpose. This identity was not primarily one of race or birthplace, but of faith. Contemporary scholars should pay attention to his self-proclaimed identity as part of a pile of living stones, a "Haufen," collected by God as a reward for God's suffering.

The final entry of Zeisberger's diary reveals that, although he attempted to transmit meanings across cultures, he embraced the ambiguity of conflicting or unreliable messages from others as a challenge to act in the knowledge of the faith he embraced rather than in the certainty of a message he might deem clear and reliable. Zeisberger wrote:

> The 25th. . . . Brother *Sensemann* led the Congregational Service about the Watchword, Lo, this is our God; we have waited for him, and He will help us. He will indeed do this now, though things once again do not look very *favorable* in Indian country.
>
> Some warriors came here. We learned from them that many parties of warriors have gone into the White people's *Settlements*. They were on their way to the *Fort* and said that there are already many of them there, and the road to *Pittsburgh* is thus not very safe. Despite this, Brother *David* decided to go on with his journey there. (553)

Rather than wait for a human messenger to deliver a verifiable message, David Zeisberger reinterpreted his life to fit the idiom of Luther's Bible.

I began this essay with Gogol's image of an ideal translation as a transparent window. I conclude with a *Moscow Times* review of a 2004 English translation of Gogol's *Dead Souls*. The reviewer regrets that the translation lacks such transparency, and that Gogol's fans will have to continue waiting for a translation that actually "captures" Gogol.[21] Goethe, I believe, would respond that readers

---

21. Timothy Westphalen, "A Question of Style: Richard Pevear and Larissa Volokhonsky Translate Gogol," *Moscow Times,* December 31, 2004, http://context.themoscowtimes.com/story. "Gogol

waiting for such trophies are wasting their time; they would do better to pick up the translations they have and reexamine what the "imperfections" reveal about their own assumptions and interpretations. Luther might simply say they should try their own.[22] In the conclusion of his book *The Experience of the Foreign*, Antoine Berman heeds their advice and proposes a new interdisciplinary approach to translation that recognizes it as a model for intercultural communications, as the very substance of human knowledge, and as an object of reflection, in addition to its function as a limited tool for accessing information or meaning in a foreign text.[23]

This translation of Zeisberger's diaries may delight or disappoint historians seeking answers to particular questions; it may shed light on or obscure the specific details of Moravian missions and of the Delaware people. But the translation and publication of Zeisberger's diaries has already united a small group of German and American scholars from a variety of academic disciplines by engaging us in dialogue about how we use particular words, what texts are worth translating, and what questions are worth asking. Sadly, one of the key voices in the discourse surrounding David Zeisberger's diaries has already become difficult to distinguish, although it is certainly not lost. Carola Wessel passionately guided work on this project for years, but her untimely death has merged her personal voice into the collective voice of "the editors" in this translation. I would like to express my sorrow that all of our communication took place by e-mail, and I never had the honor of talking with her personally about the many people, places, and ideas that occupied so much of her life.

---

has eluded capture in English to this day, with the hunt for his 1842 novel, 'Dead Souls,' invariably resulting in the lifeless carcass of the text, rather than the living, panting animal, itself. The laughter that rings out like a bell in Russian is inevitably reduced in translation to garbled mumbling."

22. In his public debate with the Lutheran pastor J. M. Goeze of Hamburg, published in eleven pamphlets between April and October 1778, Gotthold Ephraim von Lessing redefines the identity of a "true Lutheran" in a way that not only excludes Goeze himself from the fold but also traces Lessing's own subjective approach to the truth to his Lutheran roots: "Der wahre Lutheraner will nicht bei Luthers Schriften, er will bei Luthers Geiste geschützt sein; und Luthers Geist erfodert schlechterdings, daß man keinen Menschen, in der Erkenntnis der Wahrheit nach seinem eigenen Gutdünken fortzugehen, hindern muß. Aber man hindert alle daran, wenn man auch nur Einem verbieten will, seinen Fortgang in der Erkenntnis andern mitzuteilen. Denn ohne diese Mitteilung im Einzeln, ist kein Fortgang im Ganzen möglich." Gotthold Ephraim von Lessing, *Werke*, ed. Karl Eible and Herbert G. Göpfert, 8 vols. (Munich: Hanser Verlag, 1970–79), 8:161–62. Lessing's definition of a true Lutheran upholds Luther as a champion of the individual right to pursue the truth. It also boldly claims that the progress of society depends on each individual's freedom to disseminate the results of his search.

23. Antoine Berman, *Experience of the Foreign*, 54.

INDEX

aboriginal peoples. *See* Native Americans
Academy of Sciences (Russia), 23
acculturation: French missionaries and concept of, 68–76; impossiblity for Native Americans of, xx; music as tool for, 127–42
Acosta, José de, 21
"Age of Revolutions," historical references to, 77–78
Ainslie, George Robert, 93–94
alcohol addiction of Native Americans: Catholic missionaries' concern over, 107–14; Moravian missionaries' struggle with, 5, 118–24
Alden, Timothy, 189
Algonquian tribes: colonial dispossession of, 153; Moravians and, 145; Munsee nation and, 147–52
Allemewi (Munsee clan elder), 160
Alsted, Johann, 130
Anindamonwoágan (Munsee leader), 158–59
Anouaren, Joseph Teorogaron (Mohawk chief), 89
anthropological research, on acculturation, 73
apartheid, Western view of Amerindians and concepts of, 68–69
apodemic literature, ethnography and influence of, 20
Apostles, mission tradition and influence of, 72–76
Arab scholarship, ethnography and influence of, 20
Archaeology of Knowledge, The, 204–5
Argenti, Giovanni Giuseppe Vincenzo, 88
Asselin, Charles-Joseph, 92–93
Audisio, Gabriel, 72n.10
Augustin, Stefan, 30
authority, missionaries' delegation to Native Americans of, 99–100, 105–14
Axtell, James, 15, 99

Badin, Étienne-Thédore, 94
Bailly de Messein, Charles-François, 91
ball-play (Cherokee sport), 120–21
baptisms: by Catholic missionaries, 81–82, 84–85; gender differences in rates of, 170n.9, 171–74; of Munsees, 154–55, 157, 160. *See also* conversion of Native Americans

Barnes, Carol, 55
Belleau, Ferdinand, 94
Beninga, Anna, 3, 15
Berman, Antoine, 205n.20, 207
Beschefer, Thierre, 97
Beschreibung und Naturgeschichte von Grönland, 25
Bethlehem, Moravian missionary in, 115–24, 153–55
Biard, Pierre, 98n.4
Bible: English translations of, 198; Goethe's translation of, 195–98, 205; Luther's translation of, 198, 202–3, 207
Bigot, Jacques, 100–101, 103–14
Bigot, Vincent, 101, 103–4
Bilodeau, Christopher, xxii, 97–114
Black Robe, 67
Blanchard, David, 15–16
bookkeeping, ethnography and influence of, 19–20
Bossart, Johann Jakob, 25–26
Bourdieu, Pierre, 103n.15, 106n.16
Brackenridge, Henry, 142
Bretennière, Charles, 94
Briand, Jean-Olivier, 78, 82–83, 91
British colonists: Catholic missionaries and, 78–79, 90–95; Delaware Nation and, 168; Dunmore's war and, 6–7; Moravians and, 8–11; Munsee nation and, 147–52, 156, 158–59
Broadhead, Daniel, 11
Brown, Kathleen, 165
Buckagahitas, 125
Buffalo Creek, Haudenosaunee perspectives on, 175–92
Bulletin of the Archaeological Society of New Jersey, 49
Burke, Edmund (Bishop), 87, 93–94
Burnaby, Andrew, 87

Campanius, Johan, xix–xx
Canada, Catholic missions to aboriginal peoples in, 77–95
Captivetown settlement, 12–13
Capuchin missions, in North America, 79–81
Carroll, John, 79–80
Carver, Jonathan, 29, 128

Cass, Lewis, 23; Delaware succession dispute and, 39–42
Catholic Church: Canadian missions of, 78–95; French missionaries and, 71; Holy See and North American nations, 77–95; Native American youth as priests in, 89; Wabanaki view of, 97–98, 102–14
Catholic missionaries: allowances paid for work by, 91–92; attitudes toward aboriginal peoples of, 85–95; cultural exchanges with Native Americans, 67–76; delegation of authority to Wabanakis by, 103–14; distance from Roman hierarchy of, xxii; ethnographic descriptions of, xii; ethnohistory of, 70–76; Native American exchanges with, x, xvii–xviii; Wabanaki and, 97–98
Cayuga Nation: land losses of, 187–88; Munsees and, 151, 162
Chafe, Wallace L., 186
Chelloway, Job, 173
Cherokee Nation, Moravian mission work among, xxii–xxiii, 119n.16, 120–24
Chippewa Nation: Catholicism and, 92; clan structure in, 150; Munsees and, 162
Christianity: conversion of Native Americans to, xx, 77–95; government policy toward Native Americans and, 184–88; Haudenosaunee spiritual crisis in context of, 190–92; mission tradition in, 71–76; music as bridge to, 127–42; Native American culture in context of, xv–xvi; validity of Native American conversions to, 15–16. *See also* conversion of Native Americans
Church of England, Native American cultures and, xviii
"civilization" program for Native Americans, Jefferson's proposal for, 181–82
clan structure, in Native American tribes, 147–52
Clement VIII (Pope), 76
Clement XIII (Pope), 82
Codignola, Luca, xx, 77–95
Comenius, Jan, 130
Conner, Richard, 40n.21, 53
Conner, William, 40–42
conversion of Native Americans, xx, 15–16; Catholic missionaries' efforts for, 77–95; Munsee resistance to, 154–55, 162–64; music and syncretic approach to, 133; Wabanaki conversion of, 101–14
Cook, James, 30
Cooper, James Fennimore, 145
Cornstalk (Shawnee chief), 9, 35n.9

Cosmotraphices, ethnography and influence of, 20
Council of Trent, 71, 93
Cranz, David, 19, 24–25, 28, 30
Crews, Daniel, 197
Croghan, George, 32
cross-cousin marriages of Delaware, 63
Crow Nation, kinship structure of, 54–55
culture of consent, Delaware Nation and, 31–48
Custaloga (Munsee leader), 156, 158; negotiations by, 159

Dahlonega, Georgia, gold in, 119n.16
dance, importance in Native American culture of, 127–28, 134–42
Danckaerts, Jasper, 56–57
Dead Souls, 206–7
Dean, Nora Thompson, 149
De Andreis, Felice, 88
DeFoe, Marvin, 148n.12
De-hae-hiyawa-kho (Earth Grasper), 186
DeKay, Edward, 59
Delaunay, J., 88–89
Delaware Indians: A History, 44
Delaware Nation: American massacre of, 15–16; culture of consent in, 31–48; descent principles of, 55–56; as endangered culture, 145; family households in, 56–57; Glikhikan as leader of, 1–16; head chiefs of, xxi; internal structure of, 43n.32, 45–48; kinship system of, 2, 53–55; lineages within, 57–59; location of, xiv; Moravians and, 5–16; Munsees and, 148–53; music in, 133–42; Muskingum Valley Great Council of, 159–61; naming practices of, 52–53; phratries of, 59–60; political alliances of, 168; social control in, 62–63; sociopolitical organization in, 49–63; song as cultural mediator in, 125–26; succession debates and chiefs of, 32–48; towns and tribes of, 60–61; Wolf phratry in, 32–34, 59–60, 150; women of, xxiii, 165–74; Zeisberger's observations concerning, 31–48
Dellawaerisches Gesang-Büchlein, 134–35
De Peyster, Arent, 12
Descartes, René, 76n.15
Deslandres, Dominique, xxii, 67–76
diaries: ethnography and importance of, 19–20; of French Catholic missionaries, 67; Springplace diary, 116–24. *See also* missionary narratives
Discalced Carmelites, 80
dogiques (catechists), Native American hierarchy of, 103–5

dream songs, cultural importance of, 128
Dubourg, Louis-Guillaume-Valentin, 88
Duche, Joseph, 135
Dugnani, Antonio, 80

Edict of Nantes, 76
Edmunds, David, xxi, 1–16
education, Haudenosaunee views on, 179–80, 183–84
Egede, Hans, 25
Eliot, John, 127, 131
Elliott, Matthew, 9–12
Émery, Jacques-André d', 87
endangered Native American cultures, missionary descriptions of, 145, 154
Enlightenment philosophy, ethnography and, 23–24
eponyms, tribal names and use of, 148
Erie Canal, Native American land losses and, 185
Ernestus, John Gottlieb, 120n.18
Esopus Wars, 147
Ethnography, Delaware Nation sociopolitical organizations, 49–63
ethnography: definitions of, ix–x; Delaware succession accounts and, 42–48; Moravian missionaries and development of, 19–30; Zeisberger's observations on Delaware as, 31–48
ethnohistory, Munsee nation politics and, 147–52, 162–64
ethnology, ethnography and, 23–24
Ettwein, John, 5
European religious leaders: ethnographic research of Native Americans by, xiii–xiv; Zeisberger's identity as separate from, 205–6
Evans-Pritchard, Edward E., 50
Experience of the Foreign, The, 207

faith, inconvertibility of, for French missionaries, 72–76
family structures, Delaware Nation, 56–57
Farmer's Brother (Seneca leader), 175, 179
Fauvel, Jean-Baptiste-François, 88–89
Feest, Christian, xxi, 19–30
Fontana, Francesco, 87–88
Fort Laurens, 10
Fort Stanwix Treaty, 156–57
Foucault, Michel, 204–5
Fowler, David, 131
Franciscan order, Native American exchanges with, xvii–xviii
French and Indian War, 155

Gambold, Anna Rosina Kliest, 116, 121–22
Gambold missionaries, xxii–xxiii; of Bethlehem and Salem, 115–24; Springplace diary of, 116–24
game-playing: in Cherokee culture, 120–21; in Delaware culture, 133–42
Gatterer, Johann Christoph, 24
Gekelemukpechünk, 127
Gelelemind (Delaware leader), 9; kinship terms used by, 54–55; Netawatwees' selection of, 62–63; succession issue and, 33–35, 37–39, 47
Gendaskund (Munsee leader), 9
gender issues: Cherokee intermarriage patterns and, 121–22; Moravian and Native American relations and, xxiii. *See also* women
geography, ethnographic research and role of, xiii–xiiii
Geschichte der Mission der evangelischen Brüder auf den caraibischen Inseln S. Thomas, S. Croix und S. Jan, 19, 25
Geschichte der Mission der evangelischen Brüder unter den Indianern in Nordamerika, 19, 26
Gibault, Pierre, 83, 85–86
Girty, Simon, 9–10
Glikhikan, Isaac, xxi; baptism of, 5; betrayal of, 14–16; conversion to Christianity of, 4, 158; family of, 3–4; military and leadership qualities of, 3–4; negotiations by, 159, 161; validity of conversion experience by, 15–16; Zeisberger's encounters with, 1–16
Gnadenhütten settlement, 5, 8, 10–11, 14
Goethe, Johann Wolfgang von, 195–98, 205–7
Goeze, J. M., 207n.22
Gogol, Nikolai, 195, 205–7
Goschachgünk settlement, 6–8, 10–11, 157; Delaware succession dispute and relations at, 38–39
government policies toward Native Americans, land losses as result of, 184–88
"gradual compliance" policy, Haudenosaunee-missionary relations and, 177–84
Granger, Erastus, 185
"Great Council" of Delaware People, 41–42
Greenland, Moravian mission to, 24–25
Greer, Allan, xii–xiii, xvi
Grey Eyes (Delaware chief), 32
Grumet, Robert S., 49–63
Guswenta (Two Row Wampum), "gradual compliance" policy and, 177–84
Gutkigamen, 56

Haidt, Valentine, 130
Half-King (Wyandot leader), 8, 11–13
Hamilton, Henry, 7–10
Handsome Lake (Goskukkewaunau Konnedieyu), 189
Hankins, Jean, 132
Harrington, Mark Raymond, 58–59
Haudenosaunee Nation: "Christian-Pagan split" in, 176–77; "gradual compliance" policy of, 177–84; land losses by, 184–88; location of, xiv; missionary relations with, 175–92; Munsees and, 151, 153–56; Presbyterian missionaries and, xxiii; spiritual crisis of, 189–92; thanksgiving principles and rituals of, 185–87; Treaty of Big Tree and, 178–79
"Haufe," translation in Zeisberger's diaries of, 200–204
Hauptman, Laurence, 185
Heckewelder, John Gottlieb Ernestus, 7, 10–12, 14–16, 42–48; Delaware Nation sociopolitical organizations and, 49–50; Moravian music and, 132–33, 141; observations on Munsee nation by, 145, 148–49, 161
"Heckewelder Error," Delaware Nation sociopolitical organizations and, 49–50
Herodotus, ethnography and influence of, 20
Herrnhuter Wörterbuch, 197
Hewitt, J. N. B., 186
Heyrman, Christine, xv
historia genre, ethnography and, 19–20
Historia natural y moral de las Indias, 21
historicity, Delaware succession accounts and, 42–48
Historie von Grönland, 24–25, 28
historiography: Munsee nation politics and, 147–52; Western acculturation concepts in, 67–68, 74–76; Western view of Amerindians and, 68–69
"History, Manners, and Customs of the Indian Nations," 49–50
History of Curiosity, 20
History of the Northern American Indians, 19, 31, 35–48; Delaware Nation sociopolitical organizations in, 49–63
Hoffer, Peter, 126
Holland Land Company, 178n.9, 184–85
Holmes, Elkanah, 175–77, 179–80
Holy See of Catholic Church, conversion of Native Americans and, 77–95
Hopocan (Delaware chief), 32, 60
Hubert, Jean-François, 79
Hulbert, Archer Butler, 42

humanism, ethnography and influence of, 20
Humboldt, Wilhelm von, 196
Hunter, William A., 49
Hus, Jan, 115
Hutchinson, Thomas, 91
Hyde, Jabez, 183–92

Indian Removal Bill, 119n.16
Indians' Helpers' Conference, 167–68
Inglesi, Angelo, 88
Iroquois Confederation: Fort Stanwix Treaty and, 156; location of, xiv

Jackson, Andrew, 119n.16
Jansenism, 72n.10
Jefferson, Thomas, 181–82
Jennings, Francis, 15
Jesuit Relations, xii
Jesuits: Canadian missions of, 78–82, 84–85; cultural exchanges with Native Americans and, 67–76; French-speaking Roman Catholics and, xii–xiii; Haudenosaunee and, 175–76; Wabanaki missions of, 97–114
Johnson, William, 32, 156
Johnston, Darlene, 147–48
Johnston, John, 179n.11
Johnston, William, 179n.11

Kaiser, Siegrun, 145–64
Kakwah (Turkey leader), 158
Kamchatka expedition, 23
Kansas, Munsee settlement in, 163–64
Key into the Language of America, 22
Kieft War, 147
Kiminitchagan, Augustin (Native American priest), 89–90
King James Bible, 198
King Philip's War, 97
kinship relations: in Delaware Nation, 53–55; in Moravian communities, 172–74; in Native American culture; Sulpician manuscript on, xiii; of Wabanakis, 102–14
Kirkland, Samuel, 131, 176
Kishentsi (Hardman), 6
Kohlmann, Anthony, 84
Koychezetel (Cherokee chief), 121
Kraft, Herbert C., 42–45

La Barre, Joseph-Antoine Le Febvre de, 97, 108–10
Lafitau, Joseph François, 22–23, 29, 31
Lahontan, Baron de, 21
La Mahotière, Jean de (Oneida leader), 79–80

land cessions by Native Americans, government policity and Christianity and, 184–88
language of Native Americans: Delaware kinship terms and, 53–55; European studies of, xvii; music translations into, 134–35; translation and editorial issues with, 195–207
Law, Andrew, 135
Leatherstocking Tales, 145
Lefèbvre de Cheverus, Jean-Louis-Anne-Madelain, 79–80
Le Jeune, Paul, 70, 86, 127
Lenni Lenape: internal subdivisions within, 44–48; location of, xiv; Moravian histories of, 42–43; Swedish Lutherans and, xviii–xix
Leo XII (Pope), 89, 94
Lessing, Gotthold Ephraim von, 195, 207n.22
Le Tonnelier de Coulonge, Jean-Louis-Victor, 79–80
Lichtenau settlement, 7–8, 10–11
Little Billy (Haudenosaunee leader), 189
liturgical rituals: as bridge to Native American culture, xxii; female imagery in, 166; music and song in, 129–42; Wabanaki interest in, 97–114
Logan, James, 55
Long, John, 127
Loosungen (Moravian song), 130
Lord Dunmore's War, 6–7; Delaware Nation negotiations during, 160
Loskiel, Georg Heinrich, 19, 26–27, 29
Luther, Martin, translation of Bible by, 195, 198, 202–3, 207
Lutheran Church, 207n.22

Maccatebinessi (Maccodabinasse), William (Native American Catholic priest), 89–90
Máchtapasseèk (poison), 156
Mack, Anna, 167
Mack, John Martin, 118
MacLeod, William Christie, 55
Mahican Nation: as endangered culture, 145, 154; intertribal villages with Munsee, 159; Wolf phratry of, 150–51; women of, xxiii, 165–74
Mancall, Peter C., 107
Manhattan Confederacy, 146–47
manitous (spirits), 98
Map of Virginia, With a Description of the Countrey, the Commodities, People, Government and Religion, 21
Marchand, Jean-Baptiste, 85
Mariauchau d'Esgly, Louis-Philippe, 78

marriage: Cherokee intermarriage patterns, 121–22; cross-cousin marriages of Delaware, 63; mixed marriages, Catholic missionaries performance of, 81–85; phratry system of Delaware and, 60; Zeisberger's comments on, 167–68
Martin, John, 14, 137–38
materialism, religion and, 70
Matignon, François-Antoine, 79–80
matrilineal structures of Native American nations, 52; descent principles and, 55–56; family households and, 56–57; kinship terms and, 54; lineages and, 57–59; Munsee practices, 154–55
McClinton, Rowena, xxii–xxiii, 115–24
McClure, David, 132
McKee, Alexander, 9–10
McNally, Michael, 126, 128
McSweeney, Michael, 93
Membertou, 102n.13
Merritt, Jane T., 43n.32, 132, 165–74
Meulles, Jacques de, 97
Meurin, Sébastien-Louis, 82–83
Meyer, Matthias, 26
Michael, Hendrick, 157
Mi'kmaq Nation, 101
Mingo Nation, 7–8; Delaware allegiance to, 168
missionary narratives: of Catholic missionaries, 67, 70–76; Haudenosaunee spiritual crisis described in, 190–92; as literary source, 145; Munsee cultural resistance in, 146; Native American women in, 166–74
Moeurs des sauvages ameriquains, comparées aux moeurs des premiers temps, 22–23
Mohawk Nation: Haudenosaunee and, 188; land losses of, 180; Wabanakis and, 97–98
Monroe, James, 187
Montagnais Nation, 70
Morain, Jean, 101
Moravian Meanings, 197
Moravian missionaries: attacks on settlements of, 13–16; in Bethlehem and Salem, 115–24; Delaware succession disputes and, 33–48; ethnographic research and, 19–30; gender issues in, 165–74; Glikhikan's relations with, 1–16; governmental system of, 116n.4; Haudenosaunee Nation and, 175–92; historical roots of, xi; Munsee Nation and, 9–10, 145–64; Native American relations with, x–xii, 168–74; Native American women and, 168–74; song as cultural mediator for, 125, 129–42; women's role as, 167–74

Moravian Mission Diaries (Zeisberger): ambiguous terms in, 200–204; Bethlehem and Salem settlements in, 116–24; ethnographic observations in, 51–52; translation and editorial issues with, 195–207
Morgan, Lewis Henry, 53–54; Delaware lineages and, 58–59
Mt. Pleasant, Alyssa, 175–92
Mühlenberg, Henry (Heinrich Melchior), 136–37
Müller, Gerhard Friedrich, 23
Munsee Nation, xxiii; cultural resistance by, 146; deterioration of, 162–64; disease and starvation among, 152–55; exile of, 61, 152–55; Glikhikan as leader of, 1–16, 7; kinship terms of, 54; Mahican intertribal villages with, 159; Moravian interaction with, 9–10, 145, 152–64; Ohio Valley missions and, 157–64; political function of phratries in, 146–52; rise and fall of Papunhank tribe, 155–57; sociopolitical organization of, 50–51
Murdock, George Peter, 57, 148
music in Native American culture, 125–42
Myatakawkwha (Munsee leader), 158

naming practices: of Moravian missionaries, 52–53; Munsee nation and, 147–48
nationalism, Moravian Church and, 116n.3
Native Americans: Catholic Holy See and conversion of, 77–95; Christianity as viewed by, xvi–xvii; conversions of, 15–16; French missionary cultural exchanges with, 67–76; gender issues among, 165–74; impressions and exchanges with Europeans settlers, xii; internal dynamics of groups of, xxi; Moravian interactions with, 116–24; song as cultural mediator for, 125–42. *See also* phratry system; *specific Native American nations*
naturalists, ethnography and, 24–25
neolocality, Delaware social order and, 51–52
Netawatwees (chief), 5–7; kinship structure of, 54–56; phratry system and, 60; social control exercised by, 62–63; succession issue following death of, 32–35, 47; widow of, 170
Newallike (Munsee leader), 9, 161
New Light missions, music in, 131
New-York Missionary Society, 175–76, 183–84, 190–92
Nimham (Oping leader), 59
Nimho (Shawnee leader), 35n.9
noble savage myth, Catholic missionaries dismissal of, 85n.31

Nouveaux Voyages, 21
Nutimus (Delaware chief), 55–56

Occom, Samsom, 131
Ogden, David, 184, 187
Ogden Land Company, 184
Oldendorp, Christian Georg Andreas, 19, 25–26, 30
Oneida Nation: French missionaries and, 79–80; land losses of, 180
Oniem (Wolf spiritualist), 156
Onondaga Nation, land losses of, 187–88
Oping Turkey tribe, 58–59
Osage nation, Catholic missionaries and, 89
Other, French missionaries' concept of, 67–68, 71–76
Ottawa Nation, Catholicism and, 92

Pachgantshihlas (Delaware chief), 11
Packanke (Munsee chief), 1, 3–4, 60
Papunhank (Munsee leader), 149, 150n.23, 155–57, 159, 162
Parrish, Jasper, 187
Passamaquoddy nation, French missionaries and, 79
Paul, Vincent de, 72n.10
Peach War, 147
Pelewiechünk, 161
Penobscot nation, French missionaries and, 79
Peucker, Paul, 197
phratry system: colonialism and, 162–64; of Delaware, 59–60; of Munsees, 146–52; totemic identity and, 148–52
Pietists, Munsee nation contact with, 145, 156
Pipe (Captain) (Delaware chief), 9, 11–13, 32, 60, 125, 168; Delaware succession dispute and, 39–42; Pontiac's Rebellion and, 156
Pirouakki (Wabanaki leader), 101–2
Pius VI (Pope), 79–80
Pius VIII (Pope), 77
Plessis, Joseph-Octave, 88, 92–93
policing activities of Wabanaki missions, 104–14
political organization among Native Americans, xiv; phratry system and, 146–52
polygyny, Moravian prohibitions against, 51–52
Pomoacan (Wyandot leader), 8, 12–13. *See* Half-King
Pontiac (Chief), 85
Pontiac's Rebellion, 2; Catholic missionaries and, 80–81; Munsee Nation and, 155–56
Post, Christopher Frederick, 2

Potawatomi Nations, Catholicism and, 92
Preface to the Old Testament, 198
primogeniture, Delaware descent principles and, 56
Printz, Johan, xix
Proceedings of the English Colony, 21
Propagation de la Foi, 87–88
Protestant Churches: importance of music in, 131; mission work of, 93–95
Provencher, Joseph-Norbert, 84–85, 94
Pueblo Revolt of 1680, xvii

Quakers, Munsee negotiations with, 155
Québec, aboriginal mission activities in, 78
questionnaires, origins of ethnography and, 23–24

race, historical definitions of, ix–x
Rath, Richard, 126
Rauch, Heinrich, 153
reciprocity, Wabanaki concept of, 98, 102
Red Jacket (Seneca leader), 175–84, 189, 191–92
Reichel, Johann Friedrich, 26
religious beliefs and practices: cultural capital and, 103n.15; historiography and, 68–70; Otherness and, 74–76
Revolutionary War: Munsee survival during, 160–62; Native American women and, 166–74
Richard, Gabriel, 94
Richter, Daniel, xxiv, 67
River Indian Confederacy, 147, 151
Roeber, A. G., xiv–xxiv
Romig, Joseph, 163–64
Rouchouze, Étienne, 84
Royal Society of London, questionnaires of, 23
Rush, Benjamin, 139
Russian Orthodox Christians, Native American culture and language studied by, xvii

Saami people (Lapland), xix
Sabathy-Judd, Linda, 53
Sacred Congregation de Propaganda de Fide, 87–88
Salem settlement, 10; Cherokee land negotiations, 120n.17; of Moravian missionaries, 115–24
Salisbury, Neal, 15
Sassoonan (Delaware leader), 60
Sayre, Gordeon, 20–21
Schlözer, August Ludwig, 24
Schmick, Johanna, 167
Schönbrunn settlement, 5–8, 10
Schoolcraft, Henry Rowe, 23–24, 127
Schutt, Amy, 171
Schwarze, William Nathaniel, 42
scientia genre, ethnography and, 19–20
Second Great Awakening movement, 176
Selekis, Benjamin, 157
Séminaire de Québec, missions of, 80
"Sendbrief vom Dolmetschen," 198
Seneca Mission Church, 192
Seneca Nation, 32; land losses of, 179–80, 184–88; missionaries and, 158–59, 175–76; Munsees and, 151–52, 162; Presbyterian missionaries and, xxiii; thanksgiving principles and rituals of, 185–87
Seneca Thanksgiving Rituals, 186
Sensbach, Jon, xv
Sergeant, John, 132
Seven Years' War: Canadian Catholic missionaries and, 77–78, 81; Native American migrations following, 168
shamanism, Swedish missionary targeting of, xix
Shawnee Nation: Delaware allegiance to, 168; hostility to Moravians of, 5–9, 12–13; musical culture in, 140–42
Shoemaker, Nancy, 16
Six Indian Nations, 32; clan allegiance to, 168; Munsee supported by, 153
Smith, John, 21, 127
social control, in Delaware Nation, 62–63
Society for Propagating the Gospel, 164
sociopolitical organization, ethnographies of Delaware nation and, 49–63
song, as cultural mediator, 125–42
Spangenberg, August Gottlieb, 118n.12, 166
Spangenberg, Maria, 167
Speck, Frank G., 55
Spicer, Edward H., 50
Spiritan missionaries, 80–81
spouse service, in Delaware nation, 52
Squash Cutter (Munsee leader), 156
Squaw Campaign, 9, 161, 172–73
Stagl, Justin, 20
statistical studies, ethnography and influence of, 20
stereotypes of Native Americans: Catholic missionaries use of, 86–89; Moravian perceptions based on, 118n.12
Stonor, Christopher (Kit), 81
Strachey, William, 127
Strong, James, 185n.28

INDEX

Sullivan Campaign, 161
Sulpician missions, in Canada, 79, 87–88, 94
Swedish Lutherans, Native Americans and, xviii–xix

Tacitus, ethnography and influence of, 20
Tecamthi, 152
Tekakwitha, Kateri (Mohawk saint), xii–xiii, 89
Tenskwatawa, 152
Tetapachksit, 63, 152
textual sources, overview of, xxi
thanksgiving principles and rituals, 185–87
Thirty Years' War, xi, 115
Tooker, Elisabeth, 148
totemic identity, historiography and, 148
translation of Zeisberger's diaries, interpretations of, 195–207
travel literature, ethnography and influence of, 20–30
Travels Through the Interior Parts of North America, 29
Treaty of Big Tree, 178–79, 184–85
Treaty of Easton, 155
Treaty of Fort Meigs, 92
Treaty of Paris (1763), 90
Tridentine missions, 68
Trigger, Bruce G., 69
Trowbridge, Charles C., 50
Troy, John Thomas, 88
Turkey phratry, 59–60; Delaware internal structure and, 43n.32, 168; Delaware succession dispute and, 34–35; diplomatic negotiations by, 158–64; lineages in, 58–59; Munsee nation and, 148, 150–52, 155, 162–64
Turtle phratry, 59–60; Delaware Nation structure and, 42n.43, 168; Delaware succession dispute and, 33–35; Munsee nation and, 159–60, 162–64
Twenty Canoes (Haudenosaunee leader), 189
Tyger (Cherokee leader), 121–23

Unilachtego, exile and emergence of, 61
United States Middle Department for Indian Affairs, 161
Unity of the Brethren, xi; Bethlehem and Salem settlements of, 115–24; Elders' Conference of, 26–27; ethnographic research of, 19, 26–30; history of, 115n.3. *See also* Moravian missionaries
Universal-Lexikon, 197
Urban College, 89, 90n.45

van der Donck, Adriaen, 56–57
Vaultier, Jacques, 100–102
"Virginian," Zeisberger's concept of, 203–4

Wabanaki Nation: Catholic missionaries and, 97–114; policing in missions of, 104–14; succession hierarchy in, 112n.22
Walking Purchase Treaty, 153, 155
Wallace, Anthony F. C., 42–44, 55–56
Walter, Thomas, 135
Wangomen (shaman), 2–3, 157–59
Washington, George, 87, 181
Weber, Julie Tomberlin, xxiii–xxiv, 195–207
Weiser, Conrad, 118, 136–37
Welapachtschiechen, 34, 63, 150n.23, 169
Wellenreuther, Hermann, xxi, 31–48; on Moravian music, 130
Weslager, C. A., 40n.21, 42–44
Wessel, Carola, ix, 195, 207
West, John, 94
Western historic tradition, acculturation concepts in, 67–68, 74–76
Wheelock, Eleazar, 131
Whitaker, Nathaniel, 131
White, Richard, xiii–xiv, 117
White Eyes (Delaware leader): diplomatic negotiations by, 160; Moravians and, 6–7, 9–10, 168; succession dispute and, 33–35, 47; in Turkey phratry, 150n.23
widows (Native American) in missionary colonies, 168–74
Williams, Roger, 22
Williamson, David, 14
witchcraft, Munsee concept of, 145–57, 159
Wolf phratry, 32–34, 59–60; Delaware internal structure and, 43n.32, 168; diplomatic negotiations by, 158–64; Munsee political structure and, 147–52, 154–57, 162–64
women: in Native American cultures, xxiii, 165–74; role in Wabanaki missions of, 105–14
Woodward, Walter, xxii–xxiii, 125–42
Wyandot Nation: Delaware Nation and, 168; Dunmore's War and, 6–7; Moravians and, 8, 10–13; Munsees and, 161

Young King (Haudenosaunee leader), 185n.28, 189

Zeisberger, David, xi, xx–xxi, xxiii–xxiv; adoption by Munsee of, 161, 206; Bethlehem and Salem missions and, 115–24; Broadhead and, 11; on Delaware Nation sociopolitical organizations, 49–63;

Delaware succession issue in writings of, 32–48; ethnographic research and writings of, 19, 24–30; Glikhikan and, 1–16; Munsee relations with, 145–46, 152, 157–64; on music as mediator, 126; Native American women in journals of, 166–74; observations on Delaware by, 31–48; Ohio Valley missions and, 157–64; translation of diaries of, 44–48, 195–207

Zinzendorf, Erdmuth Dorothea von, 201

Zinzendorf, Nicholas Count von, xi, 24–25, 115, 117; hymns of, 201–2; missionary activities of, 153–54; musicial influences of, 130; on women's role in mission work, 166–67